Utrecht

Rotterdam

Voorne

Over Flakkee

Tilburg

Westkapelle

Antwerp

Bruges

Ostende

0541

Dunkerque

0521

Ghent

51°

Brussels

Liége

Lille

Level A.5.

Charleroi

POLARIS 0550

JUPITER

FIX 0530

0806

2356

Abbeville

Climb A.5. 155

Amiens

23.25

St. Quentin

2349

0509

0509

VSC 7°

400 m

DESCEND 0540 A.5.

04.59

04.59

VSC 8°

0459

Reims

288 m

280 m

Chalons-sur-Marne

0445

0435

228 m

Paris

CW01468352

HIGH ADVENTURE - NAVIGATOR AT WAR

HIGH ADVENTURE - NAVIGATOR AT WAR

By

R.L. Austen,
B.Sc. (Lond.) F.G.A. F.S.V.A.

Chichester
Barry Rose

HIGH ADVENTURE

BARRY ROSE, Chichester

Typeset by:
Countrywise Press Ltd.

Printed by:
Entaprint Ltd., Cranleigh, Surrey

FOREWORD

I felt very honoured when Dickie Austen asked me to write a Foreword to his book. The war ended forty-four years ago now, so that nobody aged less than about sixty is likely to have taken any active part in it, and memories of it are starting to become dimmed; but a book such as this brings us back to the time when Britain was engaged in a life-or-death struggle against quite the nastiest foe in the whole of history.

If we had not won "the war in the air", this book would never have been written. The RAF operations were team efforts, but it is not always that the navigators receive the honour to which they are entitled. Without them, Bomber Command could not have operated. Navigating an aircraft needs as much skill as piloting it; the skill is not the same, but it is just as important.

What Dickie Austen has done is to tell his story, quite calmly and without any mock heroics. He takes us through the training, some of the early boredom, the first operations, the raids and the massed attacks which did so much to bring the Germans to their knees; as you read his words, you feel that you are part of the action. It is a story which needs to be told, and he has told it well. I admire him for his courage, his skill and his modesty; let us give our best wishes to his book - and to Dickie Austen himself.

PATRICK MOORE

Contents

ILLUSTRATIONS IN THIS VOLUME

The end papers show actual flightpath to Dresden

NAVIGATOR AT WAR

R. L. AUSTEN

Introduction

The pilots will not like this! However, the Air Ministry in a war-time publication emphatically stated: "The key man in a bomber aircraft is the navigator".

This story underlines the training and techniques that went into navigation in the 1939-45 war, as practised in Bomber Command and also to some extent as practised on the ground in Control, concerning the operation of night interceptor fighters. Comment has been made in some quarters about the sparseness of information dealing with RAF training, which was an intense period of arduous study and physical training for those who underwent it, and which in many cases took a man halfway across the world. It took a tyro from the first principles that might well be understood by the competent yachtsman to the complication of radar that enabled a target to be obliterated without anyone actually seeing it. Not a few fell away in the process and some lost their lives during training.

So far as bombers were concerned the Ministry statement was only partially true. Each crew member was indispensable and each carried the lives of all his fellows in his hands. A strange discipline evolved because air operations from Britain were always in a situation where some contact with home and friends was possible and yet the battle line was only a short time away. There is no need to comment on the fierceness of the air battles. The losses speak for themselves.

It is certain that warfare will never witness again masses of heavy bombers plastering a target. Technology has seen to that. The missile, with its vast destructive power, will probably supersede the manned aeroplane entirely but even if that doesn't happen the explosive power of the weaponry has made numbers irrelevant. The heavy bombers of the second World War will then appear in the pages of history like some ancient horde that came on the scene for an instant in full fury, to vanish almost as soon leaving behind only destruction and death.

HIGH ADVENTURE

Glossary of some RAF
abbreviations used in the text

AFU	Advanced Flying Unit
API	Air Position Indicator
ASR	Air-Sea Rescue
ATA	Air Transport Auxiliary. The aeroplane delivery organization
CO	Commanding Officer
CTO	Chief Technical Officer
DF	Direction Finding
DI	Daily Inspection (of aircraft)
DR	Dead Reckoning. Alternately - a calculated position
DR Compass	The distant-reading Gyromagnetic compass
ETA	Estimated Time of Arrival
Form 2330	A routine weather forecast
Gee	Grid Navigation. A radar position finding system based on ground stations
GH	Grid Homing. A blind-bombing device
HCU	Heavy Conversion Unit. A training school for heavy bombers
HE	High Explosive
H2S	Airborne Radar Navigational System
IFF	Identification Friend from Foe. A radar device for establishing friendly identity
Joes	'Victim of circumstances'
MF	Medium Frequency wireless
MU	Maintenance Unit
OTU	Operational Training Unit
PFF	Pathfinder Force
PPI	Plan Position Indicator. Radar display
PSI	An airman's welfare organization
Pundit	Beacon
QBB	Height of cloud base
QFE	Barometric pressure at ground level
RT	Radio Telephone (voice transmission)
SFCO	Senior Flying Control Officer
SNO	Senior Navigation Officer
	Station Navigation Officer
TIs	Target Indicators
TRE	Telecommunications Research Establishment
WT	Wireless Telegraphy (Morse transmission)

Targets bombed by the author's crew

Communications centres
Oberhausen
Duisburg
Trier
Neuss
Krefeld (three times)
Saarbrücken
Köln
Krefeld Ürdingen
Wesel (three times)
München

Oil plants
Hamborn
Gelsenkirchen (three times)
Kamen
Nordstern
Datteln
Huls
Merseburg
Regensburg

Military and naval
Bonn military airfield
Köln
Kiel harbour

Strategic
Dresden
Chemnitz
Berlin

Chapter 1

RADIO LOCATION

When, in 1938, it became obvious that a European war was virtually inevitable, in common with most young men of my generation I was compelled to consider what might be done.

Our ideas of warfare derived from the experiences of our fathers and uncles and focused on the trenches of Flanders or the cold waters of the North Sea. On the other hand we were fascinated by the air. Flying is commonplace nowadays but this was by no means so then. I had been off the ground in the 1920s when Alan Cobham had brought his rusticated first-war converted bombers, to give the public short flips for a few shillings, taking off from farmers' meadows. Also, there was the occasional chance of a flight with a wealthy friend who owned a sports plane and I sometimes went over to the Isle of Wight from Shoreham in West Sussex in a Dragon Rapide. Not much experience to go on but enough to convince me that it was better than mud or wet. Besides, there were romantic ideas of the chivalry of air combat built around the characters and reputations of former aces. So I went off and joined the Royal Air Force Volunteer Reserve. If the war didn't happen still I might learn to fly at the government's expense!

I made a few sporadic attendances at the West Sussex airfield, just outside the cathedral city of Chichester, where there was nothing much for me to do and certainly nothing whatever to do with flying, but when the war broke out I had a telegram in early October, 1939, to report to Euston House where I was enrolled as potential aircrew and told to go home until they wanted me. As I was 29 years old at that time it made it fairly unlikely that I might become a pilot and I came to the conclusion that I should be a navigator.

When I was finally summoned there were the usual months of initial training that all recruits endure. Marching, with sore feet. Endless inoculations and inspections. Incomprehensible discipline that one then resented but now realizes was so necessary. I often marvel at the magnitude of the task the Services were forced to undertake in turning hundreds of thousands of men from civilian life into fighters, particularly when one considers the multitude of backgrounds from whence they came.

In common with my fellows I endured such delights as being dumped on Wigan railway station in the early hours of the morning en route to accommodation in a disused jute mill in Arbroath in Angus, on the East Coast of Scotland, in mid-winter. Of pneumonia contracted under canvas when there was snow on the ground. Of being billeted with honest north-country housewives who fed me mounds of mashed potatoes soaked in gravy when I had acquired the healthy appetite of a horse because the RAF were getting me fit. Inevitably, there was improvization in every direction because the nation just wasn't geared to war. Finally, after the period of disciplinary training I was posted to the radio school at Cranwell in Lincolnshire, where in an atmosphere of the utmost secrecy I was initiated into the mysteries of RDF.

In the Services everything is reduced to initials. RDF implies Radio Direction Finding, the name formerly given to that which is now termed radar, which name will be subsequently used to refer to processes covering the much wider fields that opened up as the war progressed. It was the secret weapon of the RAF and probably the crucial factor in the winning of the Battle of Britain. It is now common knowledge that the air protection of the British Isles relied upon the early detection of approaching hostiles coupled with facilities for putting intercepting fighters in the right place at the right time.

The Americans used the terms "Radio Direction and Ranging" to name the system. This was shortened to radar and as they ultimately came to dominate the Allied cause, their nomenclature passed into the language.

Just before the war it was possible to see great steel towers arising in secluded places near the coast and looking rather like the electricity grid. The nearest of these to Tangmere was at Poling just east of Arundel. No one was able to satisfy curiosity as to their purpose. There were dark rumours of death rays and suggestions that motor car engines would stop mysteriously in their vicinity. In fact, a chain of these stations was built to cover the south-east of Britain where the trouble was likely to be the most significant. These stations were termed Chain Home or CH. They were the backbone of the early warning system.

Some CHs were operational by the early autumn of 1938 and were deployed to track the aircraft that took Mr Chamberlain to München for his famous parley with Hitler. Round the clock manning of the CH stations commenced very shortly after this historic event and continued until the end of the war. In fact, WAAF plotters were first tried at Poling and found to be perfectly efficient. They were invariably girls of good education and intelligence. Some idea of the size of the station construction may be gleaned from the fact that when the feeder lines iced over in the winter it took an unfortunate mechanic about an half-hour to climb the 300 odd feet to the top of the tower to clear the cables. Ice on the feeder lines distorted the picture below.

These towers, of which there were three, carried stacked arrays of transmitting elements with output up to a megawatt. These sent out a coherent beam in a fixed direction, termed a line of shoot, and were used for both transmission and reception to provide range data. A cluster of much shorter wooden towers carried conventional direction-finding antennae coupled to a manual goniometer which is a coil system mounted below a bearing ring which would provide azimuth information when manipulated. The massive matrix so formed was linked together with feeder cables.

It was found that transmissions should be in short bursts, called pulses, only microseconds in duration and when these impinged on a target a small amount of radiation was reflected back. In the case of an aircraft, a small object, the received signal would be very weak and amplification in the receiver had to be provided. Since the velocity of wireless waves can be equated to the speed of light the target distance could be derived as half the time elapsed between pulse and echo in these terms. Everything was happening far too fast for stopwatches; the required range data had to be extracted electronically. The solution was to employ a cathode ray tube that might be described as the prototype of the television screen we all know, or perhaps more closely as an oscilloscope.

A spot of luminescence was created on the surface of the tube when focused electrons impinged on a coating of fluorescent phosphor. This spot moved across the tube at a regular rate, called the scan and the afterglow from the screen coating lingered long enough for a trace-line to be apparent. The process of scanning the spot across was repeated at such small intervals that the eye could not see any interruption but perceived a continuous line. As the burst of energy went out from the transmitter the spot on the range tube was synchronized to start its measured journey as the trace. The received echo was fed to this trace to form a vertical blip whose distance from the beginning of the trace was converted by a scale into the actual distance of the target away.

The spot was quenched at the end of each traverse and returned to its origin in darkness. Otherwise, the fly-back trace would give rise to false ranging data.

Bearing was derived from a second, similar tube when the aircraft blip rose out of the trace as the goniometer sensed maximum returned radiation. In fact, the traces were never good clear lines but looked rather like a wobbly grass verge, so that it was most difficult to spot a weak echo and some operators became much more skilled than others in doing so.

An over-riding consideration arose in identifying our aircraft from the enemy and it had been solved by mounting in ours a transponder which sent back a kick of energy on being triggered by the frequency of our beams. This surge appeared as an amplification on the blip at the receiving station and adequate control of interceptions would have been impossible without it. Also, without positive identification of a target, the Royal Artillery and indeed the naval gunners would loose off at any intruding aircraft - including ours!

Although I was trained on CH at Cranwell and subsequently paid visits to such operational stations my recollections of their methods are now vague. I seem to recall vast valves kept in a state of vacuum by mercury pumps and miles of wires kept in order by Post Office engineers of remarkable efficiency, and of turning the goniometer to DF the echo to maximum.

One of the most interesting things I saw at Cranwell was the prototype experimental Gloster aircraft fitted with a single Whittle jet. This was the shape of things to come with a vengeance. It was 1941. It looked like a flying stovepipe with an aircraft built around it, no airscrew of course and this was startling. As I had a stopwatch and could guess at the distance across the airfield I made rough estimates of its speed when it came over low and it certainly topped 300 mph. Although this was not up to the maximum of a Spitfire it was certainly fast for those days.

When I was ultimately posted to an operational station it proved to be something entirely different, going under the initials CHL meaning Chain Home Low. This unit was a back-up to the CH. It was small. It transmitted a narrow beam rather like a searchlight and on a shorter wavelength and its radiation filled in below the lobes of the CH. It could search an area because its aerials were able to rotate as the result of the labours of an airman who turned a bicycle pedal connected thereto. Doing this for one's period of duty was a most boring occupation, and it was called binding. Whereas the display had originally been twin tubes, the engineers of Telecommunications Research Establishment (TRE hereafter) managed to incorporate range and bearing on to one by pulling the time base through a complete circle in synchronization with the antennae. This single tube was called a Plan Position Indicator.

These TRE boffins were a brilliant lot of most ingenious scientists whose thought was generally ahead of that of their German counterparts. The enemy certainly had two types of radar station, the Freya and the Würzburg, roughly corresponding in their functions to the CH and the CHL respectively. Not much was known about them at this time. We were to find out more in the near future. The early improvization of TRE constantly improved in all directions until radar became what someone has described as the most important invention in warfare since gunpowder.

The station to which I was posted was Foreness Point. Its parent station to which it was linked by direct telephone line, was at Dunkirk (the village in Kent) near Canterbury.

Foreness is right on the tip of the Kent coast by Margate. As near to the enemy as anywhere in the United Kingdom. The radar station was enclosed within a barbed wire perimeter embracing an acre or so, with some land mines sown. However, the only defence of the place was a couple of gun pits fitted with first-war Lewis guns mounted on rings, probably taken from 1918 aircraft. Rather amusingly the RAF regiment gunners went off duty at sundown leaving the unarmed operators to their own devices. The station itself was a small hut virtually smothered in sandbags with the restless aerial array swinging above it. Personnel were billeted in a taken-over girls school which was comfortable enough for war time and the accommodation was ample. The Station Commander was a Flight Lieutenant with engineering qualifications.

Margate had been evacuated and there was hardly a civilian to be seen. It was strange to walk through a ghost town where all the front gardens were going to riot and grass was growing in the streets for the town was a prohibited area. Local fighter activity was centred on Manston, an airfield that had taken its fair share of strafing and bombing in 1940, the scars were still obvious. Since Manston was about the nearest airfield to enemy territory it was frequently used as an emergency landing field by damaged bombers returning from the Continent after a raid. Sadly, many of these crashed on touch-down, often to burn up, and I have seen wrecks in the surrounding countryside, generally Stirlings at this time. Also, it was not uncommon for sneak raiders from the other side to hop across the Channel. I have had to dive into a ditch on occasion. There was a long walk along the deserted cliff top between the billet and the station that I did not much like since in course of time I was relieved of normal watch keeping and could quit work at stand-down, usually in the small hours of the morning. One gets a funny feeling between the shoulder blades when walking home at 3 am, in an area not unlikely to be a possible venue for commando penetration.

The reason for my change of duties was Squadron Leader Mawhood.

In 1941, before the coming into general service of the specialized Ground Control Interception (GCI) units which could control fighters overland, replacing the Observer Corps with their obsolete sound equipment, someone had considered that a CHL might be employed to direct night fighters.

Mawhood had been shot down in the battle of France and had sustained injuries which had put him out of flying operations, but he had lost none of his aggressive spirit. Doubtless, he had been retrained as a controller and he descended on Foreness in a small sports car to see what he could get going. Of course he outranked our mild and technical CO.

An ex-pilot acting as a controller had the edge over the general run of that breed who had been recruited from the civil professions but did not know from personal experience what happened to an aircraft in a tight turn or a spin and perforce had no first-hand experience of air fighting. Mawhood knew instinctively the value of such natural phenomena as the evening afterglow that persists at altitude long after sunset on the darkened earth, and of the visibility conditions created by the position of the moon. Also what could be expected of the engines in an emergency. In the coming months I came to have a great admiration for his grasp of tactics and his split-second decisions.

The basic theory of our interception control was that our plotters should report the blips of both the enemy and our fighters and that the controller should vector our fighters into a position for a kill.

This entailed a certain amount of navigating.

Since I was wearing the white cap flash of potential aircrew he detailed me to undertake this task. Indeed, I had some elementary idea of the art but a great deal to learn. We were to employ the Beaufighters of No. 29 Squadron who were based at West Malling and our main area of interception was the approach to the Thames estuary, that road to the heart of London that no raider could miss. Our radiation could see as far as the Dutch Islands below the Hook and since we swept over the sea our picture was uncluttered by geographical obstacles. Our wavelength being short meant that our beam was tangential to the earth and disappeared into the stratosphere in due course, which put a limit to our range.

There could hardly have been a more significant part of the English coast than our corner of Kent. Our plotters were ordinary RDF operators, generally of good education, particularly in view of the secret nature of the work. Still, they were not versed in combat operations as was Sector to which our plots were normally fed for filtering and display on the operations table. The plots were read in terms of the British Modified Grid and we devised a graticule to fit over the PPI tube, allowing for its curvature towards the edge.

We received a plotting table of about the size and appearance of an architect's board, to the side of which was fitted a course-and-speed calculator connected to a moveable ruler. A grid corresponding with the map of our area was covered with a sheet of transparent perspex.

As the operator at the tube called out the aircraft plots the man at the board quickly positioned a mark and time against his position on the perspex with a chinagraph pencil.

It seems to me that our method was more efficient than the German Seeburg table which was essentially a glass surface with two men placed underneath it shining coloured lights to represent the fighter and its quarry. Our controller was able to see the track of both in relation to each other, which made vectoring that much easier. Of course, the accuracy and quickness of the plotter on the board were crucial.

Perhaps this is the point at which to begin explaining the behaviour of an aircraft in relation to its environment. We shall take this in easy stages throughout this narrative because the understanding must be more and more comprehensive as time goes on and one technicality builds upon another.

The wind bloweth where it listeth. This is one of the main snags. Of course, a seaman is in somewhat similar circumstances since wherever he steers he is borne along by the movements of tides and currents and if he stands still he may well be drifted on to a lee shore. Should an aircraft set off from base for a point due west on the globe in entirely still air he will point his nose at 270 degrees true. But if a howling gale is coming down from the North Pole he will not get to his destination unless he heads off to the right by a significant number of degrees. The right-hand side is starboard and the left is port in nautical parlance, adopted by the RAF.

Naturally, if the wind is blowing directly towards him it will push him backwards relative to the ground; if behind, forwards.

These facts lie at the root of the navigator's Triangle of Velocities of which the components are:

(a) The direction of the machine through the air, called the course,
(b) The speed of the aircraft through the air,
(c) The direction over the earth, called the track,
(d) The speed over the ground,
(e) Wind Speed and
(f) Wind Direction.

There are a number of complications in ascertaining the parameters of these four items, arising from such considerations as the behaviour of the instruments used in measuring these velocities under the influences of height, pressure and temperature and from the nature of the globe itself. They will be explained later. Sufficient to say that the Air Ministry had long ago devised a mechanical navigational calculator small enough to be strapped to the leg and from which could be ascertained (c) and (d) above if (a) and (b) together with the wind conditions were known, and not too difficult for a pilot to operate on top of everything else.

The calculator attached to the plotting board at Foreness was a modified instrument of this type. The calibrated ruler moved the dial of the calculator so that when this ruler was laid along a track on the board the dial would record the bearing.

Modus operandi was to set up the instrument with the wind conditions of the time as pontificated by Met. When we became experienced we found our own winds. As the plots from the radar were ascertained the track of the incoming aircraft soon became apparent and when this had been charted for a few minutes the ground speed could be read from a slide rule. Then immediately the airspeed. By laying the edge of the ruler along the track plots the corresponding course of the aircraft could be read from the calculator on which the wind had been set.

If the operators were quick and accurate the controller knew he had a hostile coming in at a certain airspeed and on what course. He had the delicate task of putting our fighter in the proper position to shoot it down.

The question of altitude was one of our difficulties. A CHL had no height finder and we had to get such information from Dunkirk. Unfortunately, the radiation lobes of this station were subject to fade points where the echo disappeared entirely from view for short periods. However, even this was put to advantage since over a period of calibration flights it was possible to draw fade diagrams which showed, for instance, that an aircraft at a range of, say, 50 miles would fade at an altitude of 15,000 feet.

The other piece of equipment that had to be installed was a VHF voice transmission radio so that the controller and the pilot were in immediate speech communication. Before the war messages were passed to an aircraft in buzzer morse, as indeed they were throughout the war at long range, and part of the training of aircrew, as I subsequently learned, was to read both keyed and Aldis lamp transmissions at moderate speed. This method of communication was far too slow and ponderous for fighter interceptions. The VHF set in the aircraft had various push-buttons each corresponding to a crystal controlled frequency, one for us, one for West Malling control tower, one for Group and one for emergency. And so forth. All the pilot had to do was to press the appropriate button and speak.

Towards the end of 1941 we commenced the process of mastering the deadly chess game we were to play in the coming months.

Chapter 2

"ONE FOR 29"

The Bristol Beaufighter was a most formidable aircraft and No. 29 Squadron was the first to employ it operationally as a nightfighter. It mounted two powerful Hercules engines in circular nacelles that dwarfed the rest of the front of the machine and although its ceiling was only about equivalent to that of a Lancaster and its speed to that of a Ju 88 its main feature was its powerful armament.

Four 20 mm cannon ran along the fuselage to fire through the nose and six .303 Browning machine guns of the usual type were placed into the wings. When this devastating broadside was fired the machine virtually juddered to a momentary pause. The cannon had to be reloaded by the observer if they were emptied in flight and this, I am assured by my friend Robert Wright, was no mean task.

The other feature was that it had airborne radar, AI Mark IV at the time when Foreness was involved. The two-man crew consisted of pilot and observer and the latter sat at the set during the final stages of an interception to give the pilot directions that would end up with a visual identification of the target and an attack. The set had two screens, one for combined range and relative bearing and the other for elevation. The existence of airborne radar had to be kept from the enemy and as night interceptions started to become frequent ridiculous stories of the efficacy of a diet of carrots and pilots with exceptional night vision were put about in the hope that they would reach enemy intelligence. It is doubtful if anyone was deceived as the Germans developed their own airborne radar in due course. Nevertheless, we were forbidden to vector our fighters over the enemy coast in case an AI set fell into their hands.

The Beaufighter, however, had no rearward firing armament and therefore it was necessary to control the placing of an interception to a nicety by controlling the closing speed so that the fighter should not overshoot its victim, which had forward firing guns. The trick was to more or less match airspeeds a mile or two from closure and at slightly lower altitude so that when the actual attack was made the interceptor was masked from the crew of the victim by the body of the latter aircraft.

The range of the AI gear was probably three miles but at this distance its pulses would be uncertain. As the fighter closed in and the responses increased the pilot would report "contact" and the control of the interception would then be in the hands of his operator. In fact, the blips on our PPI would virtually merge at this stage. There was no evidence for expanding the range scale as was done latterly with H2S so we could not be of much help when the planes were close together. By this time, hopefully, the fighter pilot could actually see the bomber.

By the end of 1941 we were learning the ways of the Beaufighter. It soon became obvious that some pilots could hold a course and airspeed much better than others. We asked them to do calibration runs on definite headings and checked the results on our own PPI. One of the most reliable was Bob Braham who was ultimately to become one of the top scorers of enemy destroyed. We played the game of telling him what his compass and airspeed indicator should be reading when we had been plotting his track for a few minutes. The results were surprisingly good and the exercise assisted in speeding up my work at the same time. Another excellent pilot was a slightly built Canadian named Pilot Officer Pepper who became the first of our pilots to shoot down three enemy in one night but, unfortunately, was later killed in a landing crash.

The airspeed indicator does not show the actual speed of a machine through the air because the instrument, which is of the nature of a barometer, is affected by the temperature and the air pressure. For instance, if height is 20,000 feet and temperature zero an indicated air speed of 300 mph would be 330 in reality.

Also, if the course were being read from a magnetic compass in the aircraft there were two complications to be taken into account. Firstly the magnetic field of the earth, which the compass needle follows, bears no alignment with the geographical meridians because magnetic north is many degrees off true north, either east or west and its direction varies by large amounts according to that part of the globe where one is. This aberration is called "Variation". It alters slightly from year to year but fortunately it has been well plotted by the chartmakers. Secondly, local magnetic fields set up in the aircraft, or ship for that matter, by wiring carrying electrical circuits, for example, cause disturbance of the compass needle. These latter particular errors are known as "Deviation". They can vary with the heading of the aircraft. The amount of deviation on any particular heading is ascertained by a process called swinging and a deviation card was placed in proximity with the compass.

Far more sophisticated instruments are available to aircrew today, radar altimeters and gyro compasses make for an easy life.

Naturally, we did not want to tell a pilot to steer a true course. We had to tell him what to put on his compass. Also he must be given Indicated Air Speed after we had made the necessary corrections. Fortunately, it was always possible in a pursuit to feed minor corrections to an aircraft under control as "so many degrees port" or "increase angels by one".

"Angels" is patter for height expressed in thousands of feet. The CHL set had no height-finding array and this information on a hostile was fed to us by the CH at Dunkirk.

There was a deal of RT patter to be learned. Communication between ground and air is a matter of discipline so that instructions are instantly understood. For instance there were four operational airspeeds.

Saunter ... for comfortable idling
Liner ... normal cruising
Buster ... open up and get going
Gate ... full bore emergency only to be maintained for a few minutes before the engines would suffer damage.

Mawhood would only order "gate" in an extreme situation. Another command was "flash your weapon" which meant we had placed the fighter within range of his contact. We could hardly say "turn up the AI old chap" in case the enemy was listening in.

In the process of familiarization I went to West Malling for a flight in a Beaufighter. This was very exciting. I stood behind the pilot and did not realize at the time that I was on the door of one of the escape hatches which was secured, I assume, by a single bolt. I also visited the meteorological office at Manston in Kent.

In due course I gave the benefit of such experience as I had to Johnnie Brewster who doubled up with me on the plotting board and who remained a friend until his death a few years ago. Also a second controller, Flt Lt Roles, came as a deputy to Mawhood.

The winter weather did not help operations. The moon state was important because it gave the pilots some chance of a visual essential if a friendly machine was not to be attacked. So we logged the time of moonrise and set every night. Some success began to be achieved in January of 1942 when I noted two enemy shot down on the 14th. On the 17th, Wing Commander Evans had to land at Manston on one engine only and for some reason without the benefit of the flarepath. Probably there were intruders about. It must have been an unpleasant experience.

One taste of action came on February 12th when (the battleships) *Scharnhorst* and *Gneisenau* ran up the Channel. One of my colleagues, Corporal Rennison, who was on watch at Swingate in the early hours noticed long-range echoes in the Channel and reported them but they were probably considered by the Filter Room to be spurious. For some time before the break-out there had been a squadron of Royal Navy Swordfish aircraft stationed at Manston in anticipation of the event. I had marvelled at their ponderous slowness in the air. In fact, if a high wind were blowing in their teeth they almost stood still. They went off on a suicide mission to attack the German naval force in the Dover Strait, never to return. The air around us was full of Spitfires and Coastal Command Hudsons coming in to refuel at Manston and running battles took place between 11 Group and the Luftwaffe which was out in great strength. I was on gun liaison throughout the action. Our tube suffered jamming for the first time which made it appear that the enemy had our frequency. They had the advantage of some surprise and certainly air superiority and they deserved their success.

Our Flight Sergeant mechanic disappeared. British Intelligence had become aware of the existence of an ancillary station attached to the German Freya long-range radar, of a similar nature to our relation with the CH set up. But they wanted to know much more about it, particularly in regard to the frequency on which it operated. Our mechanic was a possible for inclusion in the party designated to raid the German station at Bruneval on the French coast. In the event our man was not selected and Flight Sergeant Cox from Dunkirk went with the paratroopers. I am sure that when he joined up he could hardly have anticipated being parachuted into enemy territory with a bunch of airborne troops and he was deservedly decorated for his exploit.

Mawhood considered that the Germans might very well launch a reprisal raid and the obvious target would be ourselves. He went off to Group to demand some weaponry and in the end came back with a Thompson machine gun of the American gangster type. However, this was not intended to defend us but was intended to shatter our apparatus in the event of attack. The secret circuit diagrams were to be thrown into a tank of acid. Presumably, the enemy would obligingly wait outside while we carried out these procedures and before cutting our throats. In the end we received a box of rifles packed in grease since the Boer war and with magazines that held only five rounds each. In fact, we could have done nothing to resist a raid such as Bruneval.

On February 19th I was called to Euston House once more. The Empire Air Training scheme was beginning to absorb large numbers of cadets and my time was obviously getting near.

Interception operations in the early part of 1942 were hampered by bad weather and my diary recorded that on most nights there were patrols and exercises only. Mawhood stuck a swastika on the wall for each enemy shot down but the numbers were not increasing very fast. The enemy seemed very often to be able to get off the ground when our airfields were closed and on one night when the cloud base was low they were coming over at very low altitude, probably pinpointing on the North Foreland light which the navy felt compelled to leave flashing because of the hazards of the Godwin sands to their vessels. Mawhood and I felt so frustrated at actually being able to discern the shapes of the enemy that we manned our vacant gun posts and blazed away most of the precious ammunition that our protectors were nurturing so carefully. The only result was a fierce satisfaction for ourselves and a rocket for Mawhood from on high.

On March 14th we were vectoring D5 who followed a bomber out as far as the Dutch coast where we lost contact with him for 24 minutes. It would have been a catastrophe if the enemy batteries had shot him down, but all was well in the end. At the end of the month there appeared in our vicinity what the poet could well term a strange device. In the form of a naval effort called "Ops Petard".

Sir Arthur Harris in his book concerning Bomber Command comments scathingly about crackpot inventions and ideas thrown up during a war. This was one of them. Possibly realizing that the RAF were better at mine-laying than they were as far as attacking the enemy coast was concerned, the Admiralty decided to turn the tables and conceived the idea of an aerial minefield. So a large convoy of lorries turned up and parked outside our perimeter, presumably on the assumption that we could provide information on approaching hostiles. The lorries were laden with iron cylinders of hydrogen gas and the sailors smartly sat in little booths. When Jerry duly approached the mariners inflated balloons to which they attached a long wire with an explosive on the end set with a time fuse. The idea was to release large quantities of these in the teeth of the oncoming foe.

By the time the gentlemen of the Luftwaffe were back in their Mess enjoying their Schnäpse the mines exploded harmlessly over the water (unless the wind had changed meanwhile!) The only outcome of this naval venture were reports of heavy firing over the North Sea and of course the distortion of our radiation due to the amount of scrap iron in the vicinity. Fortunately, Ops Petard did not last long.

Things began to warm up by the end of March. The constant patrols and exercises were relieved when a Dornier 217 was shot down on April 5, and another damaged on the 6th. On the 9th there was a fierce gale and the runway at West Malling was smothered in water but some 10 raiders managed to come in with nothing worse to face than the guns which were able to let all hell loose as none of our aircraft were airborne. At this time I had the heavy news that my brother had been lost on one of the Russian convoys and his obituary was printed in the newspapers. Fortunately, he turned up months later in a POW camp after having suffered severe hardship in the Arctic. He had been rescued from the sea by the Germans.

Symptomatic of our activity was a daylight sweep of approximately a hundred fighters, one of which came down in the sea 26 miles off the Point. We controlled a six-hour air search but, alas, without success.

One of the navigational exercises we had learned was how to conduct a search. Since an aircraft will be drifted downwind when patrolling, the area to be covered was regarded as a square. The searcher was vectored to a possible starting point and then turned directly upwind for a distance considered to be twice the visibility in the area. No drift need be allowed on this leg. The aircraft was then turned on to such a course as to give a track at 90 degrees to the first, and again flown for twice the visibility. Then downwind for four times visibility and then crosswind similarly, always maintaining track at the 90 degree angle. Next leg six times visibility and so forth. In this way nothing in the field of search should escape observation. Some time later, when I was flying in Canada, I had to put this theory into practice in the air. Nowadays a search is conducted largely by reference to radar positions.

The night bomber activity interfered with our patrols. Bomber Command sent out 350 heavies, many through our area which made interceptions virtually impossible. The flak which could be seen over the French coast was intense.

The weather now turned warm and sunny. It was mid-April and spring was on the earth.

In marvellously clear meteorological conditions the air war took an upturn. Fighter Command was sending out large sweeps, demonstrating its superiority and with a view to tempting the enemy to battle over their territory rather than ours. Some 150 fighters went out on the afternoon of April 15th and had a battle with about 100 enemy over the Le Touquet area. These numbers are approximate, being those given us by Sector, or derived from our own observations. There was an early evening battle in the Dover Strait after the machines had been refuelled and again with a superiority of a hundred to eighty in our favour. Foreness was controlling D31 when suddenly our VHF transmitter had a fuse as he was heading towards the enemy coasts. He was within four miles before he could be turned back, much to our relief. Bombers started out at midnight, hundreds of them making a direct line to the Ruhr and going in via Ostende. They were still going out at 02.00 hrs. This was before the policy of concentration of bombers into a stream and condensed in time had caused some alleviation in their appalling loss rate.

At this period, before Air Marshal Harris had had much time to make his influence felt, there was slight regard for the tactics in planning these raids. The fact that we were plotting outgoing bombers for two hours over the same route illustrates the lack of the competent directing which came in my time and which was made possible by the very high navigational skills which our training in due course produced.

Anyone who has seen intruding aircraft on a radar screen will be only too aware how vulnerable is one that is unattached because it gives ground control a sitting duck for interception.

Another hundred went out at 07.00 hrs on a fine and sunny morning and a further wave of 120 at 14.00 hrs. These were intercepted by the enemy just inside the coast at Le Touquet. Some 60 Germans attacked in waves of 20. I noted in the early evening that a convoy of our invasion barges were being towed past the Point, hoping to slip through the Dover Strait in darkness. In the night 40 enemy bombers came in overland and on the following morning we made two fighter sweeps across the Pas de Calais. German fighters came up from the direction of Lille with the obvious intention of doing battle, but they arrived too late. Probably their control was not as efficient as ours. In any case we could claim air superiority over our immediate area of Northern France, being in 11 Group of Fighter Command which had broken the Luftwaffe in 1940. Another sweep of both Hurricanes and Spitfires went out at 15.00 hrs.

Later on we vectored our Beaufighter on to an incoming X (unidentified) only to find that it was one of the few survivors of that early Lancaster daylight operation against Augsburg which resulted in over 50 per cent losses and convinced Sir Arthur that long daylight operations into the German heartland had little future at that time. It was April 17th.

I had hardly got to bed exhausted from the tensions of the past few days when I was pulled out because two suspected hostiles had been detected and was none too pleased when they turned out to be Havocs from North Weald. It was a quiet night of patrols only so for the next few days I went on leave to the glorious relaxation of a boat on Chichester harbour.

Foreness got a Heinkel 111 on the 30th with Flight Lieutenant Roles controlling. The score was 8 Certain, 1 Probably, 3 Damaged.

Chapter 3

MORE FIGHTER OPERATIONS

Mawhood and I were now given a new assignment. The powers above had discovered a disused tower at Walton-on-the-Naze which is a small seaside resort a few miles south of Harwich. They decided to install in it a CHL with motorized aerials which could be controlled by push buttons and this seemed to be quite an advance on our manual binding. We were to work up its potentiality for operations.

En route, I managed to get an evening in Cambridge where no doubt I made my first aquaintance with the Baron of Beef since I slept that night in somebody's kitchen. As I got into Liverpool Street station in the early morning with time to spare I was able to get a good look at the blitzed area around Tower Hill. It was bad enough. In particular, I noted with regret that the church of All Hallows was virtually destroyed since in my idealistic youth I had been an enthusiastic member of Toc H, that worthy relic of the first war.

Most individual journeyings on posting or leave were by train, usually very overcrowded, but the railways were performing a very good job. There was invariably an officer called an RTO at big stations, with military police to check on passing personnel.

On arriving at Walton I was billeted, as usual, on one of those good seaside landladies. Nothing was really ready at the tower. The apparatus was installed but not lined up and there were no trainees for our instruction. We were rather like Frankenstein in those old horror films, shut up in a tower full of weird apparatus and waiting for the lightning to strike. We therefore settled down to maintenance which in my case was a euphemism for sweeping out the place.

Although the radar was already installed only now were the architects testing the tower for safety. When we succeeded in getting an aircraft for calibration runs we found that it could only be worked at three thousand feet altitude. At other heights it disappeared from the tube. We were wasting our time and Mawhood decided to go back to Foreness where at least we could do some good. He took me back in his car and allowed me to go home for the night.

Upheaval had struck Foreness. With postings away of male operators who were bound for North Africa and the arrival of WAAFs to take their places. We were in for another period of patrols and little enemy activity which made training possible. The girls proved very conscientious and made excellent operators. Several days of thundery weather put a limit to operations and all was quiet except for the regular procession of invasion barges around the coast.

In the estuary of the Maas are various islands well known to British aircrews. One named Overflakke was the subject of the rather sick joke "Flak over Overflakke". Another was named Schouewen.

On May 16th our nightfighter was sent after what was obviously a patrolling German interceptor. They both twisted and turned for a quarter-of-an-hour but there was no engagement. Our pilot knew that he was being deliberately employed as a possible target for the enemy. The operation was set up by command because the enemy was definitely under ground control because "Y" service of British intelligence had picked up the radio patter. The Germans were busily engaged in replacing sound locators with radar in General Kammhuber's famous line and there seemed little doubt that a fighter box was working at Schouewen. By deliberately drawing their fighter out on different vectors and then noting the plot at which he turned back we were able to guess the range capability of their installation, ours being superior. It was a most dangerous operation for our Beaufighter and a critical control situation for us.

On the 19th there was a big bomber programme. Enemy flak and searchlights were very visible across the Channel. D33 reported seeing the wreckage of a bomber burning on the sea and D26 was sent chasing after the Schouewen fighter who was stalking one of our ingoing bombers. He attacked to break it up and reported a large explosion and we saw something on the tube that might have been a smash-up. Finally, alas, a returning Beaufighter crashed at West Malling, killing the pilot.

Enemy jamming on our frequency was resumed. Also on the 23rd the weather closed suddenly just after midnight. D21 and D23 who were practising interception on each other had to be recalled to land at Manston along with every other aircraft in the area, fortunately with safe touchdown.

Our duel with the Schouewen fighter was renewed and took a new turn when D31, fitted with the new Mark VII AI having a rotary scanner and a PPI type tube, was weaving with the enemy for twenty minutes without success. When we brought up reinforcement in the shape of D40 equipped with the old Mark IV the enemy broke off and turned for home.

Bad weather and patrols for the next few days. More barges going round the Point. We chased an unidentified coming in and lined up a perfect interception but our pilot ran into cloud so there was no visual contact. The enemy came out to attack a large northbound convoy off Dover in the early hours. We had no patrol but a Beaufighter was scrambled into the air as dawn was breaking. He was recalled to leave the job to the Spitfires as the light grew. The convoy came past the Point in due course.

Canterbury was raided on May 31st. D12 attacked a Dornier 217 but his cannon jammed after the first burst so he was only able to claim a probable even though strikes had been observed together with a glow in the cockpit of the target. There was evidence of the raid to be seen all around Canterbury railway station as I saw when I had occasion to pass through the next day. That night I saw an enormous bomber programme aimed at Essen, with our tube literally swamped with echoes. We played ducks and drakes with a few enemy mixed in among the bombers but without any success because selective interception was fairly difficult in these circumstances. The weather was uncertain but not bad enough to ground the enemy. Our bombers went out on the 16th in very bad weather and D41, flown by Squadron Leader Verity, one of our best pilots, had to ask to be sent home because conditions were so bad. They must have been! For the next few days it was the same pattern of patrols, bombers going out and barges sailing round the coast. A Havoc crashed at West Malling on the 20th and we had to divert D42 to land at Tangmere. There was a large mid-afternoon fighter sweep on Sunday involving Havocs and the Germans attacked Winchester with about 50 aircraft. Enemy jamming on our frequency was intense. TRE had provided us with a Leica camera - a German camera to photograph German jamming - I took a full spool of pictures of the interference to send up to them for they hoped to be able to analyse the sort of transmission we were up against with a view to countering it. Since the jamming continued next day a TRE scientist came down and monitored our reception with an oscilliscope. We were able to get in a chase the next night before the weather closed. The tension that always built up during these chases was too much for one of our little WAAF and she fainted away. We were all so busy that all we could do was to take her outside and lay her on the wet grass to recover.

On the 25th of June there was a big bomber effort. In all 742 machines, Wellingtons, Stirlings and Bostons, were sent out and 565 of these were routed over Orfordness. Our patrols chased a number of unidentified which turned out to be returning bombers. Another WAAF fainted. The Ops room was probably overcrowded and it had inadequate ventilation. The army had started a system of searchlight boxes to guide the homecoming bombers and as I went back to my billet I reflected on how beautiful were the reflections on the clouds. One of the strange ironies of war.

Mawhood thought he would try to vector our fighter in German to confuse enemy intelligence. Apparently Verity, who was the victim of this effort, was a bit of a linguist also as when about 20 intruders made for Norwich he stalked them until he went off the edge of our tube. Then D76 was vectored on to an enemy going home and after a quick chase the Beaufighter shot him down. He was seen burning on the water.

Whereas no German worthy of his salt would have been deceived for very long by Mawhood's linguistic efforts it is well known that very able lady operators of "Y" service did engage in confusing broadcasts and even in slanging matches with their opposite numbers on the other side.

On July 5th a queer meteorological condition developed. Large cumulus clouds worked up in the early evening and these resulted in hailstones of exceptional size, with diameters of up to half-an-inch or more. I counted five distinct layers in a broken one showing that it must have gone up and down often in the freezing zone of the cloud before becoming heavy enough to escape the updraughts and fall. To get an aircraft involved in such a cloud would be dangerous enough to become fatal. By 22.00 hours the pressure had dropped to 1006 millibars and a general thunderstorm started, visible as interference on our cathode tube. D18 going out for a patrol found himself surrounded by storm centres with excessive lightning and we found it prudent to send him back home. At 21.30 the following night an excited operator came out of the plotting room yelling that two enemy were making a beeline for our station. I tumbled into a gunpit and cocked the weapons in hope but they were probably at Angels 5 when they appeared. It was not dark, being July, so two Spitfires were scrambled from Manston to chase them off.

Jamming and routine patrols both continued and an attempted duel with two enemy nightfighters was tried off Ostende where there must have been another control box. We gave nicknames to both the Schouewen and Ostende patrols. Obviously, they were some sort of counterpart to our own and under very similar operational conditions. For instance when D61 encountered severe icing which forced him back in impossible conditions the enemy nightfighter merely poked his nose out and promptly returned home.

The July weather continued uncertain. The enemy appeared to be sending over Dornier 217s judging by their airspeed of approximately 240 mph. On the 14th D18 ran into thunderstorms off the French coast and was recalled. D33 came out and braved the elements for an hour but Sector called him in at 01.49 hours. There was lightning in plenty out east but this did not stop six enemy raiders. Pilot Officer Pepper in D76 was airborne and we vectored him on to an enemy. The chase lasted 20 miles and they both came right over our station. Anybody not on duty rushed out to hear them. Then there was the noise of Pepper's guns and we were able to claim a Ju 88 which intelligence confirmed as destroyed.

So things went on. The enemy suffered the loss of seven out of some two hundred that went in North of the Estuary into 12 Group territory. We worked a Mosquito for the first time on July 24th. The Mosquito was destined to supersede the Beaufighter because of its superior performance. Our aircraft came from Debden since West Malling was weatherbound. Our results were not brilliant, probably because we were used to the tricks of the Beaufighter. Things hotted up on the 27th when D42 had a combat and shot down an Heinkel. The rear gunner of the Heinkel damaged our fighter badly around the wing roots and he had to go back to base in a hurry. The Wing Commander came out next and had three or four contacts but no combat. Then D32 took over and we put him on to a homegoing He III who was obviously aware of his danger as he took avoiding action. Still D32 stuck to him and got in an attack as they were about to cross the French coast at Dunkerque. A big explosion was seen and a probable claimed. Sector subsequently confirmed a kill as the wreckage of the enemy was seen burning off the hostile coast. We now had eighteen successful certains to our credit. We were lucky again on the 29th when D51 shot up another Heinkel which went down in a spiral dive from 2000 feet and was claimed as damaged. It was usual for homegoing enemies to loose height and gain speed in a long dive for the French coast. After all, the distance was small and they knew very well that our interceptors broke off any chase at this point. How different was the situation for our own hard pressed bomber crews coming back hundreds of miles over enemy territory.

A large bomber programme cluttered up our screen and we were back to abortive chases and patrols only, but in the early hours of August 2nd a Dornier 217 was shot down. Pilot Officer Mason was doing the controlling and Johnnie Brewster was navigating. We managed to control the rescue of a Kenley fighter pilot off Ramsgate one morning. Two Messerschmitt 109s got mixed up with the operation and the AA batteries on the coast let off a lot of ammunition, a thing they seemed very delighted to do on the slightest excuse. On the 7th the weather forecast was bad and 29 Squadron decided not to fly. However an enemy plane, considered to be a reconnaissance, came out and we got D31 airborne. As our Beau was closing in on him Group ordered us off and a fighter from Trimley had a go but overshot, which was not a very desirable thing. We were then allowed to have a stab at the enemy as he went home but he got over the coast before we could close. The weather reconnaissance enemy came out on the 8th at 21.30 hours and we plotted him into the estuary. Braham got D42 airborne with celerity but the target turned over land where we could not see him. However, Pilot Officer Pepper shot him down under the control of the GCI at Willesborough.

GCI stations were coming increasingly into service to monitor fighters against enemies that had crossed the coastline.

The fun started early on Sunday. Three enemy came in just before midnight and Braham D42, shot down the first of them. He radioed back congratulations to me on the exactitude of my airspeed calculations. We quickly turned him to have a go at the second intruder and contact was established. Braham got a visual as he crossed the coast at Felixstowe when unfortunately our searchlights opened up and completely blinded him. He then had to break off the chase. It was another Dornier. We had several chases later resulting in one visual and several AI contacts but no combats. In the intervals, we tried to intercept the Schouwen fighter but he seemed to be able to turn on a hair and invariably escaped. Perhaps the Würzburg crew were as good as we thought ourselves! The problem of jamming, now code-named "visitors" was still with us and the Leica was kept busy.

The 16th was a particularly long day. I was map-drawing from ten in the morning to half-past ten at night and then on operations until 3 am the following day. In order to check the limits of our coverage we took Pilot Officer Pepper out to 100 miles range. When he disappeared from the tube I was navigating him by Dead Reckoning, in fact for some 120 miles of the trip and with very satisfactory results. There were very active fighter sweeps. Squadron after squadron of Spitfires went through our area, 390 of them being out. More calibration flights for us and plenty of work. I had put in 26 hours of duty in the past two days.

August 19th 1942. The Dieppe raid. This disastrous attempt at landing on the enemy coast was a chastening experience for the Canadian army. Chester Wilmot mentions casualties of over three in five and goes on to say that the high command learned useful lessons so that the sacrifice was not entirely in vain. The RAF, as usual, provided air cover. Five hundred fighters went out in the morning. The CH at Dover was jammed out of operation as the enemy realized what was going on. I was in our operations room all day and returned again in the evening after a hasty meal. A significant air battle developed with all the consequent tensions. This was not unlike the *Scharnhorst* affair, the enemy having some advantage from the proximity of their airfields to the scene of the action. By the time it was over and the remnants of the military withdrawn the RAF had made 2,400 sorties under ground control with 91 enemy destroyed, 31 probables and 140 claimed as damaged. We lost 98 machines and I do not know the extent of the damage sustained to aircraft that managed to limp home. So the odds were about even.

These were the figures I ascertained from Sector at the time. As with those of the Battle of Britain they would be subject to some revision in retrospect as Intelligence derived additional information, but they give some idea of how vital a contribution the RAF always made to the other services, when necessary.

At this time my friend, Corporal Rennison, who was the watchkeeper who maintained he had picked up the *Scharnhorst* at long range, was posted from Swingate to go to Initial Training Wing as aircrew. Poor Rennison! He was killed two years later at the end of his training when the Anson he was in crashed on to a mountainside as they were letting down through cloud.

The enemy sent over about a dozen minelayers but we could not catch them although we had two fighters under control because their speed was calculated at 270 mph and this was too great to allow a Beau to close the gap before they were over Europe. The 27th and 28th of August witnessed heavy bomber programmes. Three hundred on the first night, with a 10 per cent loss rate and 600 on the second. As usual, we chased after a number of "Xs" which turned out to be homecoming bombers. One

Lancaster took a pot shot at P/O Pepper when he closed in for a visual. Fortunately, there was no damage. Braham under Beachy Head control got one enemy and then promptly overshot another which plastered him. One engine caught fire. He was 20 miles out to sea but managed to crash land near Littlehampton. He and his observer, Pilot Officer Gregory, were unhurt. One likes to think that Mawhood would not have allowed the overshoot. He would have ordered wheels and flaps down to put on the brakes.

I noted that eight Stirlings crashed on attempting to land at Manston that night. Also D21 crashed on take-off from Manston for a dawn patrol. Squadron Leader Parker and his observer were unhurt but the machine was a write-off. Enemy jamming, which had been absent since Dieppe but had now started again, was very heavy.

Now the sad tale of Primer Blue 2. On one of the odd occasions when Sector asked us to vector day fighters our latest controller, Pilot Officer Mason, had two Spitfires for the dawn patrol and they were shot at by the Dover guns because of inadequate liaison. The German reconnaissance plane that was almost a daily visitor was a stripped down Heinkel having no armament and a very high ceiling. It was planned to intercept him with these two Spitfires. Under Willesborough control they were waiting for him at thirty thousand feet. We were just about to take the fighters over when the enemy entered our airspace but fortunately for our reputation we didn't move. There was an 80 knot wind at Angels 30. I noticed from the board that the enemy was climbing and Blue 2 radioed that he was above 35,000 feet and still trying to climb, being behind the target but still below. Suddenly Sector said the pilot was baling out. I dashed outside to see the Spitfire come screaming down in a vertical dive. There was a horrid smoke puff and the sound seemed to persist after the machine hit the ground. The parachute could be spotted at about Angels 8 drifting out to sea on the south-west wind. In fact, the pilot splashed down about three miles NNE of the Point and two crash boats from Ramsgate and also the Margate lifeboat were sent out but it took an hour to find him even though we gave all the help we could. The reason given for his bale-out, as I understand it, was that no petrol cooler had been fitted to his fuel system and the fuel had boiled at the low pressure at the height, cutting out the engine. Blue 1 had the same trouble but managed to retain control and glide into Manston. Operations at this high altitude were quite exceptional at this stage of the war and one has to learn by experience.

We were glad to learn that Pilot Officer Pepper had been awarded a well-earned DFC.

Since Braham and Parker were both temporarily without aircraft we found ourselves working comparatively freshmen which we didn't like very much. Another of 29 squadron's aircraft crashed on landing at base and also a Stirling came down very near us with the loss of the entire crew.

There was a plaintive song among airmen at this time which included the words

"If I only had Wings
Oh what a difference it would make to things!"

My posting to Initial Training Wing for aircrew came through on September 10th. At last I was going to find out the reality behind my longing. My final night in Foreness operations room was one on which 29 Squadron did not fly. Debden lent us a Mosquito as the enemy came in with a few minelayers. Mosquitoes and newer AIs were the shape of things to come. But that is another story.

Chapter 4

"PER ARDUA"

Whereas I might well claim to have had some small part in the destruction of Foreness's thirty enemy aircraft it was to be two years before I should be engaged in conflict again. This period would cover the long process of flying training up to operational standards.

Surely never in the history of warfare had a military machine undertaken such a mammoth educational task as had been devised by Bomber Command. Sir Arthur maintained that the cost of training a member of bomber crew would have sent ten undergraduates to university for three years. The bomber offensive required a constant stream of replacements to make good the horrific losses but the increasing sophistication of the machines and equipment and the advances of associated technology meant that it was impossible to get men up to operational standards in a short time. Without the wholehearted co-operation of Canada and Rhodesia and, in no small measure, the United States the training programme could never have been carried out. Britain was a combat zone and it would hardly have been feasible to allow numbers of freshmen to stooge about in her skies. Moreover, whereas the early stages of education were well served by academics, these gentlemen, on the ground, could not possibly teach one to fly. It takes a pilot to train a pilot!

One doubts if the lesson of that war-time experience has been learned. The time taken in training is crucial. Professional soldiers spend a great deal of their time in learning their trade and one of the arguments often advanced by military men is that two years of National Service may be morally good for youth but at the end of that period the recruit is only just beginning to master the job and off he goes. Seven years in the volunteer forces as territorials would seem to be something that should be encouraged and considered as almost an obligation by honourable young men. Particularly since in the future we may not be so fortunate with either the time available or the facilities that we had at that time.

The minor odyssey of my training adventure commenced prosaically enough for me in St John's Wood in London where we were accommodated in sparsely furnished but comfortable middle-class blocks of flats requisitioned by the Air Ministry. We were paraded for endless inspections, inoculations and the like in such exotic places as Lords cricket ground and the Zoo. Whereas remustered airmen like myself had been through it all before many of the cadet intake were raw recruits, scarcely more than schoolboys, needing to be brought up to scratch and indeed we all had to go through the same processes of discipline.

Here we spent some weeks doing nothing in particular but collecting instructional leaflets and mounting guard duty to protect nothing and complaining about the food. We were, of course, waiting to be slotted into the next stage of the programme. It would have required some superhuman critical-path analyst to ensure that there were no interruptions in the progress of the individual. In war-time this is an impossible aim and all through one's service there were times of delay, followed by intervals of intense activity. In the early stages of one's military career the disciplinary NCOs are apt to hand out such jobs as peeling potatoes in the cookhouse. At the same time providing a generous amount of physical exercise in the form of drill and sport.

As part of the toughening up process in October, we were sent off to the town of Ludlow on the Welsh border. There we slept under canvas in bell tents and spent our days digging with pick and shovel in a reservoir. As the winter drew on conditions became hard. For instance, washing water was often frozen and sanitation was of the most primitive character. Ironically, later on in our training we received lectures on the laying-out of camp sites having had the practical experience of how not to do it beforehand.

The training of civilians to become military is similar in all the Services. If the trainee cannot stand up to its rigours he is out. In fact, right up to operations, some of our companions fell by the wayside at every stage and disappeared when they found the pressures too great.

The rather boring preliminary phase was over on January 9th 1943 when I reported to Initial Training Wing at St John's College, in Cambridge, in D Flight. I was roomed in the Victorian-Gothic New Court, an obvious afterthought to the mellow early-brick originals, with another cadet named Neville Parry. Certain sections of the University had been requisitioned by the RAF and we were able to enter into some of the phases of student life almost as though we were undergraduates. Our meals were taken in the dining hall at Magdalen which is adjacent to St John's. Our lectures were in college classrooms or in the School of Divinity which struck me as rather incongruous until I came to the conclusion that our mission in life was going to be to put the fear of God up the Germans. The bath-house of the college was sheer luxury compared to Ludlow, with quantities of beautiful hot water. The intellectual atmosphere was obviously stimulating and in such time as we could muster it was easy to find good inns in Cambridge and there was the Green Man at Trumpington. The college skiffs were available to us and there were punts on the river. We might attend the Union if we were lucky. Although we were not allowed out after lights-out when my wife Kathlyn, whom I married before the war, was able to come up for a week-end at a local hotel, at the risk of being caught by the Service Police I went over the wall.

Since, in theory, any cadet could end up with a commission the instructors set out to instil a sense of elitism without in any way making it obvious. For example, we were issued with belts which we industriously pipeclayed to a virgin white. Our brass glinted like gold in the sun and our boots would have done no discredit to a Guardsman. Also we marched everywhere at a fast pace, the sergeant being equipped with a pace-stick in the best army tradition. When at the end of our course we were grouped for the final photograph on passing out the picture was a masterpiece of applied discipline. Every cap at the same angle, every hand and arm aligned and the line of belts on the four tiers of men looking as though they had been ruled.

Cambridge was frequented by operational aircrew from the many East Anglian bomber bases. We were able to admire this haughty breed from a respectful distance and sometimes they would condescend to enlighten us as to our rather slim hopes of ultimate survival. In order to convince us that we had not yet sold our souls to the devil, which indeed we were pretty certain we had, on Sunday January 17th there was a church parade of the entire Wing, that is to say of all the cadets in the University. A column half a mile long led by a band provided quite a show for the townsfolk.

We settled into the routine of learning and it is quite necessary if one is to appreciate the niceties of navigation that some explanation of the fundamental principles is grasped. There is the nature of maps and charts and of the plot. All RAF work in the air was done on the One to a Million Mercator chart which is ideal for plotting in European latitudes. A map is essentially a flat piece of paper representing some portion of the globe which is itself a sphere. It is what is termed a projection and is often explained by assuming a glass model of the world has a light in the centre which throws shadows on to the paper sheet. The paper might be wrapped around like a cylinder touching the girdle of the globe and indeed this is the basis of the Mercator. Or the sheet might just touch at, for instance, one of the poles and this principle lies at the root of the gnomonic. There are obviously going to be distortions however the projection is devised. With the Mercator, the graticule composed of lines of latitude and longitude will expand as the chart gets farther from the lines of contact and indeed this map has hardly any use at all in high latitudes. We recalled that maps of the world in our school atlases made on Mercator's projection made Greenland look about the size of India which is by no means the case. On the other hand with the gnomonic projection the distance will expand in every direction away from the point of contact.

The world map is always latticed by lines of latitude and longitude and the position of any place can be referred to these co-ordinates which are numbered in degrees in the case of latitude, north and south of the equator and in longitude east and west of the Greenwich meridian because the British did most of the donkey work when world maps were first being drawn. On the Mercator chart the intersection of these lines of latitude and longitude, termed the graticule, are at right-angles. Not so on the globe itself. Distances between lines of longitude appear the same. The distances between the latitude lines expand towards the top of the chart. From the navigator's point of view his track can be drawn as a straight line, called a rhumb line, which cuts all meridians at equal angles. Actually, an aircraft on a rhumb-line course flies a curve over the earth but for short distances this does not matter very much. Straight lines on the actual globe are arcs of circles and their resolution is a matter of spherical trigonometry - from which it is as well to shy quickly away. Since the chart expands evenly from bottom to top it is necessary to measure distances by stepping a pair of dividers evenly either side of a middle point, that is to say the mid-latitude and evaluate them against a scale suitably expanded and printed at the side of the chart.

Angles were measured with a square Douglas protractor made of transparent plastic on which one could draw a line if necessary. So the fundamental requirements for keeping the plot were a chart, a ruler, a pair of dividers and a protractor. Also a supply of well sharpened hard pencils because they had the habit of breaking at crucial moments. One soon learned to take into the air a good supply together with two or three erasers.

The basis of good navigation whether in the air or at sea is Dead Reckoning which involves drawing on the chart the direction of the true course and laying off the effect of wind or current in order to ascertain the actual path of the craft. In order that anyone taking over the watch may immediately evaluate the maze of lines there are conventions of arrowheads, one for a course pointing in the direction taken, two for a track similarly and three for a wind velocity. Also various symbols to indicate positions real or assumed, these being called fixes when derived from actual observations.

It is essential to keep the plot going all the time and to correct its assumptions by actual observation at every convenient opportunity. In order to do this it is necessary to have an accurate timepiece, in the RAF a wristwatch of famous Swiss make which the navigator was required to rate, and synchronize before take-off.

Certain aids to navigation were always available except in the most extreme circumstances. For instance, one could look at the ground when this was visible. Special maps, called topographical, showed ground features. Even the coast could be drawn as a position line. Bearings on radio stations might be ascertained for the same purpose. Drifts could be measured in a variety of ways. Before the development of airborne radar navigational systems the RAF crews depended very much on such methods and the rather unsuccessful bombings of such places as the railway station at Hamm gave testimony to the need for much more sophisticated techniques.

Meteorology played an important part in the curriculum. We had to have a sound working knowledge of the uncertain nature of the upper air, of cloud formations and frontal systems and the wind conditions associated with them. Even in a trip of only a few hundred miles the wind can shift dramatically and of course it changes its direction and speed as an aircraft climbs to height. One had to be able to interpret the synoptic chart, now familiar to most television viewers as part of the weather forecast. Isobars and fronts were rather less known about in those days.

Other matters included such subjects as the theory of flight and aircraft handling, engineering, armaments, including an actual amount of shooting and the principles of ballistics and bomb aiming. Signals, with practical experience of the morse buzzer and the Aldis lamp. Aerial reconnaissance and photography. Of much importance was aircraft recognition so as to be able to tell friend from foe in a matter of seconds. Indeed this was part of the business of survival in which we were duly instructed. Aircrew could well be called upon to fly in any part of the world and if the machine came down would have to look after themselves in the jungle, the Arctic, on the sea after ditching or on a mountain slope or within enemy territory where it was particularly important so far as our operational future seemed likely. Dinghy drill was laid down in detail in such instructions as that entitled "Life in a rubber dinghy in temperate climates" which sounds rather like a jolly lark at Brighton. It was practised in a swimming bath where duly blinded by dark goggles we splashed about until we located an overturned inflated dinghy which the instructor had thoughtfully thrown in upside down. As one was clad in a flying suit and Mae West, just shed by the previous victim, soaking wet and cold this particular exercise was really not much fun.

Sport and gymnastics played an important role. The standards of physical fitness were high. Some of my fellow cadets had already made names for themselves. One was an international rugby player (Billy Liddell) and one a Scottish international (whose name, to my shame, I cannot recall), while our physical training instructor (Cyril Washbrook) was an England and Lancashire cricketer. Keeping up with such men in the gymnasium made demands which were not easy to achieve, nevertheless the physical standards built up in such periods have undoubtedly served one well.

In one's snatches of spare time it was possible to enjoy the University. Its beautiful buildings and surroundings, the Backs with their lawns running down to the river where punts and skiffs still used the water. To study in such an environment itself puts a student well along the road to learning.

When the final examination results came out in April I was pleased to find that I had done well, particularly in the navigational subjects and I was classified as an Observer. What then followed was the usual period of waiting before the next stage of the game and the only notable happening was a bit of psychoanalysis. One of our fellows, a chemist named Colton, maintained we were given pills the object of which was to sustain aircrew in stress situations and indeed operational aircrew had access to caffeine tablets to ward off sleepiness at night. Also there was the all-pervading notion that bromide was put into the NAAFI tea to suppress sexual urges and this has given rise, forty years afterwards to the joke perpetuated in aircrew reunions that it is just beginning to work!

In May, we were posted from Cambridge which we left with much regret. We landed in Manchester at Heaton Park but with sleeping billets in the town. More waiting and filling in time. One of my previous colleagues had managed to get himself commissioned in the administrative branch and he found me a congenial occupation in the entertainments section, which illustrated the old saying that it is not what you know but who you know that gets you on in life. I knew very little of the entertainments business but since I still possessed a suit of tails at home I was able to appear on the stage of the Manchester Hippodrome at a fund-raising concert. Several of my previous friends were gathered at the Park having been to other ITWs. One very pleasant gap-filling activity was that of being sent on goodwill visits to armament factories in the neighbourhood on the assumption that our presence might stimulate increased production on the part of the young ladies working there. Finally, embarkation leave and detailed instructions from my wife on how to purchase minor luxuries in wherever I was going. So to the Clyde and the *Aquitania*.

The ship was not overcrowded although provision had been made for the transportation of some thousands of men. On her return, of course, she would be packed with American troops. She sailed unescorted, steering a zig-zag course at a fair speed calculated to outrun any submarine. We were unaware of our port of destination but could tell we were heading south-west by the position of the sun at mid-day. However, we duly turned west and in the early morning light of August 23, amid great excitement, there on the starboard side was the skyline of New York. We docked alongside the half-turned French liner *Normandie*, disembarked, and boarded a train that headed up through New England towards Canada.

Chapter 5

RIVERS

Arriving at New York is an experience under any circumstances, particularly if the city is seen from the river where the skyline is awe-inspiring. To come to it from war-time Britain after years of black-out and to see the lights shining unashamedly once again gave an impression almost of unreality, of unworldliness, emphasizing how Britain had changed since 1939.

Ashore, the American Red Cross were waiting to welcome us with that ever-present generosity that all visitors to the USA seem to receive. However, there was no time for delay or sightseeing. We were marshalled on to a train and proceeded up through New England. As the train threaded its way along the valley bottoms of a wooded landscape I could visualize the red-coated soldiers of the army of King George being picked off by the colonial sharpshooters up in the timber. Across the Canadian border we proceeded to Moncton, in New Brunswick, which was the reception area for cadets arriving before dispersal to the various training schools. Here we were re-kitted to some extent and had a short period of idleness in largely unspoiled surroundings. Moncton itself was an uninspiring small town but the surrounding countryside was idyllic.

Aircrew training on a scale sufficient to meet the demands and casualties of the RAF would have been impossible in war-time Britain and therefore both Canada and Rhodesia and to some extent the USA had co-operated in the vast task involved. Apart from any other considerations these countries possessed vast areas of flat open country where flying hazards might be reduced to a minimum, and also fairly long periods of stable weather. I found myself destined for No. 1 Central Navigation School at Rivers on the Manitoba prairies. Two vast railways crossed Canada from coast to coast, the Canadian Pacific and the Canadian National and upon the latter we made our journey westwards. Parry and I shared a compartment in some comfort as the seats converted to sleeping bunks and there were washing and dining facilities of adequate nature. As we left it was late September and the woods were already turning to the blazing autumn colours, orange, red, yellow and purple which make the Canadian fall such a wonderful sight. Our route took us through Montreal and Ottawa and then for hour after hour past the Great Lakes and on to Winnipeg where we arrived on the fourth day. Here we had a break, to be welcomed by Canadian matrons and their daughters, but this was only a brief encounter for we were at Rivers by the afternoon.

It is interesting to reflect that nowadays one flies from London to

Winnipeg in some seven hours, with the obvious reflection also that any government that neglects to provide troop carrying aircraft for battlefield reinforcement in an emergency will learn a very nasty lesson!

One other reason for being grateful to the Canadian railways was that when flying over the featureless prairies, if one got lost one had only to turn south, pick up the line for an east-west axis and go down to read the name on the boldly marked grain elevators for a pinpoint. This was cheating of course, but better than failing to make base.

Rivers itself could hardly be called anything more than a hamlet, being a collection of dilapidated wooden buildings, rather like a Western film set, clustering round a railway halt. This depot, as befitted the only place of consequence, was the centre of life of the community in that it possessed an eating place. In those days the liquor laws of the Canadian provincial governments were inclined to vary from little to none and any possibility of calling in to a bar in off-duty time simply did not exist. Not that, as we were to find out soon enough, there was going to be much off-duty time. The RCAF station was a hutted camp, the buildings wooden. The sleeping berths were double-tier metal frames. Food was ample and the discipline tight.

The aircraft were yellow painted Ansons, probably the Canadian-built Mark V, and I was soon to learn that the first task of the student navigator was to manually wind up the undercarriage on take-off with some 140 turns of a crank. The instructors were invariably Canadian personnel, our Flight Commander being a large and genial Flying Officer Scott.

Any elation we might have felt at the prospect of getting airborne was very rapidly doused when only two days after our arrival, around midnight, one of the aircraft coming in on one engine hit another in mid-air. There were no survivors of the nine men aboard.

Settling in and classroom work, and then a first flight in daylight, which was described as familiarization, and map-reading. This was to introduce us to the elementary part of making our way in the air by identifying pinpoints on the ground. It is obvious that some features, such as the shape of a river or lake, are easy to identify and give a positive position to the navigator.

The Canadian maps presented no problems, being almost simple by comparison with the British equivalent. The featureless prairie was divided into sections, usually delineated by dirt roads orientated to the four points of the compass as they were laid out by the Government's surveyors. Since these had had the advantage of dealing with empty land they had been able to be methodical and even in the cities the buildings appear to be arranged in rectangular blocks. Prominently marked were the radio ranges which were then the chief aid to air navigation. These operated on the well-known Lorenz system of a dot-zone and a dash-zone received into the pilot's headphones. In the centre of the zones the two systems overlapped to give a continuous note. This was the beam he rode. There was a cone of silence over the actual transmitter that gave an accurate pinpoint. By riding from one transmitter to another in a simple, uncongested airspace as it was then in the New World it was possible to traverse the entire continent on the beams. I feel that the existence of these beams gave a feeling of comfort to the pilots who were flying with student navigators!

Such navigation as the pupil attempted in the early flights, which were entirely in daylight, was related to ground pinpoints derived from the topographical maps and to endeavouring to ascertain the angle of drift from a sighting instrument.

My first flight lasted an hour-and-a-half. The second was over three hours. By the end of October we were trying our hands at aerial photography, taking a series of overlapping oblique shots with a large hand-held camera, from which photographs a mosaic called a "line overlap" could be built up.

The basis of all navigation at this stage was dead reckoning which involved the keeping of a plot. Essentially, the plot involved drawing on an appropriate chart the route to be followed, and after calculating the various parameters involved in solving the triangle of velocities, marking the actual position of the aircraft over the ground to enable any corrections of direction and time to be effected. In order to standardize the procedure a set of symbols had been evolved which anybody with knowledge could read. For example, the course was marked with one arrowhead, the track with two and the wind direction with three. An air-position was a triangle and a fix a cross. All flying in November was by day and was concerned with actual plotting of course and track. At this stage the methods employed varied very little from those used by the navy for centuries. Indeed, such techniques are basic essentials but the speed at which an aircraft moves made it essential for the air navigator to work as quickly as possible and the Air Ministry had been compelled to quicken up things. For instance, the calculation of Astro-shots had been assisted by the provision of a new almanac.

The winter cold of the prairies when an almost permanent polar air mass straight from the Arctic settles over the land for months made flying in the draughty Ansons a numbing business. I had icicles forming on my moustache from my condensed breath and it became extremely unwise to touch metals with an ungloved hand for fear of losing some skin. Nevertheless, the cold was dry and exhilarating, particularly as one was fit and well fed. When the snow came it was dry and powdery and the propellors of a machine being warmed up on the ground would throw up rings of refracted light as the sun glistened through the crystalline curtain.

The curriculum at Rivers was not by any means confined to navigation but embraced subjects that might be useful to commands other than bomber, although no one had much doubt as to where we should eventually end up, and probably in the literal sense of the word. In line with this generalized training we took signals and armaments, being able to strip down the .303 Browning gun and even the old Lee Enfield rifle which I had used as a schoolboy. Aircraft Recognition was an important subject, speed and accuracy being essential in combat. There was plenty of strenuous sport and the occasional intelligence lecture.

Plotting in the air tested our ability to draw accurately on a very small and very cold table in a bucking aircraft which was not all that easy by day, but in December, after a very welcome week-end in Winnipeg, we were airborne at night.

One had become so used to the blackout since 1939 that even the small communities of the mid-west with all lights showing seemed like jewels when seen from the night sky. The length of our trips had become to be about three hours, during which time we would cover up to about 400 miles, with the routes becoming more complicated, involving such items as "avoiding prohibited areas" which later had some relevance to flak positions in Europe. There had been no more fatalities but at the end of November one of the machines could not land because of ground fog so the crew baled out and the Anson crashed.

Although I was familiar with airborne radar from Beaufighter days I knew nothing about the new aids such as Gee and H2S. These were to come later. Now the next extension to Dead Reckoning was to be Astro. Nelson in his sea battles, moving at eight knots could readily find where he was by a two or three line fix from star shots. Even if this procedure took six minutes to work out he would not have moved a mile. Also, when he took his sights with a marine sextant he had a fairly stable platform and a defined horizon to help his shots. This condition did not apply as far as a bucking aircraft over cloud was concerned and the Air Ministry were compelled to speed up matters and to provide some form of artificial horizon to enable a navigator to read the altitude of a star. They had acquired the bubble-sextant which substituted a spirit-level style bubble for the actual earthly horizon. This bubble, faintly illuminated, could be seen in the centre of the eyepiece of the instrument and by rotating a knob the star to be observed could be held within the circumference of this bubble. The sextant was designed to take sixty shots automatically over a period of two minutes and the average of these was shown on a veeder-counter.

To keep the bubble as steady as possible the pilot had to fly straight and level and at a constant speed. The average pilot when over Germany strongly objected to this!

Accurate Greenwich time at the moment of observation is essential and to this end we were issued with high-grade wristwatches. These we had to rate for any timekeeping error, the maximum requirement being six seconds a day.

By calculation, which in the early days involved a trigonometrical formula, it was possible to derive a position line from the altitude of a heavenly body. The Air Ministry reduced the need for mathematics by producing an instrument called the Astrograph. This was a projector which threw a series of shadow curves on to the navigator's chart so that he could read off the appropriate point in relation to the observed star altitude. However, the device had to be fixed at a precise height above the chart and its film was limited to two stars and the Q correction for Polaris, so if these were not available because of cloud cover, which can be patchy, the apparatus was a dead loss. Although I came across the Astrograph in the obsolescent Stirlings that I later flew it never seemed to me to be very effective. Of far greater use was the Astro-compass which enabled a navigator to give the pilot his course derived from bearings taken on a star, the instrument having been set up with appropriate astronomical data.

I was interested to master as much as possible of Astro navigation and on being issued with a sextant and tables took innumerable shots, the best of which I logged in my Sight Log Book, a volume decorated on its cover with the hopeful slogan "Man is not lost". I noted over 20 shots on some days including meridian passage of the sun which is a good way of getting a quick latitude. It was necessary to spend time at night gazing at the heavens to familiarize oneself with some of the lesser known stars whose constellations were observable at appropriate altitudes and always keeping an eye on Polaris. Sometimes there was a ghostly flickering of the aurora in the skies towards the Magnetic Pole which is located in northern Canada. This display, which the Indians call Palefaces Dancing, was very frequent.

On the first of our December day exercises the authorities played a little game with us. Parry and another pupil were flying with me and the first navigator was an instructor. The idea was that the pilot set his own courses and we had to work out the complete plot from our own observations. Somehow or other we found ourselves over the United States before turning back to base. However, there were no international repercussions. Since the latitude of Rivers was fifty degrees and thirty seconds North it was not difficult to trespass over the border if one were not careful.

As December progressed the flying conditions became more difficult. High winds from the Arctic not only cut our ground speeds down to as little as 100 knots but also brought down the temperatures. I recorded minus 25 degrees Centigrade at 6,000 feet. Nevertheless, the flying pressures increased and I did two night trips totalling 5 hours and 50 minutes. The temperature had now dropped to minus 32 degrees Centigrade and it was so cold that both compass and sextant froze. Even with the Canadian flying clothing which was well padded it was difficult to persuade one's numbed fingers to record the plot and that at a slow pace.

We had our first experience of the Astrograph in the air on a trip over Winnipeg. I took the shots and Parry plotted them. The view of Winnipeg by night was far more satisfactory than the results of the astrograph.

A poor Christmas came and went. Cadets were not even allowed a glass of beer and the only bright spot was no flying, probably because the instructors were all enjoying themselves elsewhere. Parry and I managed to get out of the station on Boxing Day and skated down the river to the railway station where we had a square meal. However, we were given a few days leave over New Year where we had a pleasant time including dining in the famous Pallisser Hotel, in Calgary, with such unheard-of luxuries as finger bowls en suite. Also we managed to get a trip in an RCAF training aircraft over the foothills of the Rockies.

Back through an all day snowstorm to Rivers and the beginning of what was to be one of the most eventful years of my life. Flying again in January on a Coastal Command exercise, flying various courses and deriving wind velocities from observation of drift. Over the sea an aircraft would be taking back-bearings on a smoke float with a drift sight. This exercise was not very successful and we had to come back on a QDM which meant that we had to ask Base for a course to steer to return home. Next night was another exercise with the Astrograph. I took a number of shots under very cold conditions and didn't think they were all that good but on the next day trip repeating the drift-finding exercise my log was well marked by my instructor. The next exercise was what was described as a low-level one, obviously in preparation for the sort of trip that 617 Squadron did against the dams. Navigation by map-reading and course correction from pinpoints. The pilot was a mad Yankee who delighted in the opportunity of beating-up everything on the ground and at the same time scaring the daylights out of the navigators who were trying to revise ETA. Another night trip with the Astrograph on which I made the turning point satisfactorily after some 1½ hours flying. There was one heavy snowfall which caught the afternoon flight in the air. Only four got back home, the rest landing at Winnipeg and Portage la Prairie with the strong fear that one machine was lost since it did not report. However, it had come down in a remote place and was not able to establish radio contact for some time. Nevertheless, we were sent out on a square search for it.

By this time we were nearly half-way through the course and the first of a series of examinations, one for photography in which I managed to score high marks. The next day flight had to abort after 25 minutes with engine trouble and in the replacement aircraft we ran into winds of 50 knots which were significantly high compared with the airspeed of our lumbering Ansons for when the wind was on the beam the drift was as much as 26 degrees.

Night navigation continued with Astro. Also a practice at compass checking in the air. The rest of the flying until the middle of February was divided between more Astro and Coastal Command exercises. A flight on the 12th took place in another snowstorm and we got back with some difficulty. The first fortnight of February was an intensive period of examinations. My last night flight at Rivers was on the 15th when the work of the instructors was seen to have borne fruit since I achieved a mark of 90 per cent. Two days later a day flight was devoted entirely to sun shots. In the period from October to February I had logged 176 sights, had flown 65 hours by day and 43 by night and had managed to secure excellent marks in the examinations.

Now the fun began. Our instructor, by now Flight Lieutenant Scott RCAF took us to a graduation dinner in Brandon with the officers of both "A" and "B" flights in attendance. On the way from Rivers the bus blew a front tyre and for a terrifying moment plunged across the ditch and up the railway embankment running parallel with the road. However no one was hurt.

Wings parade was on the 25th with the whole course drawn up in the gymnasium for the AOC to present the brevets and myself out in front to receive the award as best cadet. Then hurried packing to go on 28 days leave with travel warrants for wherever we wished so long as we reported to Monckton at the end of it. The next batch of cadets was obviously arriving to take over our accommodation. Parry and I stopped off at Winnipeg to say goodbye to our friends there. We had been invited to stay with my cousin in New York, together with T.C. Williams who survived the war to become the Chief Constable of my home county of West Sussex where I have lived for years. While we were in New York we had telegrams to say that all three of us had been awarded commissions. A month of touring and American hospitality soon came to an end and we were back in New Brunswick.

We sadly learned that just after we left Rivers one of our pilot instructors was killed in a crash with three others.

Chapter 6

PRE-OPERATIONAL

Early in April we left Canada with some regret to recross the Atlantic to reality. We sailed in an erstwhile French luxury liner the *Louis Pasteur,* and since Parry and I were now officers we shared a two-berth cabin with bath. Some subtle changes in our life style became evident. Instead of the Crown and Anchor of our outward journey it was now Bridge. Thank goodness my parents had pointed out to me that one should eat one's food with a knife and fork, even though there were no silver napkin rings. The early April weather was bad, the vessel pitching and rolling since, being unescorted, she had to make as much speed as possible in case of the odd submarine. After the icy prairies and the heaving sea it was wonderful to sail up the Mersey and see the green fields of England once more. We were posted to the Queens Hotel in Harrogate where the representatives of a famous firm of brothers decked us out on credit with our new uniforms. The most insignificant form of life in the RAF is a newly commissioned Pilot Officer. The airmen avoid him, the non-commissioned officers lay great stress on the word "Sir" and in the mess he feels very small in the company of his be-medalled seniors. He is only too aware of the single thin ring on his sleeve, made as narrow as the tailor's needle will allow.

Here at Harrogate we were sorted out as to our future Command postings. I was sent to No. 10 Advanced Flight Unit at Dumfries in Scotland.

The purpose of AFU was to begin to familiarize new navigators with flying conditions in Britain which were far different and much more complicated than those we had so far experienced. Terrain features are closely packed and varied and there was of course the unstable English weather. The meaning of the word "scrubbed" which is slang for abandoned due to deteriorating weather soon became only too obvious. My first flight was scrubbed. The aircraft were still Ansons but we flew as first navigator all the time.

The pattern of flying was an extension of our work in Canada. Trips averaging three-and-a-half hours on cross country legs, with some bombing practice thrown in and still with emphasis on Astro. On one of these day trips which took us across the Midlands to turn over the Wash I had my first experience of industrial haze which was so thick that it cut out visibility enormously. The same conditions often prevailed over the Ruhr. We made all our turning points and my logs were being well marked with high scores. Sometimes things went wrong as instruments might become unserviceable and a certain amount of estimation crept into the plotting. By the beginning of June the weather turned very nasty. There was no flying. Only rain in torrents.

When I next got airborne the aircraft toiled up to ten thousand feet where the temperature was minus 9 degrees Centigrade. Like a fool I was not wearing a flying suit. The ascent was through virtually ten-tenths cloud all the way and the cold slowed my work down. However, we let down safely through the overcast. This was not without its dangers. Some weeks later my old friend Rennison of Foreness days but now a trainee navigator was killed when his Anson broke cloud below the summit of Criffel, the local high peak near the Solway Firth. Meanwhile the invasion of France had started.

The last two trips at Dumfries were by night with bombing runs on infra-red targets which we could not see and therefore only the camera would record our results. The implications for accurate navigation are obvious. Meanwhile, I had logged another fiftyfour sights and clocked up another thirty hours.

On to No. 11 Operational Training Unit at Westcott. This was a miserable station with 24 men in a hut and a half-mile walk to the ablutions. Here we flew Wellington Mark X, mostly machines that had been withdrawn from operations and the power of whose engines had been de-rated but they were still capable of greater altitudes than the Ansons and of course higher airspeeds which meant faster working at the plot. Significantly, also there was more flying by night than by day. Also we were on the fringe of operational flying areas and there was the small comfort of gun barrels in mechanical turrets. There was a catwalk along the fusilage, quite narrow, and since at night everything was dark one had the feeling that one might blunder off and put one's foot through the diamond-shaped geodetics of the bodywork which were fabric covered. A small torch thrust into the top of a flying boot became a necessity.

In order to provide for two pupil navigators there was a small table halfway to the rear with a compass and an airspeed indicator. Here, I performed my first four trips as second navigator, keeping a plot from such information as I could gather from my instruments and the intercom. The first night trip took us up to 16,000 feet. My first experience of breathing oxygen. The crew practised such exercises necessary for survival as banking searches and corkscrews and the gunners fired off their turrets. All very good practice. Next day another taste of the real thing. We were briefed at mid-day but hung about until 17.00 hours in the warm afternoon sun waiting for an aircraft. We had scarcely got to 700 feet when the pilot noticed that the petrol flaps had come open so we had to land again expecting the possibility of difficulty. Near Newcastle we flew into cumulus cloud. The aircraft refused to climb above 14,000 feet and the pilot's windscreen iced up. Also we could hear the squeaking of the balloon barrage around Newcastle, the balloons being fitted with a device which gave a warning we could read. However, we got home safely.

Whereas, due to my Foreness experience, I was quite aware of certain aspects of radar operations, up to the period of OTU I had had no experience of Gee. This system is well known nowadays, not least from the writings of Mr Alfred Price whose book, *Instruments of Darkness*, is a must for all students of the air war. In essence, the navigator received blips on a cathode ray tube which were pulses radiated from ground stations. The blips were displayed on two time bases and there were means of reading Gee numbers which could be referred to a lattice chart. The values of particular stations were printed in different colours and superimposed on a one-to-a-million Mercator chart. By noting the intersection of two lattice lines and reading off the relevant latitude and longitude the navigator had his fix. The lattice lines were hyperbolic curves drawn around the transmitter and the further one was from the transmitter the more gentle the curve. The manuals gave the range of the system as 450 miles at altitude 15,000 feet, the range increasing the higher the altitude of the receiving aircraft and certainly enough to give data from England to the Ruhr. It was possible by maintaining a pulse against an indicator, called a strobe, through turning the heading of an aircraft to fly along a lattice line of the Gee chart. This was very useful for homing to a target or indeed finding base in bad weather. A lattice line was also a possibility as a position line. In order to minimize any printer's error caused by shrinkage of the paper on which the charts were printed these were expensively backed with fabric.

The OTU Wellingtons were fitted with Gee and I applied myself to mastering the box with the same diligence I had previously employed with Astro. Astro henceforth would take a minor role in position finding. It was considered that one should take a Gee fix, ie, read the coefficients from the cathode tube, enter the Gee chart to convert these into latitude and longitude and plot the position on the Mercator in the time of six minutes. One had to become adept at interpolating, particularly when it is considered that there was rarely adequate light in which to do the work. No wonder aircrews had to have perfect colour vision to pick up the lattice lines.

The machines also had a direction-finding loop aerial with which the wireless operator might derive a bearing from a ground transmitter. However, a loop, like a magnetic compass, was liable to deviation caused by the metalwork of the aircraft and it had to be swung for a deviation chart in just the same way.

On my third trip, still as second navigator back in the tunnel, there was a sharp reminder of things to come. The aircraft fell foul of the gunners of the Royal Navy, probably because it was off track and possibly because they would shoot at anything that looked like an aircraft. We were shot at twice, once over Pembroke Docks and once over Cardigan Bay. The navigator reported that Gee was unstable and I was able to provide him with two good Astro fixes, it being night.

Now came the time for the ritual of crewing and for a short time I found myself with an Australian pilot who rejoiced in the name of "Killer" Arkens. I took an instant liking to him in spite of his nickname. I was transferred to the Pool on the assumption by the Station Navigation Officer, probably reinforced by words that I had had with the great Mahaddie, that I should go to PFF. Instead, I went on leave and on returning was pitchforked into my last second-dickie trip, a taste of the real thing. We drew special rations and aides just as if we were going to war and set off on a diversionary trip to Le Havre.

It was not unusual for OTU crews to be employed on diversions and spoofs and indeed they actually went bombing on the classical Köln raid when Sir Arthur Harris wanted to demonstrate that he could put a thousand bombers into the air at any time.

I was in my unenviable second-navigator position. The route chosen was probably pretty safe and the orders were to break off just north of the French harbour and return.

The Wellington climbed to about 17,000 feet through broken cloud. There was some light in the upper air. As we crossed the English coast the pilot ordered all lights to be extinguished. The bomb-aimer practised dropping "window" down the flare chute and a lot of it blew back over me. Window was the metallized foil which threw spurious echoes back to the enemy radar screens, and indeed one aircraft throwing it out could give the impression of a larger force to the enemy detectors.

Since I was robbed of my tiny glowlamp I sat for a few moments in the pitch-black thrumming hull of the bomber until it occurred to me that I could well stand with my head in the astrodome where I could at least see the sky and probably some stars.

I looked around. There was light enough to see. We were flying in and out of thin cloud, coming out every now and then and as suddenly plunging back in. The whisps of vapour flicked across the wing tips like whips dispelling the illusion of motionlessness suspense so usual in actual flight. Every now and then, as the pilot tilted the aircraft, one was aware of the Channel below.

Suddenly a black, fast-moving shape flashed across the tail from starboard to port. I realized instinctively after all those months of aircraft recognition that it was a Messerschmitt. There was an established drill for giving fighter alarm. I should have called into the intercom "Fighter fighter starboard quarter up ..." but I was so frozen by alarm I could only stutter "f-f-f-f ..." before anything could happen and the enemy had vanished. It was the first time I had seen one of their fighters in the air.

Soon we were within sight of Le Havre which was continually illuminated with vivid orange gun flashes and explosions indicative of the battle going on below. We turned around and gratefully made back to England. We went as far as Norwich and so turned for base. Westcott was closed in so we landed at a satellite and finally got back in a lorry. So to bed very tired after five hours night flying.

This was my last trip as second navigator since I was now taken out of the Pool to replace the navigator of Flying Officer Blenkin, the former having gone unstable. As I was subsequently to find out, the latter had a very cool head indeed. One of the more important requirements of a bomber pilot appeared to me to be lack of imagination and Blenkin belonged to the breed of those who press on regardless.

He had most of a crew and he was waiting in the Pool. As yet he lacked the Flight Engineer. As was usual in Bomber Command at this period the pilot was invariably the captain of aircraft. Frank Blenkin was a man of medium height, sturdily built, dark haired and strong in the arms as was evident when we shook hands. Resolute rather than cautious. As a result of our serving together we became friends for life, I ending up as godfather to his daughter after the war.

Turner Wilson was the wireless operator. A quiet, burly Scot, soft spoken and lapsing into his native brogue when excited. Although he looked more like a farmer he worked in a bank in civilian life and soon after the war became a manager. He was always well turned out in his appearance, particularly by comparison with the rest of us, and as we found, utterly reliable in his work. As a good navigator is indispensable to the pilot, so a good wireless operator is essential to the navigator. In Turner we were more than fortunate.

It is invidious to try to differentiate the importance of the respective roles of members of aircrew. However, it is certain that the most lonely and remote position in a crew was occupied by the rear gunner. Ours was Harry Holmes. He had been a sergeant gunner in the RAF regiment and as such was a good shot. Also excellent at aircraft recognition and quite up to the standards of the instructors. In fact, one might say that he was the only real professional airman among us, for whereas after the war Frank spent his life as a civilian pilot, Harry went on to finish up in the Canadian Air Force. They pay more! What Harry was secretly anticipating was that on operations he would get new guns that he could take to pieces, and oil and synchronize. Harry was definitely a Londoner. Our other gunner, the mid-upper was another sergeant, Roy Jago who was quiet, uncomplaining and not particularly communicative.

The most curious of our crew was probably the bomb aimer Jack Dannock. One might have been surprised that he was in aircrew at all since he seemed to be in his thirties and a confirmed family man. As such there would have been no great imperative for him to stick his neck out in a bomber. Again, a Londoner, and a business man in private life and anybody less warlike it would be hard to imagine. He was a slightly built man, which was probably an advantage, when he had to man the front gun turret in addition to his other duties. He had a habit of being very certain before committing himself which sometimes led to mild criticism from the rest of us when he insisted on going round again during bombing runs, a habit not to be encouraged over a target. He was cool and steady during operations. As for myself, perhaps I am eccentric enough to qualify for the strongest thing on earth after a mother's love, to whit the Navigators Union.

On our first flight together I had an instructor who showed me how to manipulate the Gee box in the air. I was very slow and lost the run of the plot which was a bad thing since keeping the plot going is one's last resort. Luckily it was an easy day cross country. The instructors, who knew their business, must have anticipated the sort of results they would get from these maiden assays. They had probably flown the route many times before. On the next trip we flew through a trough of low pressure which ensured a violent wind shift and pushed our ground speed up to 240 knots. As the wind was behind us I had to work very fast to ensure we did not over-run the turning point which was down in Cornwall and indeed go beyond critical point at which there would not be enough fuel for the return journey at much reduced groundspeed in face of the now adverse wind. On our first night exercise we did some practice bombing. All went well until we got home when Blenkin could not find base in spite of all my homings and ultimately of QDMs from base. However, to our great relief, we ultimately got down in one piece with very little fuel left in the tanks.

One of my friends, Ian Angus, was killed in a nasty accident at Oakley doing fighter affiliation. The wings came off during a corkscrew and all nine in the aircraft went including two ATC boys who were having a familiarization flight. The navigator had a lucky escape. As they were carrying a second pilot and gunner as instructors he was not required to fly, so he remained on the ground.

A piece of news from Foreness was that Mawhood was now a Wing Commander and so was Bob Braham who had risen to become the CO of No. 29 Squadron with similar rank.

There were more cross-country trips for us with bad weather and recalls accordingly and one bombing detail when Jack managed to put eight good bombs into the target from our altitude which, if converted to twenty thousand feet, would have given the remarkably low error for a normal bombsight of 135 yards. More fighter affiliations with mock attacks by a Hurricane, the gunners using cine-cameras instead of bullets, and the corkscrews making my stomach somewhat uneasy. Another minor torture was the decompression chamber, an iron cylinder in which we sat while they reduced the pressure to the equivalent of 28,000 feet. One scribbled on a sheet of paper during this performance while the boffins watched to see how much we could take before we passed out. The restoring to normal was done so quickly that I had some pains and bleeding from the nose. However I managed not to pass out.

After a couple more night cross-country trips involving as many as nine legs and more practice bombing our period at No. 11 OTU was over. I had flown just over 50 hours there in Wellingtons and it is significant that of these more than thirtyfive were at night.

We arrived at No. 1653 Heavy Conversion Unit at Stradishall which was the parent station of No. 31 Base and well into Bomber Command's operational territory. Here we were to obtain experience with four-engined bombers in the shape of the Short Stirling. Stirlings were awe-inspiring things. I could remember them from 1942 when it was no uncommon thing to see them limping into Manston, crippled and burning, and I could recall going to inspect one that had force landed and come to rest in the garden of a house. Some idea of the size of the machine may be gathered from the fact that the cockpit was level with the bedroom windows. The machine looked for all the world like a railway carriage mounted with wings which seemed too short for it and perched on great stilts of undercarriage with large tyres bulging under the weight. Inside one crawled between successive bracings of tubular spars to get to the cockpit but once there could not fail to be pleased with the roominess of the crew accommodation. In fact the navigator had almost an office in which to work. The machine was fitted with four radial engines, stood 23 feet high, was 87 feet long and weighed nearly 30 tons. Of course these dimensions have been dwarfed by modern-day aircraft but then they were significant. Stirlings preceded the other four-engined bombers in service and were being phased out of front-line operations, being given such odd jobs as trainee flying.

However, we were not at Stradishall for flying but for a series of lectures each in his own sphere. We picked up our engineer, Johnnie Wortley, who was admirably suited to his job having been in the motor business, and whose skill got us out of several tight corners in the next few months. Stradishall, in contrast to Westcott, was a permanent establishment built before the war to the comfortable standards of the then RAF messes. The weather was beginning to show signs of autumn and since I had not been in the air for a month I began to wonder whether the war might not end while we were still doing this eternal training. We were not left to wonder in our comfortable surroundings but were suddenly packed off one day to a satellite airfield called Chedburgh, to Nissen huts and the usual unfinished style of a war-time aerodrome. We were now well into the fold of Bomber Command.

The first few days were given to familiarization flying, circuits and landings usually referred to as circuits and bumps still in Stirling Mark III, when the remainder of the crew prayed silently for the tyres and sweated while Blenkin put the mighty machine down on the runway. There was little real navigation for me to do but plenty of practice with the instruments. Chedburgh was accessible to Cambridge and I was able to revisit that town on an off day. The RAF no longer had St John's College and there were few cadets to be seen. All the signs were that the ITW was closing down. When one had the chance one might cycle to Bury St

Edmunds with its ruined Norman Abbey, and the surrounding towns often possessed architectural gems in the form of the wool churches.

On one day we took off and landed in wearisome succession from 11 in the morning until five o'clock. This circuit flying was subject to inspection of the tyres at every landing. There was the constant fear of a burst and so each time we came down we taxied to a point where an airman checked the wheels to see all was well. I had my hands full with Gee operation and instrument checking but I did find time to go and occupy the rear turret for experience. I disliked the rear turret intensely. When I craned my neck to look down I seemed to have no connection with anything tangible. There is no sense of vertigo in looking down from an aircraft, rather a sense of detachment. In the forward cockpit functional correctness and a conformity with the nature of the machine, even the physical reassurance of the wings and the spinning propellers, set the mind at rest as the eye moved in continuous search. But in the rear turret the nothingness was vaguely disturbing. The air roared constantly through the embrasures, the complication of steel and perspex moved jerkily under the unskilful hand and in spite of the reassurance of the guns there was a constant feeling of insecurity. A narrow door behind the occupant protected him when the turret was on the beam. In this position the gulf of air below could almost be felt.

Still, all experience, presumably, is valuable!

Herepath, one of the pilots with us, ground-looped while taking off at night. The Stirling was doing nearly a hundred miles an hour when she swung off the runway, ran into the middle of the airfield and there, inevitably, the undercarriage collapsed. The machine was a write-off but the crew all walked away from it.

In early October we did our first cross-country, a six-hour jaunt to the Scilly Isles. Uneventful, except that we ran into icing conditions on the way back and the propellers were flinging lumps off and pieces were thumping alarmingly against the fuselage. Three of the engines showed signs of a trouble known as "coring" caused by ice forming in the carburettors. These radial engines seemed to be rather prone to it. The engineer cured it by running up the motors to increase oil temperature, which did the trick.

We took off for high-level bombing and the port inner went dead before we had much height. We had to jettison fuel and make a three engine landing and change to another machine for the exercise. We had several trips to the range and all the time Jack was improving his group, while I was getting used to an instrument called the Air Position Indicator which took some of the labour out of keeping the plot. This instrument might be described as a primitive computer. It resolved data from the compass and the airspeed indicator in conjunction with data supplied by the navigator, and it showed an air position. If one relied on the API one might dispense with the course line and airspeed measurement on the plot. However we still kept the DR going.

On October 12th while we were flying on night circuits and bumps the cabin was lit up by a tremendous flash. I looked out and there was the ominous yellow of a large fire burning on the ground. One of Stradishall's Stirlings had hit the ground just behind our station cinema. It burned for an hour while control kept us circling in the air. Two were killed, four badly burned but the rear gunner walked out unharmed.

Navigational flying involved cross-country trips of up to six hours with a strong emphasis on Bomber Command tactics with as many as ten legs to the route and the inevitable practice bombing somewhere along the line. Of course there was always something happening. Sometimes we would do our night circuits without incident. Possibly something untoward would occur. Perhaps we would sit in the aircraft for four or five hours waiting to get airborne while Flying Control decided if the weather would be suitable. Or perhaps on returning home we would find that someone had burst a tyre and we would have to orbit until the runway was clear. On Saturday October 21st we were to do our last cross-country. We took off late but the trip went well until we were recalled because the weather was closing in. Frank had been using the automatic pilot, George to everybody, and when he took out the clutch to control the aircraft himself it refused to disengage and the ailerons were locked. The pilot could not override the robot, which would take some time to run down even if switched off. We had no time for delay so Johnnie went down into the bomb hatch and hacked away with an axe at the chains running from the apparatus but they would not part. As he had to get the aircraft down he finally prized the clutch apart with the point of the axe. I lay on the floor shining one of the torches I always carried, to give him light. So we landed safely although the first bump flung both of us away from our positions. Still we were down and two days later we were finished with Stirlings and still in one piece.

By this time I had been promoted to Flying Officer with the meagre increase of pay that went with it.

CHAPTER 7

LANCASTER

Much has been written about the Lancaster bomber. Indeed the fate of each and every one has been recorded and going on for 4,000 were lost but it may not be irrelevant at this stage to recapitulate some details.

It was by far the most significant of the British bombers in that it dropped more bombs than the rest of them put together. Its faithful performance, remarkable flying qualities and ability to take punishment endeared it to the crews. The wings spread 102 feet, the machine was about 69 feet long and although it was not so high as the Stirling it still stood to 19.5 feet. The four engines were Merlins designed by Rolls Royce, although those fitted in the Mark III, which we were now to encounter, were made by Packards in America. The all-up weight exceeded 30 tons and of course the load varied with amounts of fuel, bombs and ammunition as circumstances dictated. The range of the aircraft was given as 3,000 miles by the Air Ministry but this figure ignores the load factor which cut the distance significantly. We seldom made a trip of anything like this distance. For example, our journey to Chemnitz Operational ceiling quoted as 20,000 feet could well be exceeded and indeed when the machine was light of load and fuel, was several thousand feet higher. Serviceability was an important factor here. The normal tanks carried 2,200 gallons of fuel. Maximum speed is given as 275 mph, fully loaded, at operational height.

The bomb load usually carried approximated to 10,000 lbs, but the Lancaster was modified until it could haul Barnes Wallis's ten ton monsters. When loaded up with fuel, ammunition and bombs it was just as near to a bonfire night special as could be imagined.

Pilots were very pleased with its handling qualities. It could fly on two engines, unlike the Stirling, and for a machine of its size it was manoeuvrable although with its .303 Brownings it was under-armed. They were no match for the cannon of the enemy nightfighters. Also, as there was no ventral turret, it was blind underneath and particularly vulnerable when the enemy fitted guns firing upwards to the roof of their nightfighters.

Like all British bombers its defensive armament was hardly adequate to cope with the Luftwaffe when that was at peak strength, and its ceiling was far inferior to that of the B17s of the Americans, but it carried a much superior bomb load. Also, the time the orbiting USA machines took to get to height over base enabled the enemy radar to plot them so that the fighters could be ready.

Lancaster Finishing School was at Feltwell, a grass airfield built before the war and the village from which it took its name was delightful, picturesque, still sleeping peacefully in the eighteenth century. However, we had no time for any of this. We started work immediately.

We only flew on three days, but what flying it was. A screened pilot took us up to show us the performance of the aircraft. After the Stirling it almost seemed like a fighter, climbing like a bird and manoeuvring beautifully. The weather was bumpy and in order to show us what the aircraft would do the "screen" did a series of steep turns and corkscrews. I was standing adjusting the Astro compass in the dome when he pushed the nose down and then violently pulled up. It felt as if a great hand was pushing me down, my knees gave way, unable to support me against the gravity of the change of direction. For the first and only time I was violently sick. My sensations can be imagined. I had on an oxygen mask.

Turner and Harry were both in the same plight.

We went up morning and afternoon on the next two days and morning, afternoon and night on the third. This last was for a cross-country and diversion. We adopted the technique of climbing straight off the ground on course, to save time. There was a north-westerly wind blowing at 20,000 feet, incidentally the highest altitude to which I had yet been and the speed of this wind was 140 knots. We showed nearly 40 degrees of drift, with ground speeds varying from a mere 65 knots to 335 knots, so to say the least it was an exacting navigational trip. I had to compel myself to believe the evidence of the instruments and my chart. It seemed that Lancaster flying was not going to be as easy as one had thought.

The Air Force always moves early in the morning, clinging to the virtuous belief about early rising it sends you on your way before you are really sure you are awake. This has the advantage of suppressing idle curiosity as to your destination.

One dull morning in mid-November we moved from Feltwell to Methwold. In the uncomfortable dawn hours we found ourselves in a big steel American lorry, bag and baggage, leaving the iron gates of the airfield. The village was still asleep. We were now a trained crew going to join a Lancaster Squadron for operations. We had only flown 5 hours 20 minutes by day and just over seven hours by night so as far as the aircraft was concerned we were still green.

The prospect of operations had been engrossing our minds for some time. It loomed larger and increased in importance as we went from course to eternal course, from school to school. All the time we had at Feltwell, some twelve-and-a-half hours flying, was little enough. And while we were there we had seen the operational bombers from the neighbouring airfields as they climbed under full load at take-off day after day.

That period of apprehension which I suppose everybody experiences at some time during the final stages of training had passed long since. We understood that we were in a risky business but our confidence grew with the handling of increasingly sophisticated machines. Now the sight of fully serviceable machines on Operations was enough to fill one with a sense of excitement, even if tinged with misgivings, but the irrevocable decision had been made years before and now it would be put into effect.

When I returned from Canada and was at Harrogate awaiting my fate I had been asked to fill up a form expressing preference for employment. A noble gesture. Not being entirely oblivious to the loss-rate I put down every Command I could think of, with Bomber in small letters at the bottom. Everybody else did the same. I was immediately sent to Observer AFU and told I was booked for Heavies.

Now, my thoughts were very active, turning over the past two years of laborious, expensive training, years crowded with experiences as fascinating as an adventure book. Years crowded with the faces of some of the finest men one could possibly know. Neville Parry, for instance, who had often shared an aeroplane with me and Maxie Hill who was already on Ops with the intrepid "Killer" Arkens, my Australian intended pilot. Jolting along the country road I was speculating on what the Squadron would be like. "Things will be different on a Squadron". We had heard that often enough, so we had begun to entertain a lively anticipation of the prospect of a period freed from the excesses of discipline which we had endured for so long, and of earning our keep and becoming that alter ego operational aircrew. In fact a short life and a merry one.

None of us had any illusions, either of our own importance or of any romance attached to our job. We did not consider ourselves as possible heroes, future forgotten men, or any of that nonsense. We had long become used to the potential hazards of our occupation and sometimes half enjoyed being scared. In fact, only the gunners, not entirely unjustly, thought themselves underpaid. In any case our needs were modest, being largely inclined towards beer. Not displeased at the prospect of a fight, but not unwilling to move with the course of events dictated by higher authority, we had been carried along by a stream which was about to run into a river.

Engrossed with these ideas I hardly noticed the vehicle turn off the road along a cart track with ploughed fields on one side and woods on the other. The trees were bare in the dull November air and the ground was thickly covered with chestnut leaves, yellow brown, against which the occasional evergreen showed suddenly, almost sharply.

Presently the lorry halted at a picket point and the driver's face appeared over the back.

"You're 'ere" he said unemotionally.

We clambered down, throwing out the plethora of cases, kit bags and bicycles which comprised our luggage.

I do not know why we should have expected anything different for we had been to many other stations, but it was strangely flat and disappointing to find oneself on the edge of a wood, with a main road running through it and nothing in the way of human habitation anywhere near except for a pretentious, but deserted middle-class house and a few Nissen huts losing themselves among the chestnuts. Across the way a sentry box by a gateway with a service policeman. Beyond, the beginnings of a perimeter track with black maintenance hangers and in the far distance the antidiluvian silhouettes of the bombers. No great activity. No sound except for the sudden shattering roar of an engine running up somewhere. No one to receive us.

"Better wait 'ere", said the driver. "Someone will be along!" And he took his lorry away.

"Another of these blasted dispersed places", Frank said, voicing the thoughts of us all.

"You two are all right, you've got bicycles. What about us?" This from Harry who was never slow to voice his feelings if he thought he had any cause for complaint.

Since the average bomber airfield was considerably over a mile in diameter a little exercise with pi will show how necessary a bicycle was in order to get round the circumference of the perimeter track.

"New crew?"

We nodded.

"George sir. I'm the duty batman. You'll get no service here." The last remark being hastily added to crush any hopes that Frank and I might be cherishing.

"Too many officers and not enough batmen", said George. "On the go from morning to night."

"Where are we being quartered?"

"NCOs down in the wood. Hut No. 81. Officers in the old Mess just down the path 'ere" and he proceeded to take a small footpath between the trees.

Frank looked at me and shrugged his shoulders and we picked up a heavy case apiece. We followed our guide leaving the others to make their way to their hut.

"Two bob a day, sir," said George. "In lieu. Have to make your own beds. No bat service. No nothing!"

We came to a Nissen building of the large type. The entrance was full of dead leaves from the wood which closed entirely around. A pool of dampness lay like a stain on the concrete floor. When he opened the door we saw what had at one time been a long Mess hall. Now, like a travesty of a hospital, green painted beds were ranged down either side with the wooden chests of drawers, canvas backed chairs and brown tables which furnished any Air Force room in war time. It was incredibly untidy, for none of the beds were made, kit and equipment were littered everywhere and the place was thick with dust. Around the brick fireplace at the far end, where most of the chairs were clustered in front of the ashes of a dead fire, the floor was dry, but at our end the linoleum was blooming with condensed moisture. There was a second entrance, with a pair of folding doors, and there was an iron cylindrical stove against the wall at the near end. Two vacant beds were indicated as ours.

The batman said: "Get some sheets later on and make 'em up. Only time though. Do 'em yourselves in future."

"Where are the ablutions?"

"Wash basins next door. But if you start pinching the coke from the boiler room you'll get no 'ot water. Rationed pretty tight we are."

"Any baths?"

"None", he said, dismissing such a superfluous question. "At least, there's some in the 'ouse, but the permanents live there." This emphasis on the possibly temporary nature of our sojourn in the place was not lost on us.

"As usual!" Frank spoke rather fiercely. "Trust the penguins to get themselves well organized."

"Showers over on the site. Some of 'em work but the water's none too warm." Seeing our faces he added: "The doctor sometimes lets officers bath in sick quarters: they're up the road on the right."

"God, what a pigsty!" I said looking round in disgust. "I don't care what these other fellows think but *I'm* not living in a mess like this." I had of course ignored the fact that these other fellows were rather busy bombing the enemy.

"Look at the floor," wailed Frank.

As mournfully as he had come the batman departed, leaving us to our own devices. We finished the task of moving our luggage and began the unenviable job of making ourselves comfortable.

I found I must share a chest with the unknown occupant of the next bed. His personal belongings were littered over the top and a .38 revolver with a handful of bullets lay amid the rest. "Look at this," I said opening the chambers and noting that they were all full. "This fellow deserves a court-martial." Aircrew officers were originally issued with revolvers for self-protection if forced down, but they were ultimately withdrawn for reasons of Air Ministry policy.

"Here's a find," called Frank who was investigating an empty chest. "Box of almonds."

"Probably belongs to someone."

"Empty chest of drawers. Anyway how about a couple!" Rather guiltily I helped myself. We were always healthily hungry in those days. "Look here," I said, "let's sort this lot out later and find out where we eat. By the time we have reported it will be lunch time."

"O.K. Suppose we'd better get hold of the adjutant as soon as possible."

"As like as not, old boy, they don't even know we're coming."

The Mess was nearly two miles from the billet; a dreary journey along the perimeter track which always seemed to head into the prevailing wind and along which the wintry rain usually beat in solid sheets unobstructed by any shelter, at this time of year an almost daily happening. There is nothing more dismal and desolate-looking and wretched on the face of the earth than an airfield when it is raining.

There were two Squadrons sharing the field at Methwold, No. 149 and that to which we were posted, No. 218. Ours was called the "Gold Coast" Squadron because the kindly African inhabitants of that part of the world sent it comforts, and it is to be hoped rejoiced in its exploits. After much searching we found the Squadron adjutant and were told to come back at nine o'clock next day. Time passed. After lunch we met the rest of our crew and heard from them a tale of woe comparable to our own.

Blenkin and I set to work with brooms and dusters and devoted the rest of the day to restoring order and cleanliness to our quarters - the RAF was never short of brooms. We took down the lampshades and washed them, swept the cobwebs from the roof and did away with the litter. Being old campaigners we carried in our trunks an axe and a saw, so we were never short of the means of procuring firewood and sometimes none too scrupulous as to where we found it. We soon had a good blaze in the grate, a fire of split logs sparingly laced with the forbidden coke from the boiler room.

"You look more like a housewife than a pilot," I told him as he pushed a broom along.

During the afternoon there was the beat of a Lancaster overhead, then another, and more, and we knew the kites were coming back from the day's operation. Rushing outside like schoolboys, as if we had never seen an aeroplane before, we stood on the edge of the road watching the machines as they joined the circuit and flew round the aerodrome.

Later on Grace and Knight came in.

"Hello, a couple of new Joes."

"My name's Frank Blenkin and this is my navigator, Dick Austen."

"Pleased to meet you. I'm Tom Knight. David Grace my bomb aimer." Mutual handshaking and nodding, and that minute of reserve when each sizes the other up before deciding to be friendly.

"Where did you go today?"

"Homberg. Oil refinery in the Ruhr. I reckon there's more flak there than any other target I know. Don't you Tom Thumb?" said Grace to his pilot, who was surprisingly lightly built to handle a heavy bomber.

"I saw several go today," he replied shaking his head slowly while his face took on a set expression.

"You chaps 218 of course?"

"Lots more training to do before you go on Ops. You'll find out tomorrow. Skippers go on a couple of second-dicky trips too. One day and one night. They won't let you take your own crew until you've done them. You won't be on Ops for a fortnight anyway."

"What!" I exclaimed, having had ideas of starting within a couple of days. "Not for a fortnight?"

"No. No dice. Definitely."

"What's the Squadron like?"

"Oh ... not bad. We've done a lot of daylights lately. They're pretty easy. Our twenty-fourth today."

"Was it really? You'll soon be finished. It's still thirty to a tour I suppose?"

"Yes, but they really don't know their own minds," David replied. "A little while back they had a points system. That was when the Channel ports were being plastered. Dead easy some of them. A couple of hours flying all told. Then they changed it to a minimum number of hours flying and now it's just plain thirty trips. But", he added, "they say it's going to be thirty-five soon."

"Comforting thought!", I said ironically.

"These other fellows are away on leave," he continued. "There's Toogood just here. He's ex-CID, a big burly copper, and Tojo there and the bed in the corner belongs to a Wop-A.G.".

"That's the one with the revolver?"

"Yes, he's quite dotty. Got a twitch you know," and David sat down on the side of his bed to pull off his flying boots, singing in a tuneless sort of way ....

"I wish I were a Wop-A.G.
To fly right over Germany
But Germany ain't good for me
It's foolish but it's fun."

This to the tune of a popular song of the time.

"Pack it up Dave." Knight turned to me. "They're all tour expired. Same Crew. And when they come back they'll all be posted. Skipper is an Aussie."

"A lot of Aussies came through with us," Frank remarked. Adding "We cleaned the place up a bit. Hope you don't mind."

"Hell, we've no time for anything like that these last few days. We've been hard pressed. We don't normally let the place get so dirty. The trouble is that it's so big, and damned cold at night. Better put your greatcoats on the bed when you turn in."

So we talked around the fire for the remainder of the evening, learning some of the past history of the Squadron, what it was doing at that time and hearing those stories of general conditions which always appear so very unaccommodating in anticipation but usually become acceptable, even tolerably pleasant, as time passes in any Station.

No. 218 Squadron of Bomber Command was a war-time Squadron of No. 3 Group which had been employed on a variety of tasks. Before Methwold it had been at Downham Market in Norfolk, equipped with Stirlings, and doing such jobs as main-force bombing, minelaying and low-level dropping of supplies and agents into enemy territory. This latter was something from the pages of Oppenheim, that famous pre-war thriller writer. The Stirling would be standing at the end of the runway waiting to go, engines turning over, crew all at stations, when up would rush a vehicle closed like a black maria and the Intelligence officer would hustle out the agent and push him into the plane before anybody could see him. "Looking like some poor little grocer going up for the first time," as one of the pilots put it. As the spy sat in the darkened machine he was as much impressed by the casual efficiency of the airmen as they by his own exceptional courage. The wireless operator would fit him into a parachute harness. The machine went off into the night, flying low - quite alone - across the sea below the radar and across the fields of France or Denmark at roof-top height so as to avoid detection. Navigation by conventional methods was soon impossible and it became a matter of skilful map reading at which crews became very adept. Navigators would come into the bomb hatch rather than sit at their table keeping a plot. Only if they were absolutely uncertain would they climb high enough to take a quick Gee fix and then down again before the watching eyes at the enemy cathode tubes could be sure they had seen a blip. When the dropping area was reached the machine attained sufficient height to quickly establish position and to some 800 feet, enough to open the parachute which had been adjusted to the little man and then the bomb aimer would undo a hatch, - a sudden rush of air - and the agent rolled forward into the night.

If supplies were being delivered the guerrillas were provided with a portable automatic radar transmitter which they would turn on when the Stirling was expected. This device was called after Archimedes, "Eureka". The navigator of the aircraft brought the machine to a spot using a cathode-tube homing apparatus called, poetically "Rebecca". The strain of flying a huge machine like the Stirling to the south of France and back at tree-top height over enemy territory and at night can be imagined.

While the Squadron was equipped with Stirlings they, like their contemporaries with similar aircraft, had taken heavy punishment. In the course of overflying the Alps to bomb the northern Italian industrial cities one of its pilots had achieved a VC - posthumously unfortunately. No. 149 had also collected a similar honour. Whereas the DFC was handed out indiscriminately to pilots, the VC was a rare distinction and the number earned in the RAF during the war could almost be reckoned on one's hands.

Possibly the most spectacular of the Squadron's operations was that which took place on D Day, when its aircraft were employed in what was undoubtedly the most remarkable piece of deception ever practised against the enemy. The machines were employed on a manoeuvre which may well be described as a creeping-search forward, a patrol on a restricted front with the aircraft going across a front with restricted turns so that the front advanced at the rate of only a few knots an hour. It was the most difficult thing to manage, calling for most accurate piloting with meticulous attention to the rate of turn combined with superlative navigation and speed control. Only specially equipped aircraft such as those of 218 Squadron could possibly do it. The effect, of course, on the enemy radar screens was that of a slowly moving naval convoy since the aircraft were pushing out liberal quantities of "window", the metallized foil which gave overriding smudges on their screens.

The effect of this feint was to persuade the enemy that we would assault the Pas de Calais, and apparently it delayed the movement of vital Panzer divisions to the real invasion area.

Further south the much publicized No. 617 Squadron were doing the same thing and getting all the credit.

The expectation of convoys which never arrived delayed the Germans in the Pas de Calais for much needed hours before they could reinforce the beachheads in Normandy. It is a comment on the remarkable efficiency of air strategy that an army corps of the enemy could be pinned down in this way by two Squadrons of Bomber Command. In modern war a delay of even a few hours can be crucial.

The expressed policy of Sir Arthur Harris was rather opposed to the creation of what might be described as an elitest corps within his command and to this end he wished each Group to be able to conduct its own operations, entirely. The rivalry between Nos. 8 and 5 Groups concerning methods of target marking illustrates this point. So, when the advanced electronic apparatus known as Gee H was introduced it was allotted to No. 3 Group and with this equipment No. 218 Squadron became markers, able to locate and bomb a target entirely by radar and if necessary through complete cloud cover. Where main-force operations were involved the established marking techniques were followed but there were times when only No. 3 Group could carry out a raid because of weather conditions.

I was to find out about this in due course.

CHAPTER 8

TOOLS OF THE TRADE

Reference has already been made to the fundamental methods of navigation hitherto employed, such as our plotting at Foreness. However the emphasis now became increasingly a matter of radar. I had used Gee in OTU aircraft but was yet to achieve the rapid proficiency involved in reading the box, entering the lattice chart and plotting the fix all in a matter of two minutes which was the standard required of an operational navigator. Gee was certainly a revolution in navigation. It made target finding in adverse conditions readily possible and even more important enabled a raid to be concentrated, so swamping the defences and allowing much less scope to the nightfighters, thus reducing our own losses. Bombs started to be placed accurately where once a mere tenth of the load had found the target. A raid became a properly executed military manoeuvre instead of a series of isolated jabs, for with the earlier methods of navigation the aircraft went into the target in penny numbers, a few at this time and a few at that, simply because accurate position finding on the way out was a matter of luck and the weather, while calculation of time-on-target was to some extent based on speculation, particularly as emphasis on such matters as time of take-off and arrival at concentration points had not been particularly demanded. Even when some concentration had been achieved before the advent of the Gee box it could hardly be guaranteed.

With the coming of radar in 1942 the real bombing offensive began. At first the apparatus was shrouded in deadly secrecy, detonators were fitted in the boxes so that they could be destroyed before they could fall into enemy hands. The apparatus would blow itself up on a crash landing. The charts were printed on special inflammable paper and a destruction tube was provided for them in the aircraft. At first, unsuspected by the enemy, the range of the Eastern chain took our bombers right into the Ruhr and allowed Sir Arthur Harris to stage the great raid of May 30 1942 when for the first time a thousand bombers went to Köln. It was the success of this raid, the fact that so many aeroplanes could go through a target at night with a loss rate acceptable to the Chiefs of Staff which confirmed the long range policy from then on.

I have mentioned the appearance of that raid on our tubes in the control room. Our screens were literally blotted out by the echoes from the tremendous concentration of machines that went out in our area. When the machines were really concentrated the trace was a complete smear and the only chance of an interception would be on a straggler.

Crew members laughed heartily at the navigators with their amazing box of tricks, saying that the days of good navigation were over and observers were nothing but "box bashers". At the same time the Air Ministry was kind enough to print those immortal words "The key man in a bomber aircraft is the navigator."

Nothing can stay secret for ever. The enemy got to know of Gee and started jamming the frequencies used by the ground transmitters. A little war within the war which the signals staffs waged continuously then developed. New circuits were added to the receivers. Fresh wave bands were tried. The enemy achieved this measure of success that often enough it was extremely difficult to pick out the pulses when flying over his territory. In due course he fitted captured Gee sets to some of his own aircraft and used them to raid England. When it was suspected that the Hun was about the ground stations altered the value of the reading by pre-arranged amounts and the pulses winked at the navigator in a knowing sort of way to let him know what was afoot. The manuals put it more formally. "When coding is in force the whole of the A pulse blinks." Of course, anyone trying to work out a fix without previously applying the correction would be entirely led astray.

Further airborne radar devices came into being. By 1944 most heavies were fitted with H2S the strangely named self-contained airborne unit. This equipment searched the ground around the flying aircraft with a beam of high-frequency radiation and catching the reflections from towns, rivers and coastlines painted a faintly luminous map on a cathode tube. Not well defined except in so far as coasts and lakes were concerned. A deal of practice was required to interpret the picture. The sets were complicated and sensitive and required a lot of careful tuning. Usually the bomb aimer came and sat by the navigator to work it, for the latter scarcely had the necessary time to spare.

Of course, each aircraft carried an IFF responder to tell our plotting stations it was a friendly.

During my time a radar-controlled gun turret was fitted to some aircraft and we carried a device with the rather sinister name of "Z" equipment to identify us to the radar gunners.

The wireless operator was also provided with a screen on which he kept watch for enemy fighters. It was called, very appropriately "Fishpond" because all the bombers surrounding his own, going at the same speed, kept station with his like a school of fishes, while fast moving enemy fighters were seen to dart in and out among them. It was a most important part of the wireless operator's duty to watch out for the enemy and give the gunners due warning.

These were only a few of the multitude of radar devices that made the air war an electrician's nightmare. By the time I was flying the port side of our Lancasters forward of the mid-upper turret was a maze of metal boxes all connected with radar. They reached as far as the rear spar and in the end replaced the rest-bed, which had to be covered in. The navigator's compartment was a cramped space full of dials and buttons, with the indicators of his sets encroaching on the chart table.

A further piece of equipment which must be mentioned was the Distant Reading Gyro-Magnetic compass, a formidable name which the airforce, with its love of initials, reduced to the simple "DR" compass.

We have referred to the aberrations suffered by the usual magnetic compass, variation caused by the earth's magnetic field and deviation from extraneous fields of force. Even acceleration and turning of the aircraft will unsettle such a compass momentarily. Now a gyroscope, applied as a compass is not subject to these errors for it has the property of maintaining direction in space, but in relation to the spherical earth it seems to go off heading after a time, a property called precession.

So these two types of unit were combined into one master compass which had the faults of neither, for when the magnetic needle had taken up direction the gyro came into play to maintain it, while the navigator had a control which enabled him to compensate for his local variation as read from the chart at points of his journey. The master unit was slung at the back of the aircraft away from disturbances from engines and electrical equipment and a number of repeater dials in front of pilot, navigator and bombardier, showed true direction.

By a marvel of ingenuity the instrument makers had taken direction from this compass and speed from the airspeed indicator and fed them into another box, making corrections for the form of the earth as this is distorted to fit the charts and this box gave the navigator the latitude and longitude of his air position as he went along. This was a wonderful thing. Next to Gee, the Air Position Indicator was a navigator's best friend. It had to be watched and it had to be checked for it was no replacement for the plot, but there it was, a little black instrument screwed to the ribs of the aircraft, faithfully clocking over the minutes and degrees and keeping the air-plot going whether the pilot turned left or right, climbed or went down, and following the movement of the aircraft as no human navigator could hope to do.

A word may be said of the Astro-compass which was more of a stand-by than an instrument of everyday use.

Every heavenly body has its azimuth which is in fact its bearing from the observer. This can be worked out by the navigator using the tables provided. The instrument had a base plate with a bearing ring like the scale of a normal compass and also a lubber line. It fitted into a socket in the Astrodome.

When the details of the star had been set on the device the course required would be set against the lubber line and the pilot told to turn the aircraft until the selected body was in the sight of the instrument. By this means the navigator making constant observations and corrections could direct the pilot whose normal compass had failed.

The instrument might also be used for taking bearings. However, it was rarely used on operations. It was another box for the navigator to carry.

This, then, was our normal equipment, not forgetting the Mark III Navigational computer. In addition there were blind bombing devices fitted in some machines and operated by the navigator. No. 75 Squadron made a count of the knobs and dials under his control. They totalled one hundred and six.

CHAPTER 9

FRESHMAN ON 218

As the first few days at Methwold went by and we began to accustom ourselves to fresh faces and new surroundings, it became obvious that we should have to endure a period of waiting of unknown duration. We heard hints, dropped and quickly withdrawn, half suggestions, oblique references to equipment that was being carried in the aircraft with the banded tail-fins. There was more training to be done; that the Wing Commander had told us in his interview. We had to learn about Gee H.

No one would say exactly what it was, or what it did, but apparently it was exceptional and really top secret and the Squadron were the only people that had it, apart from No. 149 who had not been equipped until we were fully serviceable.

One evening our miserable billet seemed almost full, for the others had returned from leave. Burly Sidney Toogood lay on his bed. Used to making himself comfortable under any circumstances he puffed a pipe and contentedly eyed his substantial feet which were balanced on the bedrail.

"When you've done your G.H. training I'll tell you what we did on D Day!" he said.

David grinned. "Can't mistake a bobby, can you?" and as a pillow came flying through the air in retort he burst into riotous laughter saying "Look at those feet!"

Toogood peeled a chestnut from the tin lid that served as a roasting pan. "Never mind young Grace. If it wasn't for G.H. you bomb aimers would have to earn your money. All you are now is a window pusher. Bomb aimers ... just ballast."

All of which was somewhat mysterious. However, the conversation was interrupted when Toogood put on his slippers and shuffled off to the fuel shed, coming back with an armful of logs. These he placed in the centre of the room and began splitting them with great blows from the edge of an iron shovel, a most inappropriate instrument for the task except when wielded with much strength. Piled into the stove the wood made the fire blaze cheerfully.

"No battle order up yet. Can't understand it."

"Perhaps the weather's bad. Over Germany I mean", ventured Blenkin. "Ha, ha, ha. You'll find out! Duff weather doesn't stop 218. No damn fear. Press on regardless."

"Well Davie my boy", his skipper said as he swung his feet off the bed where his heels had been making two black marks on the blankets, "let's away to the village for a noggin. You and I can have a drink tonight."

When they had gone we carried on a desultory conversation. Presently

Tojo came in and without saying a word to anybody threw off his clothes and got into bed in his shirt, immediately burying himself in a book on Theosophy. Sidney said:

"Look at Tojo. Reading Christian Science. He was a good chap to have over a target. Knew plenty of prayers."

So this, I thought, is what ops does to them.

We began a fresh form of sporadic training. Each man reported to his appropriate section, while the pilot hung around the Flight Office where the spare men seemed to do very little all day but eat oranges provided by the Government in the pious hope of improving their vitamin content. I was issued with a large green canvas bag and a lot of navigational equipment, computer, parallel rules, astro tables, planisphere and all the rest of it. Also a book of Gee charts of the one-to-one million scale covering all the British-based chains. There were indeed Continental chains now covering the Channel and Ruhr areas. I had not used them in real practice, previously. The overprinted topographical maps we had were of the half-million scale which had been prepared in a hurry and were not quite accurate at the edge. Still they were good enough although it was a bit of a nuisance to identify a fix on them and transfer it to the plotting chart. The amount of detail on these maps was made confusing by the addition of the Gee lattice, these were printed in three colours, so that it was difficult to pick out precise details without concentration. I felt compelled to go over the whole series with coloured pencil, thickening in the meridians and parallels and marking their values in bold figures on the chart edges.

When the situation, probably in the printing industry, subsequently allowed, one-in-a-million lattice charts for fixing were produced to replace these topographical maps. They had the barest geographical detail on a white background, with the graticule boldly printed and the Gee lattice much clearer. The scale, of course, matched that of the plotting chart. It must be realized that at night there was very little light in a navigator's cabin by which to work and the clearer the chart the better, even though we had the eyes of hawks. These new charts were linen backed to reduce paper shrinkage that might induce an error of position and they enabled a fix to be taken off and transferred to the plot by eye without working out the latitude and longtitude. But at the time we joined the Squadron we were issued with a large cardboard folder with these overprinted topographicals of most of Western Europe. At the suggestion of an old hand, Warrant Officer Flavell, I prepared a sketch as a sort of atlas index and numbered each sheet. On the principle that any preparation made on the ground to ease matters in the air in action was worth its weight in gold. Or so he told me.

He was a kindly fellow. Although probably no more than a year older than me he had greying hair which made him seem very advanced in years to go on ops. I was glad to listen to his seasoned advice. He had provided himself with all sorts of individual impedimenta to help his work so that when he was equipped he looked a veritable White Knight of the air. Among other things he had a sighting device of his own invention made to fit on the head of the bombsight, from which he could get a range and bearing of a ground object after compensating for height. His fellows called it "Flavell's Dangleometer".

Anyone who is lightly inclined to dismiss such simple devices as nonsense might do well to recall how No. 617 Squadron lined up the towers on the Mohne Dam to release the Wallis bomb. Two nails stuck in a piece of board were more effective than most of the scientific instruments.

I learned from Flavell the desirability of making one's crew take the navigator's bulky equipment out to the aircraft for him. He told me to get the engineer a spare compass key and train him to line up the repeater dials of the DR compass. "In case you get out late and haven't time to do it. You can always check it when you're airborne." He also said that the bombardier should learn to verify all radar while the pilot was running up the engines. "Get the preliminary checks done as soon as possible. You can't be sure even when you've done a DI that morning, and if there is anything wrong the first chap to shout gets the fitters." I protested that I would do my own checks and he said, yes, but checking on a check was even better.

He took me out to his own aircraft and showed the plethora of dials and knobs to which I have referred. I saw the GH equipment for the first time. As we sat on the green padded seat at the chart table I felt uneasily that I would never deal with all this stuff. But all the time I felt rather operational, especially when I saw the bomb releases mounted on either side of the table..

"That one is used for H2S bombing and this one is for when you are on GH."

"What about the bomb aimer?"

"He just fuses and selects", he grinned. "Unless it's a visual job."

"So that's it! - some sort of blind bombing equipment. I've been wondering ..." the sentence trailed away.

"Don't be impatient Dick. You'll get training on it in a couple of days anyway."

I spent some time checking the sextant that had been issued to me by placing the instrument steady on a wall and taking a series of sun altitudes taking opportunity to check meridian passage. The instrument was a beauty. Between such odd jobs I put in an appearance at the Navigation Office where I remained in the background somewhat awed by those whose tour was nearly over, who sat around the stove confidently, occasionally looking at the sprog, myself, in a somewhat large manner. A pilot who had just finished his tour got all the important people on the Squadron to sign their names in Indian ink on a stuffed penguin that he had carried as a mascot. He asked me to sign, as a kindly gesture, and I did gratefully.

"This is the only penguin I know that has done thirty trips", he said. "Have you got a locker yet? You can have mine." Eked out with tea and buns from the Salvation Army the time passed quickly enough.

On the 15th of November Blenkin went as second pilot on an operation to Dortmund. This was in keeping with official policy whereby all pilots did one trip by day and one by night before being put on their own machine. Dortmund was a typical Rhur target, very industrialized, a communications centre, with an oil refinery, and it was bombed fairly regularly.

I saw him before the briefing. He looked a little worked up, not unnaturally, and I assured him that I would have a drink to his success while he was dodging the flak. He seemed to consider this lacking in sympathy and went off into the briefing hut without saying much.

When he came back to the billet late in the evening and flopped wearily on his bed I asked him what it was like. He said he saw a number of flak bursts in the Ruhr but what impressed him most was the enormous number of Lancasters that appeared to be over the target. This flying in company with a host of others was a new experience. He said he couldn't understand how collisions were not quite commonplace.

"Well, you know what it's like now; but this hanging about is getting me down. It's like waiting to have a tooth out!" I observed.

The weather went from dull to rainy and water collected in great puddles around the airfield. The grass was like a sponge for wherever one trod ooze squeezed out. Trees dripped monotonously all day, the large drops hitting the roof of our hut with dull thuds. A sheet of water formed in the entrance on the concrete and had no chance to drain away as the rain pelted down from an unbroken stratus-covered sky, and everywhere around was mud.

To occupy our time to advantage Jack, Turner and I spent hours in the radar room practising manipulating the H2S equipment, until we knew the exact location of all the church spires in the neighbourhood, these being all we could detect. Even this grew boring, for we knew how to tune the sets and once we had become familiar with the few permanent echoes that showed on the screen the only relief was when we picked up the blip of any chance aircraft. It was over a week since we had arrived and we had not even been off the ground.

So it was a great relief to be detailed to do an air test of a machine that had just come in from inspection. On Sunday afternoon around 18.00 hours we managed to get airborne. Operations had been scrubbed because the weather was down on the deck but a temporary lift in the late afternoon gave us our chance. Set free and with no particular orders we went out over the grey Wash and flew down to 300 feet before we could distinguish the grey monochrome of the sea. Even at that height it was difficult, in such a self-contained world, to see where cloud ceased and sea began. We fired the guns into the sea to test the turrets and plunged back into the blind cloud as the pilot pulled up the nose. I was glad of this opportunity for instrument flying which provided the chance of a Gee homing to the airfield, which we could never have found in any other way.

The following morning saw the aircraft off to Homberg. Another Ruhr target. David, who was on the operation, related how he saw three of our aircraft blown up by the explosion of our own bombs in mid-air. Possibly someone had failed to set an adequate time interval on the distributor box of his bomb panel, allowing an HE bomb to hit a cookie. Perhaps it was just bad luck a stick from one machine fell across that from another. Who knows? He was dispirited.

The opposition had been heavy, the blind bombing met unspecified difficulty and since there was complete cloud cover over the target it was impossible to say what damage had been done, although he thought that the bomb falls he had seen were too scattered to have made a good job of the raid. Which must have been the opinion of Command for they were sent back the next day. This time the target was easily identified and the refinery straddled to such an effect that in my experience it was not visited again. The date was November 21st, 1944.

This was the period of the Oil Plan when the Chiefs of Staff and Sir Charles Portal in particular were trying to convince Sir Arthur Harris that the war might be brought to a rapid conclusion by destroying the major German synthetic oil plants. The latter was not entirely convinced and indeed we were bombing synthetic plants well into 1945. The official historians devote quite comprehensive coverage to the exchanges between the two leaders.

By this time I was casting about for something to do to occupy my energy. I asked Flavell if he would let me swing the loop of E-Easy, his aircraft, for I had noticed that there was no correction card in the aircraft. Loop bearings are subject to deviation errors due to magnetic fields set up in the aircraft and swinging produced a correction card. Flavell was quite amused at my puerile enthusiasm: no one had swung a loop on the Squadron within memory and the Signals Officer had probably forgotten how to do it. However, there was a marked site on the field, showing true compass bearings and with the help of Turner tuning radio beacons I was able to make a graph of error for the machine.

The weather was still dull; drizzle was the order of the day and my feet were perpetually cold with the damp.

At long last we reported to the Radar Officer for initiation and training on GH.

GH means Grid Homing. The equipment was modified from Gee but differed in one very vital particular in that the ground stations were quiescent until they were "triggered" or interrogated by the aircraft sending out a pulse of energy itself. The bomber, then, carried a GH transmitter and it was its own radiation which appeared on the trace of the cathode tube in place of the normal "A" pulse of Gee, providing an index from which to start measuring. The ground transmitters sent back waves giving a blip on both time-bases on the tube and one of these was the tracking pulse and one the release pulse.

The fast time-base speeds of the aircraft equipment, coupled with the degree of accuracy employed in monitoring the transmissions from the ground at their end enabled a navigator to track along a GH line with exceptional closeness. The system of bombing was this:

Three points were calculated along the track which the aircraft must fly into the target, the direction of attack being limited by the necessity of flying along a curve which was part of a circle having the ground station as its centre. The analogy of ripples from a stone thrown into a pond is relevant. The starting point of the bombing run was chosen about thirty miles from the target where the path of the incoming aircraft cut the circle through the objective. This point was reached by ordinary navigation, coupled with homing for the last few minutes before reaching it.

In order to make the explanation clearer a homing may be described in a few words. Any place may be located on a map by the co-ordinates of latitude and longitude. Similarly, any place where there was Gee coverage could be located by two or three co-ordinates corresponding to the lattice lines passing through it. Now it was possible to set a marker, a tooth-like indentation of the trace, to the value of any required co-ordinate. In order to home the aircraft to a point the two values of the lattice lines passing through it were set up, one on the upper and one on the lower time-base on the cathode tube. The aircraft was steered so that it cut the nearer of the two lines, when the pulse corresponding would line itself with the marker. Then the machine turned on to a course following the direction of this line until the second pulse which moved gradually to its marker if the aircraft was approaching the place was lined up. With both pulses in line with their respective markers the aircraft was over the target.

To return to our GH bombing. In order to iron out several variable factors which could alter from operation to operation it was necessary to have another stage between the starting of the run and the target. The first variable was "time of bomb fall" that had to be calculated by the bombing leader according to the load carried and the height from which the bombs were released. Another was the speed at which the aircraft was covering the ground. So the warning point was determined between starting the run and letting the bombs fall; a point calculated back along the curve and given to the navigators at briefing. The release point, where the bombs dropped away was sufficiently far away from the target to allow the bombs to fall on it.

Now since the distance between the warning point and the target was known the time required to pass over these two points would depend on the ground speed of the aircraft, the reliable estimation of which would depend on the navigator's work. This time, in seconds, was worked out by the navigator. Adjustment was made for the time of bomb fall and the final figure set on a clockwork mechanism which was screwed to the bulkhead.

The navigator reached the warning point by homing his aircraft, having set its co-efficients at the beginning of the run. When this was reached, and the pulses lined up, he pressed the bomb release. The clockwork counted out the correct delay and when it had run out completed the electric current circuit that fired the bomb release from the bomb bay.

The highest standards of flying discipline were necessary in order to make a success of an attack of this kind. There must be absolute co-operation between navigator and pilot. Any miscalculation of speed or course, any failure to set the correct values of the radar pulses or to track properly would be just as fatal as if the height from which the load was released were at fault. Once the button was pressed the pilot was compelled to hold course with iron rigidity, for going off heading would fling the load aside and make it miss the aiming point, while incorrect height meant undershoot or overshoot, flak or no flak!.

So what the ground stations did where the Oboe system of marking was employed was done by the aircraft under the GH system. Moreover, whereas Oboe was limited to vectoring only one aircraft at a time some 70 machines could use GH. This explains why our two Squadrons, 218 and 149, had the equipment. Obviously, an aircraft might release a flare as well as a bomb so we were employed as markers.

So much for the underlying theory. Now the practice.

Several days were spent in ground manipulation of the equipment. The next step of the training programme was to be simulated bombing using the camera instead of practice bombs. This meant waiting for a clear day when an operational aircraft could be spared, for the equipment was too precious to be reserved for training and Command were pressing a policy of equipping as many machines as possible.

We still needed experience with the Lancaster. Frank commenced to haunt the Flight Commander to get anything that was going in order to have the crew off the ground. We did air tests in weather which kept ops on the ground, taking advantage of the possibility of doing an hour of flying where five or six would be out of the question. We took part in an exercise with No. II Group fighters. This was fun. A formation of bombers flew down to Manston and Beachy Head escorted by Spitfires and all over the south-eastern region there were dummy attacks by the new Meteor jets. It was most exciting. The sky was full of fighters above and on our level, the jets darting in and out making mock attacks almost before our gunners could start their combat patter. The graceful Spitfires wheeled and turned and thundered past our wingtips as though we were standing still, but the Meteors had the heels of them and, opening up the throttles when they approached, fled down the sky like their namesakes leaving black plumes behind their engines.

Next day we were airborne again to do a navigational exercise using H2S. We were sent to the Lincolnshire area where there were some good coastlines to prevent our getting lost. Gee must not be used at all.

It was early afternoon, one of those days when the dull earth is shrouded by a layer of stratocumulus clouds and the sky is obscured from the ground. The mounting aircraft bursts through into dazzling, blazing sunshine, so glaring that one has to put on dark glasses. The sky is full of colour, exhilarating and the newly washed clouds roll away as far as the eye can see, fluffing up here and there, touched with yellow, prismatic almost, forming a floor to a world that is all your own, and calling you to dip in and out of them like a porpoise in the sea. Who could resist such a temptation, to charge a turret and see it melt in front of your eyes, to skate along the cloudtops so that the bomber seems to be possessed with the life and speed of a fighter, and then to pull up so that you can chase the reflection of your own machine as a shadow running away before you. To glimpse the green and brown patchwork of the fields through some gap as though you were looking through a peephole into Lilliput.

We beat up the clouds for the sheer joy of doing it before going home.

The Squadron had been to Köln, where they encountered a lot of flak. We were down and parked in dispersal before they started to come in so we saw the ambulance rush out. One of 149's machines had brought back a wireless operator whose leg had been blown off. Not a pretty sight, a hopeless case, poor devil. All they could do in the air was to put on a tourniquet and give him a few ampoules of morphia. A sickening experience for the crew and for the fitters who had to clean out the machine. He was dead, of course. We stood in a group, a short way off, and watched. It is a fact that although aircrew were used enough to the presence of death they had very little experience of dead men and this sobered us up.

But we could not be serious for long. As we returned to the billet a spirit of mischief prompted me to beguile Roy.

"Do you have any metal about you, Roy?" I asked. "You sit right over the top of the H2S scanner and all the afternoon I've been getting unaccountable permanent echoes on the screen."

Radar was a closed book to Roy. He looked a little guilty and said, "Well, I've got a bunch of keys ..."

Johnnie's shrewd North Country wit had grasped the situation immediately. He took a hand. "Well, we shall have to bond 'em. You know the aircraft is bonded to prevent odd discharges. Next time we go up we shall have to earth your keys for you."

"But what about the guns and the turrets", Roy objected "I'm sure you'd get more interference from them. A bunch of keys can't do much harm, surely."

"No! Everything in the aircraft is bonded. Everything."

"It's no good Roy", interjected the skipper. "If the nav. is getting interference you'll have to do what Johnnie says. Or leave them back at the billet." Of course everyone except him had realized what was happening.

So to our sheer delight, for the next two or three practice trips we flew Johnnie would solemnly take a length of copper wire, twist it round Roy's keys and connect it to the metal of the turret. While I would pretend to tune the H2S and say "Ah ... that's better ... no interference today. Thank you Roy."

When he found out he was mad as hell.

One morning I ran into Flavell coming out of the locker room with his gear slung around him and his bulging bag in his hand.

"Where are you going chum?"

"We're doing an H2S stooge. Have to keep your hand in you know."

"I do. They had us on one. Look here, do you mind if I come along and watch you at it. I might pick something up."

"If it's O.K. by the skipper it's O.K. by me."

So I went up with him, glad to see an old hand on the job. I took my sextant and divided my time between the radar set and shooting the sun. I found the dome of the Lancaster most difficult and restricted after the capacious Stirling, and the way it was faired into the cupola restricted forward observations. Nevertheless, I got some satisfactory shots and the practice was not wasted. I found the Astro-compass mounting to be a poor sort of affair, a pity, as this instrument was potentially most useful. But crews had got to the point by now of relying on radar almost to the total exclusion of the more artistic, but less accurate, astro navigation.

Chapter 10

BATTLE ORDER

On the last day of November, in clear weather, we took off on a simulated bombing detail. The exercise involved doing runs over a target practising navigator-pilot collaboration, the camera being exposed by the same movement of jabbing the button that normally sent down the bombs. The target on this first exercise had been chosen with the charitable idea of giving the pilot something on which to align the aircraft, for although we were not supposed to know what we were photographing - the button being pressed as the pulses lined up - after we had flown over Ely Cathedral two or three times it became obvious. The aiming point was the famous lantern tower, one of the glories of East Anglia.

The rate of travel of the pulses across the screen was much faster than that of the normal Gee pulse: hence the greater tracking possible. But the pilot's flying had to be that much more precise in order to hold the tracking pulse steady, and I soon found out that last minute corrections were fatal.

We ran backwards and forwards all the morning, Frank working hard at the controls and I with my eyes glued to the green glow of the tube trying to be sure of the left-hand edge of a wobbling blip. And Jack sitting in the bomb hatch highly amused and rather sarcastic when I forgot part of the patter for getting the bomb doors open. The rest of the crew were faintly bored.

After we landed, Jack detached the camera machine and took it to the Photographic Section with his flimsy. Frank and I reported in to learn that we were flying again in the afternoon. It was so difficult to get an aircraft available for training, that when one was, the Flight Commander worked it to death. As usual it was everything or nothing.

The afternoon target was an unidentifiable field near Wisbech - unidentifiable that is to us at nine thousand feet, so there was no possibility of the comforting assurance from the front that the target had passed under the aircraft when I said "Release pressed."

It was quite interesting and a little tricky, for the place had been chosen with an awkward cut of the chart lattice lines, so that the release pulse absolutely raced in at the last minute and I had to be very wary indeed. Our procedure improved and we kept at it as long as we could. By the time we had done twenty-seven runs everyone was glad to get back to earth.

Next morning we inspected our photographs and then went off to drop some practice bombs. Anyone who has seen it cannot fail to laugh at the sight of the huge, gaping bomb bay of a Lancaster loaded up with about a dozen practice bombs the size of Indian clubs. Still they go off with quite a flash and a good puff of smoke.

There was complete cloud cover over the bombing range which was an area off the coast of the Wash. We were at 15,000 feet. When we dropped a bomb we called over R.T. to the fellows in the plotting room down below, who sighted the burst with theodolites from two or three different stations and triangulated the result. We flew a miniature cross-country at bombing height in order to be sure of the wind velocity. All procedure was as if on a raid - starting point, warning point, the cry of "bombs gone", as Jack saw the missile fall away and disappear into the cloud. Five hundred feet below us Gussie Gordon and his crew were doing the same exercise and we could hear them calling the range from time to time.

The results were waiting for us in the bombing office when we came in.

Neither Gussie nor I had passed. Both of us had registered a compact group with the exception of one stray bomb. We had been bombing different co-efficients in order to keep our groups separated and both these strays were within the circumference of the other man's bombs.

"Damn it," said Frank to Gussie's pilot, "they've given us one of your bombs, Leslie".

Harlow smiled his charming smile but he made no comment.

"You can't trust these navigators. Bomb aiming is not for the like o' they", Riley said. He was Harlow's bombardier, a Scottish university graduate. In fact, both he and Jack were highly delighted at our discomfort, while Gussie Gordon and I shook our heads and muttered.

"You'll have to go up again tomorrow!" was the comment of the instructor.

"Look here, I'm sure I didn't boob", I said. "How about coming up with me and watching me do a few runs? I'd appreciate your advice".

"Well - fair enough! I'll be glad to. See you at nine in the morning."

Which meant that next day we did the whole performance again under the eye of the instructor. When the results were plotted we passed. In fact, we had passed twice for the bombing range telephoned while we were airborne to say they had mis-plotted two bombs the previous day. One of those occasions for which Tee Emm (training manual) had invented a special order.

So here we were, trained markers, with nothing to do but try it on the enemy. Harry put the matter in a nutshell. "It's time Sir Blenkin pressed on at night."

"Don't forget to look for the pretty lights on the ground", he added, recalling the extremely graphic description of night operations given by the Wing Commander to all new crews.

We all had a keyed up feeling, a sense that now all training was done there was no excuse for any more delay whatever. As a man standing on the edge of a swimming pool hesitates while he considers the temperature and then, knowing he has to go in, takes a deep breath and plunges.

Frank did his night second dickie and on Sunday evening as we looked at the notice board in the Mess hall we saw that our names were on the battle order.

My heart gave a queer kick. "Well", I thought, "here it is at last", but I said to Blenkin: "This'll shake the boys. Let's go and have a quickie at the bar."

"Only one", he replied. "Better get to bed early." Then like a good skipper he picked up the telephone to ring the Sergeants' Mess in order to be sure the remainder of the crew had seen the order.

I suppose that any casual observer who might have seen me pedalling slowly along the deserted perimeter would hardly have guessed the confused and conflicting feelings which possessed my mind. Certainly, the fitters who clustered around the black ominous bombers, working by lamplight in preparation for tomorrow's dawn, never spared us a glance. Frank had the advantage of me, with his two sorties, and on that account he had some limited experience which was a thing to be thankful for. We said little, being full of thought and in little mood for conversation. I found myself wondering from time to time what it would be like and then telling myself that I would soon find out.

Once in the hut I set about making what preparations were possible for the morning. I laid out my warm clothing, the underwear of mixed nylon and wool; the seaboot stockings and the heavy sweater; the boots themselves with their flapping sheepskin tops that could be cut off to leave an ostensible pair of shoes if one were forced down and had to become an evader. I checked the little knife in position in the back of the boot which was provided for this purpose.

Out of my trunk came a coloured silk square to be worn instead of a collar and tie, these being prohibited by order, (due to the risk of strangulation). Then I put into my hip pocket a silver flask containing brandy which my wife had given me when I came back from Canada. It is extremely bad to touch alcohol when flying, but there was always the prospect of a dinghy when it might be handy. In the end this flask met an unusual fate and its contents were wasted.

Finally, I got out my heavy clasp knife, emptied my pockets of everything except my small black cat mascot, checked I had my identity card and escape photographs and got to bed.

I tried to compose my mind with the idea of going to sleep but all sorts of thoughts came tumbling through my mind. What a strange war it was when a man could spend the night before action in a reasonably comfortable and warm bed. This was one of the striking incongruities of air force life, that it was possible to spend what amounted almost to a normal civilian evening and then plunge into the heart of some of the grimmest and costliest fighting of the war, only to be back to normal in a matter of hours. This constant switching from one area to the other required a peculiar kind of nervous force, quite different from the soldier in the field or the sailor constantly at watch at sea.

I watched the shadows from the fire dancing on the ceiling and somehow they reminded me of Plato's cave. I wondered whether all life up till now had in some way been unsubstantial, that it had existed merely to bring me to this present, a present which could certainly be decisive even so far as life itself were concerned. I wondered whether I should write to my wife and tell her that I was on operations at last and then I decided it would be better not to write at all. Finally, as the fire died down, I went to sleep.

We were shaken in the early hours of the morning by the persistent arm of the Orderly Corporal, whose unenviable duty it was to go the rounds of all crews on the detail. Blenkin and I reluctantly jumped out of bed, because the morning was raw, and after washing in freezing water, dressed hastily, wheeled out our bicycles from under the trees and cycled off to breakfast and briefing.

Here is the pattern of briefing. They were all cast in the same general mould and it would not be out of place to describe in general terms the course of this necessary prelude to an operation.

The briefing room was a long hut, barely furnished with collapsible tables and forms. The windows were blacked out to defeat prying eyes. At one end was a small rostrum for the briefing officials. There were the inevitable round iron stoves, which must have made a substantial fortune for some shrewd Boer-war contractor, and which generally filled the room with a haze of smoke when alight, although this fug barely rose above the level of the cigarette smoke once briefing started. Behind the platform the wall was covered with a huge map of Europe on which the Intelligence staff marked the battle line, the bomb line west of which nothing might be dropped and the various prohibited areas. Big blue and red blobs showed where flak guns and searchlights were to be expected. There was also a large-scale map of the area around base showing rendezvous points. The bare walls of the room were relieved with diagrams of all descriptions, ranging from instructions for abandoning aircraft to facetious warnings about walking into propellers and a timely poster borrowed from a French squadron showing an airman standing under a red lamp with the caption *"Ne pas oubliez de vider vos poches avant de partir en operations."*

Sometimes the number of tables provided would barely accommodate the number of crews on the battle order. Navigation briefing started a good hour before main briefing and the old hands among the navigators would arrive half-an-hour earlier still. The key of the room was begged from the Intelligence officer and one by one the front tables claimed. The only time an airman shows any inclination to sit near the front.

Once a table had been claimed the navigator went to the parachute cloakroom for a Mae West and a 'chute. He then returned, using any spare time to get out his instruments and sharpen pencils, of which if he had any sense he carried an adequate supply in a suitable tin.

The Intelligence clerks would bring in rolls of charts, topographical maps for map-reading and large-scale target maps for the bombardiers. They would have a copy of the form which came over the teleprinter network from Group with details of the route and target. The Flight Sergeant would chalk up the route on a blackboard and trace it on the wall map with coloured tape.

By now the time for main briefing had almost come and the crews began to pass the policeman at the door. The navigators had already inked the route on to their charts. Meanwhile the Briefing Officer had been at the Planning Room in the Control Tower, where the Station Navigation Officer and the Squadron Commander would have received instructions over a private scrambled telephone from Group HQ. The former received all details of route and tactics for the raid, with ancillary information concerning the use of radar and countermeasures, and if it were a daylight operation of forming up, including the names of leaders of the Vic formations and their points of rendezvous with their followers.

The Navigation Officer would then go to the meterological section, usually on the same floor of the tower, where he would obtain the weather forecast, wind velocities and temperatures en route. These forecasts were from Group also, in order to ensure uniformity of Flight Plan between the various squadrons.

He would proceed from there to Navigation briefing leaving the Station Navigation Officer to work out a complete Flight Plan for the trip. Simultaneously, the Group Navigation Officer, a very exalted man, would do the same and before the gathering was over the estimate of time at each concentration point en route would be checked with that of the SNOP by four of the best navigators in the detail and in turn with the times found at Group. Thus there was check and double check to eliminate any possibility of error.

Directly the navigators had the necessary information to produce their flight plans they compiled the preliminaries on their charts, measuring directions of the various legs and distances between each turning point and set to work with their computers. Using the forecast winds and temperatures they would arrive at true airspeed from the brief indicated and decided what courses would have to be steered. They would calculate how long it would take to climb to height, the time to be spent on each leg and, working back from "H" hour when the bombs should fall on the target, calculate to the decimal point of a minute the time at which they should set course.

There were standard log sheets issued on which all this detail was entered, including the orders and the error if any of one's watch which in any case would be synchronized with Greenwich during the briefing. There were seventeen columns to each log and it was usual to complete a pro-forma for the out-ward journey and another for the return. The navigators didn't stop working at briefing. Bomb aimers, as they trickled in, would seat themselves beside their navigators and trace tracks on their maps and radar charts. The bomb aimer was the primary eye for map reading.

All quiet disappeared when Main Briefing was due as an avalanche of some 150 bodies struggled into the room. Laughter, conversation and the sound of forms being knocked over disturbed the peace. Crews positioned themselves and inquired eagerly as to the target, expressing pleasure or dismay as the case may be on being told. Gunners would want to know the temperature at height so that they could decide on suitable clothing. The Bombing and Signals leaders would walk through the room distributing instruction leaflets to their charges. The skippers would have a perspex covered miniature chart on which they would draw the route in coloured pencil. This fixed in their minds some idea of where they were going. Pleased and exhausted by such complicated work they would then go off to draw the sweet ration for the crew.

"Quiet - Quiet!" The Wing Commander had mounted the rostrum and commenced his briefing. First he called on the Intelligence Officer who detailed the nature of the target. The strategical importance and any production, if there was any. If, and when, the target was last attacked. What defences might be expected, enemy spoof targets and the nature of any diversionary sweeps. All these were in the province of Intelligence. He pinned up large maps and photographs and pointed out the aiming point and the direction of bombing. This had been decided with reference to a number of factors such as wind direction and the topography of the target area; also the possible destructive value of any undershoot or overshoot, for it had been found that visual bombing showed a tendency to creep.

Intelligence officers always struck me as being rather bloodthirsty, and the lighthearted way in which they would say "You will only find ten heavy flak batteries at this point ..." was a source of ironical amusement to crews, as was also the opening gambit: "The last time we were here ...." or "We are on at 14.00 hrs. today ...." when everybody knew he would be in the Mess bar or having a cup of tea in his office. For all that Intelligence seemed very well informed and seldom underestimated the chances of enemy fighters or the defences that might be encountered.

After Intelligence, Met. said his piece. Armed with a synoptic chart whose bold contours he displayed to all he explained what weather might be expected along the route. The upper air is an uncertain medium and forecasting a thankless task. It was the habit of Met. officers to understate difficulties, if anything, on the assumption that there is no point in making matters appear too black. However, he pointed out the types of cloud to be expected, the cover and the icing risks, and he usually got a string of questions about visibility.

The Wing Commander then went over everything again. As he talked people continued to work with one ear open in case there was anything new. Questions were invited, formation details given. Finally, he finished and the SFCO gave the pilots the time they would have to take off and which runway was in use and how they were to taxi around the perimeter.

Last of all the Group Captain, the "Stationmaster" with "Good luck chaps and a good trip."

All this had taken quite two hours. There was a surge of conversation as the crews became suddenly animated. Pilots handed round rations, gunners went off to get dressed, navigators compared charts and the WAAF of the Intelligence staff, who could be trusted to keep silent, brought in cups of tea. Personal belongings were put into numbered bags until one returned. A mild confusion reigned.

Gradually the crews made their way out to the waiting transports, loaded up with gear, and were taken to the aircraft. Only the navigators were left in the briefing room, waiting for final concentration times and for their flimsies with secret information. These must be kept from the enemy at all costs and are made of edible paper so they could be swallowed in emergency ...!

Nor was the pre-flight preparation finished when the crew arrived at dispersal. The motors had to be run up while each man checked his own equipment. Pilot and engineer tested the controls, checked fuel, oxygen and air, and looked at their multitude of dials and gauges. The navigator would have to synchronize the compasses and check the radar; the wireless operator his sets. Meanwhile, the bombardier having arranged the window load to his satisfaction, went over the bomb load and saw to his panel and sight. The gunners rotated their turrets, elevated and depressed guns, checked ammunition boxes and feeds and if possible rattled off a burst into a nearby sandpit. Everybody checked intercom and his own oxygen regulator.

Then, and only then, might there be a few moments of relaxation. The engineer could take a last look around the outside of the machine, kick a tyre and see that the pitot-head cover was off. Someone would go under the bomb-bay and maybe scribble a message on a bomb. The ground crew stood around with the trolley accumulator for starting the motors. Now and then a staff car might come up with, possibly the Group Captain with a last word. Then the navigator called "Fifteen minutes to take-off skipper". The gunners put on their outer suits. Mae Wests were checked, harnesses fastened, finally.

And last of all you might see seven bundled-up bulky figures standing on the edge of the tarmac dispersal pan together, gaily relieving themselves in unison before they climbed the ladder into the aircraft.

Chapter 11

FIRST OPERATIONS

On December 4th, 1944, the briefing was filled with a sense of urgency. Time pressed and the proceedings had to be rushed. Possibly the operation had been put on at such short notice that full details were only available at the last moment. The target was in the town of Oberhausen in the western part of the Ruhr and we were after the big railway junction where four main lines bottle-necked through one station. It was a daylight attack.

The Intelligence officer had a huge black moustache and a last-war wing. He had a long list of alternative objectives within the town that might be blasted by undershoots or overshoots. It was to be blind bombing. I found myself looking up from my chart at that moustache when he suddenly read out Frank's name as having been allotted a marker flare.

"God!", I thought. "Bit of a responsibility, having to mark our first target."

I was further perturbed when Met. handed over the Form 2330, the forecast, and I saw that the wind strength was expected to reach the hurricane force of 120 miles per hour. I hated having to work at these high speeds, firstly because I already had a little experience of them and was apprehensive of their effect on track keeping. Also the computers we used would only take a wind-speed of eighty because, when the instruments were designed early in the war, flying in winds of greater strength was probably almost unknown. So it was necessary to do proportion sums when using the computer with high winds, a nuisance and a probable source of error.

My flight planning was slow. I was over-anxious. I carefully checked everything with the veteran Flavell, who grinned and gave me good advice.

"Don't leave it too late to switch over to GH. Do it here", stubbing the chart with his forefinger, "and write your course out of the target against the tracks. You probably won't have time to work out any fresh ones, first Op."

Gratefully, for I was a trifle conscious of rawness, I fell in with his suggestions. At length I packed my green canvas bag and struggled into an overladen perimeter bus that was crowded with silent, thoughtful, men. The navigators going out to their aircraft.

I reached the dispersal with little time to spare. Harry was in trouble with the rear turret which had a door jammed and he and Johnnie were working on it. I took little notice but clambered in and went up the fuselage making my checks and talking to myself. "Master Unit says 140. 'A' minus five. Scanner heater on. H2S modulator off - VCP on. Verey pistol in", and pulling my gear heavily over the spars I sat at the table and started to unload my bag.

Directly I plugged in my helmet I could hear Harry talking to the skipper, commenting violently on the state of the turret door. New crews had to have whatever aircraft was spare, and usually these had seen some wear and tear. I checked my instruments and set out my chart. Aircraft were already taxiing along the perimeter and there was the constant beat of motors. The first took off, then the second and the regular procession began, sound rising in great screaming waves as the motors took the load and accelerated the machines down the runway.

Johnnie seized an axe and used it on the turret door in a final effort to make it work. He and the rigger wrenched at it and suddenly it came right away. There is nothing between the rear gunner and empty space but this same door when the turret is swung on the beam and Harry couldn't fly without it.

Frank gave quick orders. We should have to take the spare Lancaster.

He dashed out of the aircraft to the Flight Office to telephone for transport, while I cursed the whole race of gunners and packed my paraphernalia back into the bag.

Things happen with surprising rapidity in cases like this. A crew bus came tearing up as fast as the WAAF could drive it and we were whisked to another dispersal. Flying Control had already warned the ground crew; in the few minutes it took us to arrive they had started up the motors. The slipstream caught at my legs as I climbed in. There was no time to check anything. Frank ran her up, signed the Form 700 and taxied out immediately.

In a way this was a good thing. It was our first loaded take-off and had events taken a more placid course Frank would probably have been prey to all sorts of anticipations. As it was he whipped the thirty tons off the ground without batting an eyelid. The gyro in the master compass had toppled and my repeater dial was going round and round without any sense of direction as we climbed off the runway and I gave him the first course to set on the magnetic compass in his cockpit.

At this point No. 3 Group had not developed any elaborate forming up procedure. This was to come. At this period an aircraft arrived at a rendezvous point near the East Anglian coast, at Bury St. Edmunds or Newmarket perhaps, and set course at a given time in gaggles, following the leader of the attack. In daylight operations captains arranged themselves more or less as they found convenient and the raid went out in a loose stream. This procedure was very much the same as for a night sortie except for the fact that being able to see the other aircraft made things much easier. Navigation on a daylight raid almost reduced itself to plotting only, for the pilots followed the man in front anyway.

We made the rendezvous in time and arrived at the English coast with the others. Jack fused and selected the bombs before the French coastline passed below. We started climbing to bombing height and were forced to connect our masks to the oxygen supply. I found that we were getting much lighter winds than we expected for when we levelled out at 20,000 feet it was blowing eighty miles per hour and no more. Which pleased me although it meant asking for more airspeed.

The skipper's track-keeping left something to be desired. When I complained he snarled:

"I'm following the man in front."

"Well, he's off track too."

"For Pete's sake stop niggling, nav."

We picked up our fighter escort over enemy territory. As I told the gunners to expect them I thought suddenly and vividly that we should be in the Ruhr in under half an hour. Then, as I noticed the inked reminder on my chart I told the bombardier to start nickelling, the name given to the inane practice of thrusting out propaganda leaflets.

"OK". Jack commenced to push out leaflets. I kept one. My limited German just enabled me to make out that it was a sort of I-told-you-so to the enemy army deployed below us as we dumped the stuff overboard. It told of the destruction of Aachen after the Americans had offered it the chance of surrendering. The same fate was promised for Köln, Trier and Münster - all the cities of the Rheinland - unless the Germans turned against their leaders and gave up an unequal struggle. "*Die Wahl liegt bei Euch.*"

"Probably do more damage if we forgot to undo the bundles", was Jack's comment as he saw the leaflet storm fluttering away on all sides.

We had now reached the last leg before the run in and I commenced to set up my bombing equipment. I went through the drill in my mind saying to myself: "Let me see, turn oscillator knob until the Gee pulses are steady. OK. .... R.F. 27? Yes." Then aloud, after knocking his arm with a ruler to attract his attention, "Aerial Loading Unit to stud 7 please Turner."

Then to myself again: "Now, transmitter on", flicking the switch "Time-base speed OK? Yes! Ghost pulse on upper trace", moving the appropriate knob to see that it was. "All set!"

Since I had done nothing but practice this drill for the past week things went smoothly. There was my own pulse and there the returning signals from the British transmitters, not nearly so powerful as mine but flickering distinctly on the strobe markers just where they should be, moving gently in as the bomber approached the commencement of the run.

At this stage of a blind bombing attack a navigator had to work very quickly and methodically. He had to find a good bombing wind at his final height, so that he could calculate the last course into the target and the heading to hold as the bombs were released. He must work out the time delay between pressing the button and letting them go. He had to work out the first two short legs out of the target and the time at which to turn. And he must not for one moment relax his watch on the radar screen.

"Navigator to skipper. Pulses coming in OK ...".

"Good show, navigator."

I gave him the change of course to take us in. "Go round now; here we go chaps." Each man tracked individually from this point if he were a marker and the machine was under my direction. I reset the value of the release point and changed to a faster time base for greater accuracy. With the tracking pulse in line we would be flying a gentle curve and constant small corrections to course must be made to hold it.

"Five port!"

"Five port it is." The compass answered by moving.

"Left - left, five more!"

"OK - steady now."

"Hold her skipper, you're doing fine."

A small voice came from Frank. "Flak opening up ahead." No one took any notice.

When the release pulse was so close that it was necessary to change to extended time base, the fastest of all, I ordered ...

"Bomb doors open!"

This was the worst moment of the trip. In theory all aircraft should pass over the same spot and during thirty odd miles of run in the stream had converged until aircraft were absolutely on top of each other above and below and indeed at the sides. The flak was warming up, black puffs dotting the sky all around. Directly the bomb doors opened the rush of cold air told us that even the flimsy protection they provided was removed and the load was hanging naked to the sky.

The skipper repeated: "Bomb doors open."

I gave: "Course 109 True. Hold it." I was gripped with the intense excitement of the moment and heard him repeat the course as though he were in a different world. My whole being was focused and caught up in the release pulse now moving across the screen for the last, fatal half inch. There was nothing else but the insistence of it. I heard myself saying mechanically: "Steady - steady, hold it!" and then my heart thumped, my finger sought the button and pressed it decisively and I called:

"Release pressed. Steady."

Blenkin held her. The clockwork, upon whose perfection lay the chance of life or death in the town below, whirred away although no one could hear it. The electric relays closed; the distributor arms started their travel across the boxes in the bomb hatch. All the beautiful and diabolical ingenuity for releasing the bombs came into play. And suddenly the aircraft kicked and lurched as the load began to fall away. Fifteen bombs, comprising eleven thousand pounds of destruction, were on the way down.

Jack called: "All bombs gone. Jettison bars across."

"Bomb doors closed."

"Camera turned over."

"Course 332 True, 339 P.4. Speed 175." Answering by instinct as obedient as the working of the machine itself, the crew completed the bombing run and we turned from the target. I said: "Eight minutes to run on this course. Keep the window going."

Like a man coming out of a daze I sat back. Turner moved from his place over the cookie back to his seat, leaving the space under the astrodome clear. I got up and put my head in the dome hoping to be able to see as far down as possible. The flexible tubing of the oxygen hose held my head so I took a deep breath and undid it. There was a ring of sweat around my face. Fifteen thousand feet below stretched an unbroken undulation of stratocumulus cloud. Ahead and behind the bombers swam in the clear sunlight, those over the target shedding their heavy loads. Black bursts exploded in the air as though some giant pepperpot were being shaken over the area and when the Hun detectors managed to fasten on either an individual or a group of aircraft the predicted bursts sought too close and the bombers weaved to avoid. There were no enemy aircraft to be seen, the flashes of light way above were glinting from our own escort.

It was my first target. I wanted to see as much as possible and I was unreasonably annoyed to think that I had come all the way to Germany only to look at a bank of cloud however pretty, and a lot of flak bursts. I spared myself perhaps a couple of minutes turning my head all around and then I went back to the semi-darkness of the cabin, refixing my mask and breathing deeply.

No matter how compact the stream had been on the way out once it is through the target it always spreads and dissolves into small elements as the more impetuous pilots decide to get home first. Once out of immediate danger and the bombing orders fulfilled some relaxation of formation was possible and the machines flew as individuals for the sake of economy in engines. With the Lancaster equipped to do both day and night work formation flying was very hard on engines and even as it was the number of changes after any full-time raid was a terrible drain on the technical resources of the Command. Co-operation between pilot and engineer and a carefully managed descent would put an aircraft ahead of others not so well handled, apart from the few extra revs., which might be put on the counters.

We had not learned the tricks of the trade. Johnnie would never cane an engine anyway. Nor was there much attention to good track-keeping. Excitement, excessive concentration, left me dull when the Rhein was passed and on looking at the chart afterwards I was horrified to see how little I had done on the way back. We returned from Oberhausen with considerable dignity and landed at last. I was not a little relieved to hear Frank say: "Cut - cut", as we touched down on our field.

It was now late afternoon. The bomber lumbered into her dispersal, was marshalled into place and the engines run up and shut down. Seven weary men, grimy faced, stiff from sitting in confined spaces, collected their gear and made their way to the door. The ground crew clustered around the foot of the ladder eagerly questioning:

"Any damage to report?"

"What were the instruments like?"

"Where was the target, sir?"

These and a dozen other queries, and while some of the crew lit up their much anticipated cigarettes the ground staff lads commenced an immediate inspection of the aircraft. One set of human servants of the monster made their way to the bus while another swarmed over her, bowsers filling the tanks, oxygen wagon pumping in the gas, electrical generators chugging away and the fitters scrambling over the wings and removing the engine covers.

That evening we gathered up our belongings and packed our bags. As Blenkin remarked, we had been in one place for the duration of a month, which was by way of being a record judged by any criterion of our past. In one place was too good to last. The Squadron had been ordered to Chedburgh.

We were not sorry to leave our miserable barn of a hut in the woods; or to dispense with the rain-soaked cycle ride in the mornings to the Mess. We knew of Chedburgh where we had flown Stirlings on Heavy Conversion Unit and Methwold held no ties of sentiment for us.

The pilots agreed to give the field a good beating up as 218 departed. This was done in fine style. Aircraft took off in rapid succession, one leaving the runway, one halfway down and one turning on, a beautiful clockwork procedure which was very rarely allowed because of the obvious danger. They flew round the circuit and then, one after the other, put the noses down, aimed for the control tower and came screaming down like fighters. I was as thrilled as a schoolboy to see the ground coming up and the tower getting larger and larger until it flashed away underneath as Frank pulled out. This was one of my holiday trips. The machine we had was a brand new Lancaster Mark III lettered M for Mike that had been put down by the ATA only a couple of days before. It had no special equipment aboard and hadn't even been swung. Since the compasses could not be considered reliable we found our way to Chedburgh by simple map reading.

Johnnie O'Brien, the Flight Commander, had given us Mike for our very own aircraft that morning.

We carried our luggage with us. The body of the machine was full of cases and bicycles. All the way Frank and I were contemplating the appealing prospect of the food in the Chedburgh mess; we kept congratulating each other on the prospect of that worthy sergeant who acted as chef and was so well known to the local farmers; who always served three different meats at meals and who cut such beautiful slices from his well-cooked joints, and with such flourish.

A stand-down from operations was given for the next few days to enable everyone to settle into their new surroundings. There was an enormous amount to do, particularly for the engineering staffs who had to move in the innumerable spares required by an operational unit.

Blenkin and I made ourselves comfortable in a Nissen hut by the time-honoured practice of commandeering all the extra furniture we could lay our hands on as well as surmounting the wire of the coke dump after darkness to get hold of a little fuel. We were in a regulation hut this time, with two other fellows, and in the little room by the entrance, originally intended for the Corporal in charge of the occupants, was a bombardier who had got there first.

For myself, I was not sorry to have this break as it gave me time to digest the lessons of the first raid and get used to the idea of operations.

By the morning of December 8th, the Squadron was ready again and in order to convince us, if conviction was required, the powers that be dragged us out of bed at 3 am to brief us for Duisberg.

Duisburg is on the Rhein, at the western end of the Ruhr. It was the biggest river port in Europe, in fact the size of the port installations would do justice to most seaports. More, it was normally an important rail centre. It had its own aerodrome, was touched by the autobahn, and had figured prominently in the battle of the Ruhr since 1940.

Our target was the marshalling yards. We were in the first wave of the attack, earning our experience quickly; we carried a flare as target markers and a beautiful load of thirteen one-thousand pound bombs, all high-explosive.

There happened on this trip a circumstance, amusing enough in retrospect, that might well have cost us dear.

We had plenty of time before take-off. We had done all the checks and run up, the aircraft, B-Baker for our own was being fitted. The fellows stood aimlessly at the edge of the dishpan away from the aircraft so that they could smoke. While I was amusing myself looking at the bomb-bay a Control officer drove up and beckoned the pilot aside, saying a few words to him.

We took off comfortably. Our orders were to go to a detailed rendezvous and pick up three followers who were to join formation with us making a Vic with one in the box. They would follow closely through the target and since they were unprovided with blind bombing equipment would release their bombs as ours went down.

Climbing to the rendezvous we ran into light flurries of snow and cloud. There were heavy wintry clouds everywhere and the thermometer was low. Frank kept away from them as much as possible because of the risk of icing, and when we were forced to enter cloud he climbed as fast as possible. In the vicinity of the rendezvous we were flying in clear air although the sombre, slowly writhing heaps of cumulus stretched and piled as far as the eye could see. Alone and small, hemmed in by this monstrous pageantry, we commenced a tight orbit waiting for the followers.

After some time Harry reported: "There's a Lanc. starboard quarter down, skipper."

"Good show. That's number one!" and indeed it was, for he closed up and joined us in the orbit and his wireless operator started exchanging lamp signals with Turner.

The time went by. I commenced to advise: "Ten minutes to set course, skipper", and then "Five minutes", and there was no sign of the others.

"Probably held up because of the snow." Frank commented.

"We'll have to set course in two minutes skipper. Put 112 on your compass and go round now."

At ETA the British coast came up, where we should converge into the stream, I asked: "Any sign of the others?"

"One or two ahead. I can't see much in this damned cloud."

"Well, we're OK for position and time", I replied. "Course is 125, turn on now. Airspeed 165, height nine thousand. Better press on."

We were all surprised at not finding more aircraft about but I checked and re-checked position and time and was certain we were right.

"Ask the W.OP if there's been any recall", said the skipper.

When he came on the intercom, the wireless operator answered that he had picked up nothing at all. Of course he could not break wireless silence to call Base.

"When do we climb?" asked Frank.

"At three degrees East."

"I'll have to go up a bit now to dodge this stuff. Better go on the oxygen everybody. And give me twenty-six fifty Johnnie."

Turner unscrewed the main oxygen cock. As each man adjusted his mask he reported ...

"Rear gunner oxygen OK", and so on through the crew. Whenever this performance happened I was invariably in the middle of taking a fix. It was, I am sure, the same for all navigators.

As the Continental coast approached I kept repeating, "Any sign of the others?"

"Only our follower."

"What about those you could see ahead?"

"Can't see them now. I believe one of them turned back."

"I'm certain we're OK for time. Can't understand it."

We pressed on, clearing the cloud tops at 16,000 feet and continuing at this altitude until we were halfway across Holland. I was worried. Here we were getting near the Rhein with no sign of anyone else, when Turner came on the intercom. and remarked:

"Ah canna hear the eleven o'clock broadcast."

Frank answered almost casually, "Well you'll get it at eleven-thirty. H hour has been put back half an hour."

"God Almighty", I shouted. "You didn't tell me. We're half an hour ahead of time." I thought quickly. "Turn on reciprocal", giving him the course.

There was no doubt that the enemy radar had picked us up by this time for we were a bare twenty miles from the frontier and just about over the battle line. At our height we could be picked up a hundred miles from the detector. If the enemy had any anticipation that we were the forerunners of a raid he would have no difficulty in putting up a squadron of Messerschmitts to patrol across our route. But two bombers would not make a very large blip on a detector screen and we might very well be taken for an Allied patrol if we acted accordingly. Over to our starboard side was Antwerp, in British hands, and cloud was only about five-tenths so we could be seen from the ground. It would be an easy point to circle and a logical one.

"What do you want me to do nav?" Frank asked.

"Can you see Antwerp to starboard? I think we had better orbit there and wait for the others to come along."

"OK good idea."

"No point in putting IFF on. There's nothing thereabouts to pick us up."

"They'll see us from the ground. I say, nav., I'm sorry about this. You were out of the way when I was told of the delay and I clean forgot to mention it when we got into the kite."

So we stooged around the port for half an hour, closely followed by our faithful satellite who undoubtedly thought us mad. Then the vanguard of the raid could be picked up, making their relentless way eastwards.

Relieved and thankful we relinquished the idea of making a private attack on Germany and joined the procession, climbing up to our bombing height of eighteen thousand four hundred feet. The temperature was now down to minus 40 centigrade, equivalent to 72 degrees of frost. The gunners complained of cold in spite of their electrically heated clothing. Down below the heaped-up clouds gave way to uniform stratocumulus, with the promise of complete cover over the target. Then came the repetition of our previous bombing experience, the turning in to the target, the bunching aircraft and the tension of tracking, the danger from all sides. There was the same nakedness of open bomb doors and the excitement of lining up the pulses, pressing home the black button and feeling the welcome kick-kick as the bombs fell off.

The bomb doors shut, the camera light winked and we were through.

Jack shone the Aldis lamp into the bomb bay to check that all had gone. He said: "There are two bombs hung up, skipper." A moment afterwards and "thump" one of them dropped on to the doors of the bomb bay, which took the weight without coming apart. The releases had been choked with ice, failing to fire.

We could feel the bomb rolling about in the bay, a most uncomfortable feeling for it was fused, although all the time the vanes remained on the detonating pistol it would not go off.

"Pilot to navigator. Any likely targets coming up?"

"There's Krefeld - a couple of minutes ahead on track."

"Good enough. We'll drop it there". So we opened the bomb doors as we passed over. We dropped the other one in the jettison area east of Southwold after Jack and Turner had done a certain amount of work on the release with a piece of bent wire pushed down through the floor. We were in cloud before we crossed the English coast and had not broken through by the time we were over base. We finally came out at 300 feet which was uncomfortably near the ground, but we got in safely.

I came to the conclusion that on Ops there was never a dull moment.

Next afternoon we did a fighter affiliation exercise. After landing we found ourselves on a night detail with very little time before it was necessary to get ready for briefing. The target was to be Leipzig.

Before the war a great annual trade fair was held in this town and I knew several German business men who were regular exhibitors. They were serious, mild-mannered men; jewellers in civil life; like myself, eager for trade, honest and obliging by nature.

I experienced some pangs of anxiety as the briefing developed for Leipzig is a lot farther east than the Ruhr and you are all on your own at night. However, the operation was scrubbed owing to bad weather moving over England from the west.

"Well, we've had an egg anyway, and now we can get another supper", Blenkin remarked philosophically.

The bad weather had developed by morning. It was raining and the rain continued all day so that we did nothing but kick our heels in the Flights. Such days, called "Satan's Days" by the Air Ministry, were utilized for practical work with a broom at Chedburgh.

We made one more flight, an H2S cross-country which took us stooging around the Wash with Jack trying hard at the set but unable to say whether his responses were from Boston or King John's jewels; which legend relates were lost there. Then we went on leave.

On Tuesday December 12th the Squadron went to Witten and ran into the Hun. Harlow was leading a Vic of three with Herapath in the box. As they were running up to the target, with bomb doors already open, Harlow's mid-upper gunner spotted and identified three Messerschmitt 109s standing off on a parallel course at about a thousand yards range. The fighters wasted no time but immediately flipped over and developed a perfect curve-of-pursuit attack, picking one bomber apiece and leaving Herapath, who however put his nose down and dived straight out of the box. He was pounced on below, shot up, and was seen disappearing through the clouds leaving a great trail of smoke. Some of his crew were taken prisoner.

When the Messerschmitts had closed to 600 yards Leslie Harlow heard his rear gunner give the word to go and corkscrewed to port violently. At the same time his mid-upper let their particular enemy have it. The rear gunner only got six rounds away when an hydraulic leak stopped his guns firing. But the mid-upper shot the enemy down in spite of the fact that one of his two guns had a stoppage which he was able to clear immediately. The Lancaster on the starboard side, whose crew I knew as comrades at OTU went down in flames. The other follower was holed in the No. 1 port side tank but he stuck gamely to Harlow through the complicated movements of the corkscrew, his guns blazing away splendidly and he registered strikes on both a 109 and a Messerschmitt 140, a twin engined fighter which broke off the action and disappeared through cloud, being claimed as destroyed although proof in such cases was hard to establish.

As the German attack opened, every bomber in the vicinity fired off a red Verey cartridge, signalling our own fighters. The Mustangs came down at full bore and two of them joined in this particular *mêlée* but one was shot down immediately.

Harlow hadn't even time to close his bomb doors. The Lancaster took it without a murmur although the increased drag, particularly on the first dive of the corkscrew, must have been very great. As they straightened up with the fighters beaten off, they could see aircraft in their own vicinity trying to get back into position in time to bomb. They finished their run as well as they could. Gussie's navigation gear was all over the inside of the aircraft and his Gee charts had disappeared entirely, probably sucked through the floor of the bomb bay.

M for Mike, our brand new aircraft, was shot up and lost an engine. Fuel leaks developed. Torn between the desire to advise Base and the wish to keep the plight of his crippled aircraft from the enemy the pilot decided to make for the North Sea, send a message as soon as he left land and make every effort to reach the nearest point of the British coast. But their petrol was running away fast. They started to call the British MF direction finding stations, and finally sent an SOS as they made ready to ditch in the water.

A Mustang saw their predicament, circled them as they descended and when they hit the water commenced to patrol above them. The CHL shore stations must have noticed this.

The impact, which was sharp in spite of a skilful ditching, must have forced the carbon-dioxide bottle out of its fitting for the dinghy didn't open automatically. Stott, navigator, who was second man out of the aircraft and whose duty it was to assist the engineer in seeing the dinghy inflated, ripped open the panel on the starboard wing, put his hand in and groping for the bottle found the valve which he turned forcibly. He might have been more gentle for the expanding gas, rushing out, froze his fingers to the bottle and as he pulled his hand away he lost a certain amount of skin. He was spurred on by the water which was lapping over the wing. The little boat inflated, they scrambled in and cut the painter and pushed off.

Luckily, the sea was not running high. The fighter still circled above them. As they drifted away the aircraft sank lower in the water, the tail heaved up a little and it disappeared.

They organized themselves as they had been taught. Later the Mustang waggled his wings in farewell as he was replaced by a Spitfire.

They then knew that help must be well on the way and that the ordeal should not be for long.

Ditching in the sea had been brought to a fine art by the Royal Air Force and rescue was a triumph of organization. While Warwick's crew made themselves as comfortable as possible in their yellow rubber craft, let us glance at Air-Sea rescue.

The rubber dinghy, stored in the wing of the Lancaster, could be inflated by pulling a release in any of three places inside the aircraft, as well as one by the door outside, or it would be blown up automatically by chemical action of the salt water on an immersion switch once the aircraft hit the sea. Great ingenuity had been exercised in providing a pack containing tinned water and emergency rations, signal pistol and flares and a host of other necessities including fishing lines. The dinghy had a collapsible mast carrying an antenna and there was a small radio transmitter nicknamed the "Yellow Peril", waterproofed and made to float if it fell in. There was also a long aerial which might be hoisted on a kite.

The ditched crew could put up a sail even if they had never seen a boat in their lives, for all instructions were printed on the sheet and the cordage was of distinct colouring, red for port stays, green for starboard and so on. A rubber bag below the body of the little dinghy filled with water and acted as a stabiliser, while there was a rubber keel kept taut by the foot of the tubular mast. An aluminium rudder and a trailing bag for a sea anchor completed the rig.

Crews knew exactly what to do. They had been drilled and lectured endlessly. Once they were in they pulled the weather apron over them to keep out the sea as far as possible and they had only to turn the handle of the radio set to grind out a continual SOS on the International Distress Frequency. They could even erect the mast of an automatic radar transmitter which would send out signals to Coastal Command machines.

The North Sea is very cold in winter. Their job was to keep warm, carry out exercises of the limbs to maintain circulation, go easy on the rations and keep up each other's morale. They could wait to be picked up with fair certainty that it would not be long.

Directly the shore-based ASR organization received the message which the aircraft sent before ditching it got to work. The DF stations plotted the track of the aircraft as did the radar chain if distress signals were shown by the aircraft's IFF. As he sent his last message the wireless operator screwed down his key - the set sent out a continuous note until it failed or sank. This gave a fairly accurate last position to the shore.

The Controllers got to work to estimate how the dinghy would drift and took whatever action their experience dictated. They had at their disposal in Britain aircraft available to sweep as far out as possible, to locate the dinghy and drop supplies; even a motor driven lifeboat could be parachuted down. There was complete liaison with the navy for the diversion of vessels. There was the RAF fleet of high speed launches. The service even extended to hollow floats moored around our shores providing reasonable living room and and excellent packed rations. Since there was also brandy and rum everybody hoped that if they did ditch it would be near a float.

After all this it would be a very hard luck to be picked up by a German E boat!

Warwick's crew, then, sat tight in their dinghy. They were picked up by a launch after they had been afloat two hours. Apart from the navigator's fingers their only damage was ruined clothing. Each Mae West contained a flourescent block intended to colour the sea yellow to help identification. As the water had got at them they all looked like Chinamen. It was their first operation. They were given survivors' leave immediately. But for our being on leave it might have been us and our fine new Lancaster was gone for ever.

Weeks afterwards the army captured the Hauptmann of the German squadron that attacked our fellows.

When Intelligence questioned him he made some illuminating remarks. He said that his formation had been waiting to intercept the Americans when they saw our stream of bombers. He knew it was British because of its ragged nature, in fact even towards the end of the daylight attacks we never approached the perfection of American formation flying. He thought that the Lancasters that corkscrewed were out of control and left them alone after the initial dive. Probably he wished to conserve ammunition as much as possible for the next target. This failure of pursuit is rather surprising for one would have expected a fighter pilot, particularly, to have appreciated such an evasive manoeuvre, but if the statement were true the enemy could have had little idea of what we were doing at night and it is a compliment to the mastery of tactics which our Command had. It was rarely necessary to go through a complete corkscrew to shake off a fighter, particularly at night, their guns being fixed.

The Hauptmann confirmed Leslie Harlow's kill, but said that those claimed by the H.4 aircraft had crash-landed.

Chapter 12

ARDENNES EPISODE

Leave is a time for leaning up against a bar with a pint pot. It is also a time when one can read the newspapers over the breakfast table, a form of bad manners that I enjoy. It was in this way that I learned of the German push against the American 9th army in the Ardennes.

This was the last desperate fling of the war by Hitler and the only time after the landings in Normandy that the initiative passed temporarily to the enemy.

Undoubtedly they had taken to heart those words of Clauswitz: "The attacks should be like a wedge well driven home, not like a soap bubble which distends itself until it bursts", for the push was on a restricted front in difficult terrain and in some ways it was this restricted front which gave opportunity to the allied air arm.

The Germans either had a rare stroke of luck or their long-range forecasting was extremely shrewd for the attack came very near to achieving its objective and not a little of its initial success was due to aid from the weather. The Germans had always been fond of using fog to screen the development of their big pushes - after all, this is in accordance with well established military procedure. They did it in the first World War quite often. In 1945 fog had an importance all of its own in that it was the one condition that could really paralyse the Air Forces that were the Allies' trump card. It is unlikely that von Rundstedt gambled on the weather; credit must be given to the enemy meteorologists for seeing that the offensive could be well under way without any repetition of Falaise. One recalls the role of Group Captain Stagg before 'D' Day when he was forecasting prior to D Day.

The Times of December 18th reported German counter attacks on the Western Front under von Runstedt, preceded by the biggest effort the Luftwaffe had put out since D Day. The American 9th Air Force claimed 97 downed: "The Germans have made a series of counter-attacks on the First Army front ... between Monschau and Trier." Little news was released in the early stages of the battle although it soon became apparent that five of six armoured divisions were being thrown in.

Not that the country west of the Mosel is the best that might be chosen for tank warfare. It is heavily wooded and the most hilly ground of the northern front blocked the way to the port of Antwerp which was the prime objective of the threat. The Ardennes mountains rise to eighteen hundred feet around Bastogne and top two thousand feet further north. But the Allied front was lightly held and no doubt this factor more than outweighed the disadvantages of few first-class roads. The enemy probably expected to punch right through the difficult terrain before coming up against stiff opposition and as events proved would probably have done so but for the American stand at Bastogne.

To reinforce the attack by the German army General Galland, their fighter commander, had, with the assistance of Albert Speer, built up a fighter reserve of some three thousand aircraft and this in spite of all the bombing of the aircraft factories that had been going on.

Trier, on the Mosel, above the series of fantastic loops which the river makes before joining the Rhein, was the southern hinge of the offensive. The road from Trier runs to Luxemburg and then sweeps in a circle through Arlon to the north - the final direction of the assault. The railway from Köln comes down to Trier and all the other lines in the area feed into it. Trier, just at that time, was vitally important.

There was a battle order up for Wednesday December 19, but we were not on it as returning crews were given a day in which to settle down. Frank and I stood at the hot plate in the dining hall waiting for our breakfast sausages, chatting aimlessly about the last week. Suddenly the Tannoy blared, "Flying Officer Blenkin's crew report to the briefing room immediately."

"Curse it!", Frank shouted, to the mild astonishment of the few officers at breakfast, "We're on!"

"And I've had nothing to eat," I wailed.

At that moment the girl came out with the plates. Frank looked at me and I at him. "An army marches on its stomach", he said, "and who are we to argue with Napoleon."

We snatched the plates, pushed the food down in record time and rushed up to briefing.

The atmosphere was cold and damp. The airfield so shrouded in fog that visibility was down to between fifty and a hundred yards. A pretty fine clamp. Take-off would be impossible unless it lifted.

Something was obviously afoot. The target was Trier, we were aiming to hinder the enemy breakthrough. There must be complications for the atmosphere in the briefing room was panicky and information was changed, orders cancelled, every few minutes. Someone had prepared a chart for me. I hurriedly started work.

In the end we were sent out to the aircraft to await instructions. The fog persisted. We did all we could, then sat in the cockpit, saying very little and looking out at the greyness. An hour more passed. Nothing stirred and nothing broke the silence, not even an engine being tested. Now and then a car paid us a visit, bringing coffee and sandwiches, or the occasional duty officer. But still the fog clung to the ground.

By lunch time the grumbles were becoming audible. Nothing happened until well after one o'clock when we were instructed by a Controller to leave all our gear in the aircraft, go to the Mess for a meal and be back in an hour. We did this although the prospect looked pretty hopeless for if the mid-day sun does not clear a winter fog it is liable to deepen and last. Finally, the operation was scrubbed. The field was clamped down all day with visibility around fifty yards.

Twelve Tuddenham aircraft managed to get off and made the raid but not in sufficient strength to do much damage. Nevertheless, the Tactical Air Forces were very busy. *The Times* reported: "The German attack had clearly been timed to coincide with the bad weather which was expected to close over the Allied airfields and ground our aircraft. Until almost the last minute this seemed probable but the bad weather suddenly veered off to the north leaving the Germans exposed to the full fury of our air attack."

However, no really heavy bombing smashed at the advancing foe.

We were called early and briefed for the same target and once again we mustered in the dispersal by the aircraft waiting for the word to go. The fog mocked our impatience and wrapped its pall around everything. The temperature was below freezing point, as the moisture condensed it froze, coating every twig with a transparent film of ice, transforming the woods into a glass palace of some Northern legend. As a surface phenomenon this is very rare in England although more common in some places where there is some altitude, such as the border country of Wales, with which I was familiar. I have seen it happen when rain freezes as it falls. There is nothing uncommon about moisture freezing on the wings of an aircraft at a few thousand feet, but hardly at ground level. Now the shrubs around the dispersal were made of crystal, looking as though they belonged to an unreal world.

We stood around, waiting. Presently a party of ground crew came along and sprayed the wings with de-icing fluid. The slight interest this aroused soon faded. However, it would be impossibly dangerous to take off with rime on the wings.

The cold was raw and penetrating. One's breath was exhaled in a steamy cloud and I could feel the beginnings of ice on my whiskers.

The ground crew had built themselves a hut of odd pieces of corrugated iron and whatever other material they could collect. Inside was a good fire of chopped logs. The man in the Services has a knack of making himself as comfortable as circumstances permit, a tradition we had no wish to deny, so we crowded in with them and sat smoking, talking and waiting.

The fog still clung to the ground.

Around midday a van brought tea and sandwiches. Frank and I walked along the perimeter a short distance and stared blankly into nothingness. "Not a snowball's chance in hell!", he muttered.

The operation was cancelled in mid-afternoon.

Our airfield was peculiar in this respect, in that it was on an elevation of 400 feet above sea level in the highest part of Suffolk. Thus, if very low stratus cloud were prevalent, we would be shut in while aerodromes at or near sea level might have a ceiling of several hundred feet. Conversely, when they were clamped with normal fog we would most likely be clear and we often received diverted aircraft on this account. So the fog which was experienced at this particular period must have been of very great depth as some mid-winter fogs may very well be, and it covered the greater part of East Anglia, if not the whole eastern seaboard. In our immediate area were three fields equipped with Fido (Fog Intensive, Dispersal of - as it was apparently called) - Woodbridge, Tuddenham and Downham Market. Woodbridge was a great emergency field where the lame ducks could land if they were only just able to make England. It would not normally have a Squadron. As for Downham Market, a Pathfinder squadron was there. They had very little to do with daylight support work at this stage, the accuracy of GH bombing making their marking methods unnecessary.

So the bulk of No.3 Group had to wait on the weather, willy nilly, kicking its heels in exasperation.

Tuddenham did send off one operation employing Fido. The experiment was not repeated as it was considered too hazardous to send loaded bombers charging at a wall of flame. It is worth recalling that this method of dispelling fog had its limitations as well as its triumphs. Fido employed the principle of the blowlamp on a very large scale. On either side of the long runway a set of triple pipes was fitted in a shallow trench, each pipe being at the corner of a triangle; the lower pipes were burner pipes and the upper a pre-heater. A pumping station, with all the safeguards of duplicated pumps and valves drew petrol from great reservoirs and sent it through the system at a pressure of 25 lbs per square inch. On receiving orders from Control the manning crews lit the petrol flowing from the burners; a match did it. A great pall of black smoke went up. But soon the pre-heater pipes were hot and the petrol flowing through them became vapourized before it reached the burners, when the flame was blue and clear, the pressure was built up to 60 lbs per square inch. The enormous heat generated raised the temperature of the surrounding air and the fog, which after all is only visible water droplets, was re-absorbed into the atmosphere.

This clearance made landing possible, although the convection of the rising warm air made the approach a trifle bumpy and some pilots noticed a tendency in the final stages for the aircraft to float. The additional caution required in landing meant that the volume of traffic that could be handled in a given time was considerably reduced. Take-off between walls of flame four feet high was a desperate expedient, particularly with a full bomb load and Tuddenham, as far as I know, sent off only twelve during the war. The chief limitation was the fact that since so few airfields were equipped with Fido a really effective striking force could not be put into the air on a foggy day.

It is interesting to note that great ingenuity had been employed in overcoming the considerable technical problems associated with the equipment. The expansion of the pipes was quite enormous, not inches but feet. The brackets that held the pipes cracked continuously. But Fido developed until there were installations burning up to four thousand gallons of petrol per minute lit by remote control. And over forty thousand vent holes had to be pricked out by hand after each burning.

On Thursday December 21st, we were briefed for Trier again. There were alternative plans, A and B; either of which might be put into action depending on the weather. If the first plan were approved only the most experienced crews would take off. If the latter, everyone.

The visibility was a little better, being of the order of 200 yards. We knew the urgency of the situation for the briefing officer had given us late reports of the German drive. We were all really keen to take off.

There was a repetition of the hanging about of the last two days, only slightly more tolerable because it was expected. About midday a slight lifting of the fog, a thinning in patches, looked more promising than anything we had seen recently.

A car from control came to tell us that it was Plan A. We were scrubbed, being considered inexperienced.

I walked down the perimeter track loaded with gear, snarling with frustration at not being allowed to go after all the flight plans of the last three days. Ourselves, we were quite confident of Frank's ability to get away. Still, there was no help for it.

At the end of the runway I was stopped by a service policeman who said the perimeter was temporarily closed for take-off. Already motors were revving on the field. The noise of the Merlins can be described as shattering at the best of times. Now, heard through the fog, there was a quality of detachment in the sound, a strangeness linked with the situation as if one were on the fringes of another dimension catching the roar of another world.

I sat down on my bag to wait.

Presently Frank joined me. "It's a bit better now - a good four hundred yards I should say", he estimated.

The runway in use was lined with goose-neck and money-bucket flares which smoked away merrily for the first hundred yards and then got smaller and smaller until they were just sparks in the fog. A light stirring of surface wind carried the smoke away in long plumes. All the normal runway lighting was switched on as if it were midnight. Soon the first aircraft must have lined up by the caravan, for all at once the motor sound rose, steadied, screamed at its fullest note and moved.

Seconds later and the black shape became distinctly recognizable as an aircraft already off the runway. It passed immediately over our heads, its wheels retracting, and I caught a momentary glimpse of the crew at their stations, not the normal pleasant company one knew but taut, competent units of a team already in action against the hazard of the fog. We flung up an arm in salute, wishing them good luck. Then the machine was gone, swallowed up as the pilot gained all the height he could. Only the sound was left behind.

We saw six or eight aircraft go off. They found stiff flak at the target but all returned and all but one managed to land at base for the visibility increased to a good 2,000 yards in the afternoon. This one aircraft was diverted.

By the 22nd the enemy push was variously reported as twelve miles from Luxemburg and thirty miles inside Belgium. *The Times* of that date said: "The American First Army appears to have contained the most northerly and southerly drives of von Runstedt's offensive, though between the flanks there is a gap of some fifty miles through which the enemy has thrust deeply into the Ardennes."

We knew the target would be Trier again. Thursday's effort was very good, considering the restricted numbers of aircraft that operated, although most stations in the Group had sent some. Valuable and effective damage had been done; enough to warrant a telegram of congratulations from Sir Arthur Harris.

People were suggesting that three scrubbed briefings might be counted as an Op., and expressing strong opinions that today's would be another one, for the fog was back again as thick as ever. So it proved, for we repeated our miserable performance of sitting in the bomber all day without getting off. Even the experienced boys of Plan A had to cool their heels on the ground. It was our fourth day of waiting.

But patience, like virtue, is its own reward.

On December 23rd, in poor visibility, we took off for Trier at last. The fog was shifting and thinning and we were soon climbing in clear air. Before we reached the battle line the sun was shining and the ground perfectly visible. We flew over a snow-clad landscape which might have been painted by Brüghel, utterly beautiful and serene as it was, so unconnected with war and the necessity that hurried us on. It is doubtful if the troops down below could have appreciated this detached view of the situation, however!

In the target area flak was strong. A bomber on our port beam was hit and blew up, disintegrating in front of the eyes of our gunners. By the time I managed to look there was nothing but a ball of smoke. I had time for observation because the bombing was visual and after I had worked out the wind it was up to Jack. Besides, I was required to log aircraft casualties so far as possible. Our load fell in the south-eastern portion of the town. Someone hit the bridge fair and square for it went up in fragments, a most satisfactory piece of work because our job was to destroy communications, thus hindering the enemy thrust. There was no doubt that the town was getting hit.

We had another bomb hang-up. Not the cookie fortunately, but one of the 500 pounders. It came away well after we had left the target and were over friendly territory so we couldn't open the bomb doors to let it go but had to proceed to the jettison area in the North Sea. I had no time to worry about extraneous matters otherwise the feel of it rolling about in the bay might have been disturbing.

Back at base the visibility was down again - very poor. Blenkin couldn't make the first landing but had to overshoot. The decision to do so usually had to be made in split seconds when it became obvious that a landing would be dangerous. "When in doubt, overshoot!", was the maxim. Frank never liked overshooting but was too careful to take the risk of a chancy landing.

For all the vagaries of the English climate we had made a successful raid. We didn't go back to Trier again.

Some time afterwards I learned that one of my mates from the AFU course, Joe Veglio, was lost that day.

Christmas Eve. Peace and goodwill to all men! We were to fill the role of Santa Claus for the benefit of the Germans for we were to attack the airfield just east of Bonn: a small gesture of brotherly love to the Luftwaffe. The field was being used as a base for machines flying in support of the enemy in the Ardennes.

Morning briefing, which occupied the usual three hours, was cancelled just as our bags had been packed and crews, universally exasperated, went off to their various messes only to be recalled at 13.00 hours after a hasty meal. There was a hurried résumé of the operation with a new route to the same target. Since the attack was to open at 18.30 hours, after dusk, the usual night tactics were adopted, the route out being west of London to Reading and then over the English coast via Newhaven. These tactics gave a free hand to the defenders of the Thames estuary and the route to the capital.

Our particular crew was among those opening the attack. We carried a ground-marker flare as good visibility was predicted, together with eight thousand-pounders and the rest five-hundreds.

We set course at 15.20 hours.

In order to conceal our approach from the enemy radar for as long as possible the machines were required to remain at 4,000 feet until just on the Belgian border. So we went out low over the South Downs - the blunt bow-headed, whale backed Downs that I knew so well from my Sussex upbringing. Soon, Jack's voice on the intercom: "Brighton coming up, nav."

Smitten with nostalgia which put a lump in my throat, I slid along the seat and eased under the curtain, and there was Brighton on the starboard, with the familiar streets and the two piers, broken now, and the panorama of grey roofs. And home, and wife and all my friends and presents being packed for tomorrow's tree while we were going on our grim errand in spite of the war , I know that every time they heard the bombers go out they were sure, foolish as it might be, that I was going. Now like an invisible link with the ground I thought of them for a moment with a rather unpleasant feeling that I might be seeing Brighton for the last time. Rather sadly, very reluctantly I returned to work. War is damnable at Christmas.

The meterologists had painted a very reasonable picture of the conditions to be expected. Wind strength increased over the Continent and as the Lancaster climbed, but was usually a manageable 50 mph and never over seventy. There was no difficulty in keeping to track and schedule.

Over Bonn we ran into heavy flak. So close, that Harry and Roy could hear it bursting above the noise of the motors. It made a vicious "Whoof" and when you could hear that it was far too near for comfort.

We bombed on GH with jittery, unsteady pulses that were the very devil to line up: I did the best I could and was within the permissible margin of error when I pressed the release button.

As the load was falling away Harry shouted: "Port - go!"

Immediately Frank kicked rudder and pushed the control column forward and the machine dropped like a stone. "Diving - port!"

"OK skipper. There was a kite right up to us. We nearly got pranged." Harry's voice was scared. Indeed, his promptness had just saved us from a collision.

"Resuming course", said the imperturbable Blenkin.

Like Good King Wenscelaus of old I looked out. Although I have no wish to labour the analogy I am bound to record that the snow lay round about. Our thermometer showed minus twenty-seven degrees centigrade. The air was cold and remarkably clear, with exceptional visibility. Early evening stars glittered here and there in the sky and on the ground a neat cluster of Target Indicators glowed like fairy lights on a Christmas tree, interspersed by sudden flashes from the bombs. Instead of the wild picture of destruction I had expected, the sight was Pre-Raphaelite. An attack on Köln, fifteen miles up the river, which was developing at the same time as our own seemed at arm's length from 20,000 feet. My impression was of deepening colour in the luminosity of early evening, shot with small bright lights. Even the searchlights over Köln seemed to fade into nothing at a little height above the ground.

We crossed the Rhein having 240 mph on the clock, losing height rapidly down to 12,000 feet and with an easterly wind behind us of another 67 mph we were covering the ground at six miles a minute. Enough to make the task of any prowling nightfighter almost impossible.

"The old kite is behaving damn well!", my voice was as pleased as if I had something to do with it. "She's knocking up three-sixty ground speed, chaps."

But when we levelled out and reduced speed, Frank found that he could not clear his ears however hard he swallowed and chewed gum. They gave him pain all the way back.

Half-way home Jack came up beside me and took over the H2S set and we finished the trip using this only as an aid. I was rather pleased with the navigation. The newly appointed analysis officer, Murray Jones, who was a tour-expired New Zealander, passed the log and chart without comment.

Frank reported to the doctor after landing and was grounded for a week with inflamed ear drums.

There was something of the Roman Saturnalia about an airman's Christmas dinner, as though the Air Council were determined to make amends for the rest of the year. The cooks excelled themselves, the PSI dipped into its coffers for seasonable fare and it was the pleasure of the Officers and Sergeants to serve the men at their meal. Into a transformed Mess hall, garlanded with streamers and foliage by the WAAF came the fitters and riggers and drivers and even the humble 'erks who have the most obscure jobs - all those in fact whose toil got the Squadron into the air - to receive a repast worthy of the last century, a Chestertonian meal of turkey, ham and sausages, of stuffing and a plate piled high with roast potatoes and vegetables; plus pudding and, inevitably, with every service meal - custard! While the Group Captain beamed all over his face like Pickwick and bustled hither and thither leading a team of senior officers to pour out beer as fast as they could, which was hardly as fast as the men could drink it. Even the Station Warrant Officer unbent a little and smiled in a fatherly manner to see the barrels and jugs being emptied. The knives and forks were plied, the second helpings came and went and for a brief hour the Service laid its conventions aside and forgot the war.

There were no operations on Christmas Day.

On Tuesday the Squadron took part in a great effort against St. Vith. Normally an insignificant small town, this place came into the news for the same reason as Trier, it was a junction of roads and railways feeding the so-called "bulge" of the Ardennes. It was obliterated by nearly a thousand bombers. The RAF sent a force of Lancasters and Halifaxes large enough for a major attack on a German industrial town to bomb concentrations of troops, armour and supplies at the advanced railhead. Visibility was excellent and the crews saw their objectives clearly. When the first markers were dropped in the centre of the target area and in the brief interval before the bombing began, some columns of Germans were seen trying to get out in time. The attack was directed by a master-bomber (*The Times* December 27). The feeling of panic and terror in the trapped columns can be imagined. St. Vith was literally destroyed, as subsequent reconnaissance confirmed.

The attack shifted back to the Ruhr. Wednesday was München Gladbach, when the Squadron put up five aircraft only, after a major effort had been cancelled and the next day it was the turn of Köln. *The Times* commented that the next four days should decide the course of the battle of the Ardennes. The Germans, checked by stubborn American resistance in their attempt to work round the north shoulder of our positions towards the direction of Liege and the Meuse, were trying to see what else they could do and for this purpose were sending columns of tanks to investigate in the region of Middle Meuse and Dinant.

As a matter of fact, the tide was turning. The Americans were holding on grimly at Bastogne and on the 29th American counter attacks captured two Belgian towns. We had a briefing which was scrubbed through bad weather and the Wing Commander relented to the extent of giving the crews a stand-down for the remainder of the day. We, personally, as a crew, were still grounded but Benkin's ears were better and we expected to start flying again.

Saturday saw the commencement of a thaw after the severe frosts of the past few days. The Germans, only ten miles from the Meuse, had definitely been stopped and were "generally withdrawing out of artillery range to regroup and refit".

I was delighted to learn that Neville Parry, who had been converted on to Halifaxes, had been posted to Mildenhall which was the next base to ours and where there was another of my friends, Maxie Hill.

The easier situation in the "bulge" permitted our bombers to attack a target well behind the front but still tactical in nature. Vohwinkel. This is right in the Ruhr. *The Times*, whose excellent dispatches cover the course of this battle, reported that the weather was better on December 31st and both the USAAF and the RAF were out in strength. In an afternoon attack, Bomber Command sent Lancasters to continue the offensive against von Runstedt's supply lines. The target was a marshalling yard near Solingen and on the main line between Wuppertal and Düsseldorf at the southern end of the Ruhr.

The attack on Vohwinkel was not altogether a success for the aircraft ran into head winds of 130 mph, higher than forecast, so that the timing of the raid was upset, many crews bombing late. There were collisions over the target involving two of the Squadron's aircraft that failed to return. One crew was doing its 29th sortie, next before finishing the tour and getting a rest. It was terribly bad luck.

The Times report continued:

"Last night Lancasters attacked a marshalling yard at Osterfeld near Duisburg. Before dawn yesterday a strong force of Lancasters attacked concentrations of enemy troops and armour in a narrow river valley with steep, almost precipitous, sides in the Ardennes. The aiming point was a junction of main roads at Houffalise, about ten miles north-east of Bastogne. As soon as this gathering of troops was reported in an area where dispersal should be difficult it was regarded as an excellent opportunity for heavy bombers and the attack was made as early as weather allowed. This meant a night attack and a clear sky could not be expected. There would be no great difficulty in marking the aiming point but crews were told to make sure that they could see the target indicators clearly through cloud or haze before they dropped their bombs. Many crews found gaps of clear sky and were able to bomb the markers through fairly thin cloud but a few had to leave without bombing. Several crews reported large numbers of bombs bursting right on and close around the markers."

Although No. 218 had nothing to do with this attack I have quoted it because it provides such an excellent illustration of the "target of opportunity" that the army could confidently give the heavies for liquidation, expecting a destruction comparable with that of the Falaise Gap. In fact, snatching at the weather, the Command was pounding tactical targets along the roads and railways feeding into the Ardennes from as far back as Köln.

New Year's Day saw the last spectacular fling by Luftwaffe fighters against our forward airfields. Very heavy destruction of aircraft was suffered on both sides, the only difference being that as the overwhelming proportion of our machines were destroyed while still on the ground the Allies did not lose valuable aircrew and the Germans could not afford to do so.

Our Squadron went to Vohwinkel again, this time determined to finish it off.

One of our Squadron aircraft was knocked out, the sole survivor being the bombardier who subsequently made his way back to the squadron and told his story. They were hit over the target and began losing height. They came down to ten thousand feet by which time they were, in fact, over Belgium. They must have become detached from the main stream for unexpectedly they found themselves being attacked by heavy anti-aircraft fire, actually from American guns. Considering the strafing that the Luftwaffe had been putting up that day with all types of aircraft the Americans can hardly be blamed if they failed to recognize a Lancaster. In any case, their aircraft recognition was not always of the most critical nature. The shooting was extremely accurate and it put our aircraft out of control.

There was a great confusion of noise. George managed to force his way out. He had been hit by a small piece of flak but he managed to land without further hurt.

Uncertain of his exact whereabouts and knowing the fluid nature of the front line, and with the impression of his recent experience sharpening his sense of danger, he decided to take cover in a ditch where he spent the rest of the night. In the morning he was stiff and sore. He was considering what he should do when a small child passed by. George was not sure that he had been seen for the child displayed no emotion at all but continued on its way perfectly composed.

A few minutes only passed by when suddenly the child returned with soldiers. To his great relief they were Americans.

They got him back to England and he managed to make his way back to our station to the surprise of everybody.

None of Chedburgh's aircraft could land when they returned for the weather was completely down over East Anglia. The machines were diverted to Yorkshire. Nor were they back in time to be included in the effort of the following day. The doctor had pronounced Blenkin's ears fit for flying so after a week spent kicking our heels we were on.

As early as lunch time the rumours started going around.

"The petrol load's 2000 gallons - must be a long one."

"Did you notice the armourers putting cans aboard?"

There was a sardonic note in my jest. "Never mind, Frankie my boy. You'll probably get the Big City in your log book after all!", for he often expressed the wish to go to Berlin at least once. An ambition that I did not share.

"Joes again!", he replied. "We haven't flown since Christmas and we get landed with a long night stooge."

It was Nürnberg. Since the best of the Squadron's machines were in Yorkshire and our own had recently been lost we were detailed to fly in C-Charlie. When 218 had been at Methwold the third flight "C" had been created for training purposes and apportioned for that end were aircraft that had already done as many operations as might reasonably be expected but at Chedburgh "C" flight became operational in order to provide the biggest possible battle strength for the Squadron. In spite of the efforts of the CTO and his hard-working staff several of the aircraft of this flight were scarcely serviceable from the point of view of operations. We were, at this time, an "A" flight crew but none of "A" flight aircraft were available.

Doctor McFall, a broad grin on his face, stopped me by the door of the briefing room as I was going out.

"Want any wakey-wakies, Dicky?"

"Not I, Doc", I laughed. "Don't believe in 'em."

"Better have a couple. You navigators haven't anything to do but go to sleep."

"No. No sale."

"Well, take a couple for Blenkin."

Pilots and gunners found these tablets, which were caffeine and similar drugs, most helpful in keeping their eyes open and alert in the long hours of darkness. I had no inclination to doze, with the chart in front of me. I was fully convinced that fatigue during an operation was best stalled off by as much sleep as possible beforehand, coupled with carefully disciplined living and hearty meals. To this end I had long given up smoking and drank moderately except when the occasional party provided a certain amount of colour to the otherwise grey pattern of Station life. Being a married man I had no desire to indulge in the encounters with the fair sex which seem to embroider so many accounts of aircrew life. I even got to enjoy the morning PT on the perimeter track.

But crew members who have no positive work to occupy their minds and who stare into the darkness for hours on end seeing shadows that have no real existence, these needed the drugs to stall off sleep.

It was still daylight when we took off. We had reached longitude 8 degrees East when Johnnie reported trouble in the starboard inner engine, which almost immediately spluttered audibly and showed a rapid falling off of revolutions - a magneto had sheered. "Feather starboard inner". The skipper's voice was curt.

"OK feathering", and Johnnie brought the engine to a standstill. We were around 6,000 feet and with very little chance of getting above 10,000 loaded.

Frank said: "We shall have to return to base. We'll jettison the cookie and save the incendiaries. Course please, navigator!"

"OK skipper. The Channel area is the best one. Rough course 290 true". I commenced to plot position and work out the correct course as the aircraft turned.

The cookie was dropped "safe" in the Channel but it exploded of course, for the impact always set off a cookie. The newspaper reports of sharp naval engagements heard by people on the South Coast were always received with amusement by our fellows, particularly when several machines had been forced to jettison.

Johnnie estimated our all-up weight at landing. Presently he announced that we should be forced to get rid of some of the petrol to get down to a safe landing weight. Orders were to save incendiary bombs if possible. Frank decided that if we had to jettison fuel we would do it over base, recalling an earlier attempt on a Stirling when once the petrol started running away it refused to stop.

But the hydraulic valve of the system was stuck, as these valves usually were from lack of use. Frank received permission from Control to bring the aircraft in "passing the buck in case we prang" - and made an excellent three-engine landing, two thousand pounds overweight.

The target had been Nürnburg. The emphasis now shifted back to the Ardennes, with an attack in which the Squadron took part on a railway target at Castrop Rauxel. The place is well to the north-east of the Ruhr, it might almost have been one of the strategic bombings.

The Ardennes was over for us. The Americans had begun pushing in the salient from the south. On January 4th the Germans admitted American attacks on the north flank and mentioned the use of British tank formations. Von Runstedt's gamble had failed and the Allied air forces could be utilized elsewhere. In fact, the briefing that day was for Ludwigshaven. Ushered in by fog, the Ardennes episode went out with snow, for this latest briefing was cancelled on the promise by the meteorologists of heavy snowstorms over the continent.

CHAPTER 13

MAINLY FRUSTRATION

Clausewitz rightly said: "Everything is very simple in war, but the simplest thing is difficult. These difficulties accumulate and produce a friction of which no one can form a correct idea who has not seen war ... action in war is movement in a resistant medium."

On January 6th we were briefed for Neuss. Neuss is a communications centre and river port west of Düsseldorf of which it is almost a suburb. It contains heavy industry. A typical Ruhr target.

It started badly with early calls at 5 a.m. on a bleak wintery day. There was the preparation of two complete flight plans each of which was cancelled in turn. These took up the entire morning. Some navigators accepted the wasted work with resignation, writing it down to experience. The less patient, myself included, were inclined to annoyance and cursing.

There is no doubt that Command would have got the aircraft away if it were at all possible but when one is in the briefing room at home, with everything ready, it is easy to overlook the cumulus snow clouds towering over the Continent or being borne down on the area by an incoming front. There was no help for it, the work was in vain.

We went back to the briefing room after lunch with night tactics now and a different route but the same target. The aiming point was a marshalling yard, to be attacked with high-explosive bombs. We, ourselves, to be on at seven minutes after the opening of the attack carrying ten thousand pounds of HE bombs and a marker flare. We were "backers up." The first ground markers would be burning out by the time we arrived and the role of backers up was to keep the target marked continuously.

Ill luck still dogged our steps. When I reached the aircraft I found there was trouble which arose from the fitting of night tracer ammunition to the rear turret.

Ammunition for the four Brownings, to the tune of several thousand rounds, was contained in large tanks positioned nearly as far back as the mid-upper turret and on either side of the fuselage. It was fed through light metal guides down the side of the aircraft until the belt reached the turret. There the cartridges passed between a system of rollers and guides cleverly designed to allow smooth, uninterrupted feed while the turret was in rotation.

Nevertheless, these rollers were extremely awkward obstacles to loading. It was customary at this period to fit several hundred rounds of special tracer at the beginning of the belt and this was done by removing the cartridges at the breech of the guns, drawing them back free of the turret, securing in the fresh length of ammunition and then reloading,

pulling the slack in the belt back to the reserve tanks. This operation was
performed by an armourer with the help, and under the supervision of, the
gunner, whose turret it was.

Harry had a jammed feed. Somewhere in the system the belt was
refusing to move in the guide and he, Roy and the armourer were pulling,
tugging and working to correct the fault and get the guns loaded. This was
one of the disadvantages of being liable to change from day to night
operations at a moment's notice. A Squadron engaged in night-flying only
would have been loaded with the appropriate ammunition all the time.

I realized there would be a late take-off. I warned the skipper and then
sat down to work out a route and course if we had to get away at the last
minute.

At length they finished with the turret. Harry's temper was frayed and
the skipper was darkly angry. The atmosphere of the crew was strained.
We took off well after everyone else.

Then followed a hectic period with the engineer and pilot working to
get the maximum out of the loaded engines and I cutting corners and
snatching minutes from the route until we were on time with the stream.

Conditions were good at the target apart from the flak. We dropped the
load on navigational instruments as ordered, although the ground could be
seen for it was hardly dark. Johnnie watched our load of bombs go down
right into the middle of the cluster of Target Indicators burning strongly
on the ground. I was too busy to look out.

We came home without incident, although everyone else was not so
lucky.

One of the Squadron's aircraft was hit but managed to limp back to
friendly territory before the pilot decided to order the crew to bale out.
The lights had failed in the crippled bomber. As they were groping about
in the darkness, with nothing but a couple of torches and the possibility of
the machine plunging to earth at any minute the engineer must have
caught his rip handle of the parachute on some projection, pulling the
chute and leaving the unfortunate man with the choice of jumping with the
unfolded canopy that might or might not spread, or of coming down with
the aircraft.

Frozen into acute fear the engineer would not jump.

Then the wireless operator volunteered to take the engineer on his
back. They made their way to the escape hatch. In the darkness the
ripcord of the wireless operator's parachute caught. He felt the tug, and
although the handle came out he was able to clutch the cover of the
parachute and prevent it from unfolding. The engineer clung to his back.
Spurred on by their desperate situation they jumped together.

Clear of the aircraft the wireless operator let the parachute go. There
was a sudden jerk as the silk spread against the double weight. It was too
much. The engineer - poor fellow - fell off.

The other came down into a tree, fell to the ground and damaged himself. When his effort became known he was immediately awarded the Conspicuous Gallantry Medal. His courage and unhesitating effort to aid his comrade at his own risk were the admiration of the whole Squadron. His name was Flight Sergeant Longley.

All the rest of the crew got down safely. The pilot had the nightmare experience of slipping in his harness as he opened his parachute. He made the descent head downwards and landed in a very shaken state but physically unharmed.

The following day brought an attack on München. This target, often visited, was always greeted with some glee on account of the Beer Garden. One felt there was a certain personal touch about it - that even if we were after the railway there was always the chance that a stray bomb might spoil the Fuhrer's beer. An unforgivable insult in the eyes of most aircrew.

It was a long trip, where one might expect seven hours flying and the briefing was correspondingly long.

Not yet having our own aircraft we were detailed for one of "C" Flight's veterans - G-George, an old warrior of fifty-nine trips.

The Met. man painted a particularly unpleasant picture of the conditions to be expected. Between Suffolk and München there were two frontal systems with great variations in the types of weather. Winds aloft above base were around eighty miles per hour while over Germany they were mere zephyrs. There was risk of severe icing. Cloud below would veil the ground, high cirrus would obscure the stars, so neither pinpoints nor Astro could be expected.

When Met. said it was going to be bad it almost certainly would be.

We were circling base preparatory to setting course when Turner came on the intercom. "Hey, skipper, ma set's packed up."

"OK. See what you can do."

Which the industrious wireless man was already putting into effect, for he stripped off his harness and Mae West, being a heavily built fellow, and crawled under my table. In that confined space by the navigator's seat there was no room for me to work with anyone as big as him under the table so I edged away impatiently and for want of occupation stretched over to steady the pulses on the Gee indicator. As I looked at the screen the lines of the emerald-coloured time bases suddenly commenced to jitter, expanded violently, collapsed and faded away.

"Navigator to skipper. Gee's packed up now. When Turner gets back I'll have a look at it, but it looks to me as though a valve's gone."

"When do we set course?", he asked. I told him and added "We'd better press on, at least until we know where we stand."

"Ma set's all right", said Turner, wriggling out and getting back to the seat.

We set course. I attempted to rectify my trouble and although I ran through the few checks it was possible to make, there was no doubt a valve had gone and the set was out of commission. On a night such as this to lose Gee was a major tragedy.

My voice must have betrayed my anxiety. "We've a valve gone, skipper. There's H2S silence as far as six degrees east, two fronts through the area and no stars. I strongly advise turning back."

"Shouldn't turn back for Gee failure!"

"Press on if you like, but DR will be no good tonight. I'll do my best and we'll have to take pot luck."

"We'll have to go to the Channel anyway", said Frank, "See how you get on."

"Hello, Jack", I called.

"Bombardier answering."

"Give me every decent pinpoint you can. I must have pinpoints while you can still see the ground." I wanted whatever shreds of data I could obtain.

"OK. There's Reading coming up. I'll tell you when we pass over", and a few minutes later, "Over now."

We changed course for Beachy Head. Jack had been checking his bombsight. He came on the intercom. "Bombardier to skipper. My sighting head will be useless. There's gyro trouble that I cannot rectify."

"These bloody C flight kites", Blenkin was really fierce. "They should be on the scrap heap!"

Before Beachy Head the radio had died again beyond Turner's powers of repair. Blind and deaf the veteran flogged out the miles to the jettison area where we ingloriously dropped our load and turned back to base.

To the casual observer this may seem a sorry picture of inefficiency and lack of foresight. The truth is not altogether so. At this period the serviceability of the Squadron's aircraft was at a low level. The machines were being flown on operations nearly every day: on training when they were not operating. They were standing in open dispersals and had been through the worst of the winter exposed to all weathers and to damp that does so much damage to electrical circuits. The ground engineers were hard pushed to keep pace with the work, work that had to be carried out in such conditions of cold and exposure that I have known Doctor McFall go the rounds of the dispersals late at night issuing tots of rum to combat the hardships of their situation. Cold was particularly severe that winter in Suffolk, itself a cold spot, and Doc. McFall is dead of some obscure disease.

We were not alone in turning back from München. Of the thirteen aircraft detailed one could not even take off, one other, beside ourselves, returned with Gee failure and another had to land on the emergency runway at Woodbridge without any pneumatic pressure at all. Fortunately, the three-thousand yard runway gave plenty of space to run to a standstill, for the brakes were useless. So many things were worked by compressed air in a Lancaster that when the pressure failed one just couldn't go on.

Nor is it possible to trace many of these faults before take-off when the equipment is tested on the run-up or in air tests before operations, if time allows, and in war some risks must inevitably be taken with equipment.

Our one satisfaction in this abortive trip was that with three returns and one non-starter, the Wing Commander couldn't possibly pass on to crews the rocket that he undoubtedly received from Group.

It is possible also to take into account something of the psychological condition of our own individual crew. We had now done, in a period of just over a month, three daylight and two night operations and had turned back twice. Not really an impressive record and yet during this month we were beginning to get the taste of it and to slough off the initial nervousness which does not necessarily amount to actual fear but which permeates all action with a sense of uneasiness and which may lead to over caution. It is probable that, had we done ten trips we might have taken an unjustified risk and tried to get to München and take a chance of finding our target and dropping our load, the odds on success being long ones. It is difficult to say whether we were trying to find an excuse in our own inexperience and it is probable that turning back at this stage of operational immaturity was the wisest thing. As time went by we became more certain of ourselves until we became so much more capable from the operational point of view that when next we went to München some months later we were the leaders of the entire raid.

Over the airfield during the night the weather broke and when we awakened the ground was blanketed in snow. All morning the snowploughs were busy on the runway and the khaki-clad figures of the Regiment were dotted over the field putting down salt and shovelling snow. The job was too much for them alone and during the morning the Tannoy called for everyone on the station to give a hand.

Frank and I put on our gum boots. We were not the first on the scene, naturally! Some of our friends had made really good heaps of snowballs against the arrival of tardy folk. We were forced to run the gauntlet on our bicycles down the long runway with snowballs bursting on our wheels, on our backs and in our hair. I had a fine old bone-shaker of a Station-issue bike that hit on a piece of icy snow and slid away from under me amid a chorus of laughter, delighted shouts and repartee. Fun that would have gladdened the heart of Charles Dickens, had he been there. Indeed the cheerfulness that so readily came to the surface at the slightest provocation was typical. There was no point in concerning oneself about tomorrow. Sufficient for the day could well have been our motto.

The snowploughs were not able to clear the edges of the runways, (a huge triangle made by the three), for fear of breaking the flare-path lighting. The last yard had to be cleared by hand. We worked away as the day passed until with tired, glowing limbs we finished in the evening and went off to kill our enormous appetites.

Flying was out of the question on the Wednesday also. A few of the pilots fixed up a detail to take their crews to Cambridge, ostensibly for dinghy drill in the Leas school bath but really for a night out. The weather was dirty. Snow swirled down all the time, making the lorry journey as cold and unpleasant as could be. The swimming bath was warm and pleasant by comparison. It was all rather reminiscent of my ITW days. We spent the entire evening in the Cambridge pubs finding out those that had some beer.

However, social life could not continue indefinitely. On the 11th of January we were sent to attack Krefeld marshalling yards with high-explosive bombs - a four-thousand pound cookie and fourteen five-hundreds. Once again we had a marker flare. We were in C Flight K-King.

The weather was about as bad as it could be, the sky loaded with snow clouds and in order to keep the machines out of trouble as far as possible three changes of route had been made. We dodged in and out of cloud at the rendezvous where we were supposed to pick up three followers from other units not equipped with blind-bombing gear. However we could find only one.

Over France the Gee box failed, with trouble in the receiver. I told Frank.

"OK - never mind. I'll follow someone in front." He sorted out another leader by the yellow-barred tail fins and joined in behind. I commenced to lay off dead reckoning positions to check our whereabouts.

Presently we ran into very strong and unexpected winds, that I had no means of checking. My Estimated Time of Arrival was very near.

"ETA five minutes", I called.

"Fair enough."

As the time ran out: "A minute to go!"

"It's all right, nav," the skipper said. "This bod in front hasn't opened his bomb doors yet - hello Jack."

"Bomb aimer here."

"Disconnect the marker flare". With my apparatus out of commission we would be forced to release simultaneously with the man in front without any positive radar check of our own.

"ETA is up." I was getting worried. "What's it like outside?"

"Come and have a look!" Since there was nothing positive I could do I pushed aside my curtain and looked out. At twenty thousand feet we were flying in cirrus cloud, hedged in everywhere with the visibility restricted to such an extent that one could see perhaps half a dozen aircraft of the whole stream. Every now and then the plane in front would vanish into the dry wispy vapour; then this would flick across our windscreen, blinding us completely and then we would clear and pick up the other aircraft once more.

I scrambled back and looked at my watch. We were five minutes over my calculated ETA. I felt particularly helpless. I read the Air Position Indicator and laid off a DR position which, false as it was, showed us heading south-east of our objective towards Bonn.

"Nav. to skipper. I think we're off to starboard. Any chance of having got mixed up with another attack? We're six minutes over ETA."

"Don't worry," he said rather fiercely. "I'm sticking to this chap."

"It's all right," Jack sang out. "Flak ahead!" and then - "God!" A fragment of metal came through the nose and stopped dead beside him. He touched it and it was red hot and burning. He kept it as a souvenir.

"Bomb doors open!" The load was released eight minutes after our stipulated time.

Much relieved I read the Air Position Indicator and using the target as a fix found much higher wind strength than had been anticipated. I reset the API and altered course for home.

Now, knowing my whereabouts and being past the target I was able to switch on H2S but tune as I would the temperamental instrument could give me no help. We returned on a mixture of Dead Reckoning and keeping in sight of other aircraft as far as possible. We were in and out of cloud all the way and when we descended to a few thousand feet the stratocumulus still rolled below us all over Britain, unbroken to the horizon. ·

When the calculations showed that we were in the area of base: "We'll have to break cloud now, but be damned careful and don't go below 800 feet. If we're not clear better go back to sea and break there on an HF fix."

"There are some Lancs going down to starboard," he answered. "We'll try it."

"QBB 1,000 feet. QFE 1,000," from Turner who had been picking up a weather report.

I watched the altimeter needle falling back. After anxious minutes of flying blind we came out of the cloud over the large wood which is an unmistakable landmark of East Anglia. We found Brandon and map-read to base without further ado.

Both Frank and I had come to the conclusion that if everything did go to plan, and if an operation could be carried out after only one briefing it was singularly fortunate. So much the reverse was expected that when the early call dragged you sleepy-eyed out of bed you dressed in a cynical frame of mind anticipating a morning of fruitless briefing. Thus the alarm clock broke the peace of the morning of the 12th, finding me in just such a frame of mind as soon as I had collected my thoughts.

"Away to briefing, Austen!" Jock Stark had the bed in the corner, opposite Frank. "But dinna' forget to put some wood on the fire."

Sammy came in with a couple of buckets of water.

"What's the visibility like, Sammy?"

"Pretty grim - another scrub coming up."

"Why the hell can't they make up their minds instead of dragging us out of bed!"

"Anyway, it's one way of getting an egg for breakfast. Met. haven't a clue these days. Why doesn't someone tell them."

Frank turned over in bed, half opened his eyes and said to me: "Reset the alarm, will you Dick." I'll see you up there," for he could sleep for another hour.

"Lucky old so-and-so. Bye-bye. See you later then." And so out into a raw, dark morning.

The early briefing for a Ruhr target was cancelled. There was an afternoon preparation for a flight to Hanover but the weather intervened on behalf of the citizens of that locality for, as anticipated, there was no hope of going. Met. was impossible.

Per ardua ad astra.

Chapter 14

EXPERIENTIA DOCET

Yet when we did manage to get into the air again on the 13th for a daylight attack on the marshalling yards at Saarbrücken, we were favoured with a particularly easy trip.

The sun shone. We were running due south at a few minutes past one o'clock British Summer Time. Something prompted me to turn the pages of the almanac to see the time of Meridian passage of the sun. What a golden opportunity for a latitude from a shot of the sun, with practically no working out. I took the shot and congratulated myself on a particularly artistic piece of navigation that was perfectly unnecessary.

It must be obvious how easy the navigation was that day, when I had time to play about with Astro on the outward journey. We were flying in a particularly steady airstream from the south-east, almost in our teeth, that cut ground speed down to approximately 150 mph. From Tonbridge to a position way down in France below Neufchateau, there was the usual luck of a straight three-hundred mile leg with no complications except a rated climb to 19,000 feet, with the target just over the battle-line, the easy southern sector of the front.

In broad daylight with no cloud obscuring the target we made an instrument run up. GH was good. Better than visual bombing. The rail yards were in the north part of the town, the selected target being at the junction of lines running east-west and north-east/south-west. On a heading of 050 true we passed over the river as our bombs fell. There was practically no opposition, just a few bursts of fire. Harry was able to keep his eyes fixed on the bombs and had the satisfaction of seeing them go down and straddle the yards, a dead bullseye. "Good show, nav. Right on the dot. They've just burst smack on." It was like doing practice bombing at Rushford range.

This is the pattern of a successful operation, when the raiding force can catch the enemy unawares, exact their price and retire undamaged. Those who, half contemptuously, referred to such an attack as "a piece of cake" ignored the spade work of the Staff and the labours of Intelligence. There were some who felt that unless a dozen aircraft were shot down and the flak were like hail a raid was half failure. But it was really singeing the King of Spain's beard.

The aircraft was over the Channel, homeward bound, when Turner handed me a diversion signal. East Anglian weather had deteriorated to the extent of being impossible. I notified the skipper and gave him the course for St Mawgan in Cornwall. We map-read our way on the television screen of the H2S set and landed just as dusk was falling and the light was getting bad.

We found a great modern field, with a long, clean, runway set in the Cornish turf on the very edge of jagged cliffs. The landing was to provide a delightful and unexpected break from our normal routine.

It was a Transport Command field, a trans-Atlantic ferry terminal. The Station Commander himself in his gold braid received us and, kindness itself, did everything possible to make us comfortable within the limits of hospitality imposed by the war. We were Bomber Boys and they gave us the best they could.

So many Lancasters had come in, from various Squadrons, that many old friends met again for the first time for months. I was delighted to run into Trevor Peek on the perimeter. Peek, a New Zealander had been with us at HCU.

"Well - if it isn't Pit-borne Peek himself!"

"Hello son!" He laughed all over his face. "Managing to keep on track?"

"Listen, boy. Have you ever heard of the pilot who was so dumb even the other pilots noticed it!"

We called him Pit-borne because, in popular opinion, he much preferred staying in bed to getting airborne. No one can question the sound common sense of his preference. A bed was always a "pit" in the RAF.

"Hell, chaps, we'll have Sir John Moore tonight!" When Trevor was in his cups he was given to reciting a version of this mournful poem.

"Where's little Willie? Hey, Willie, how's your love life?"

This to his navigator.

"Don't make the boy blush. He's going to get engaged."

Laughing and drinking passed the evening away and laughter saw us into bed when men took off their outer garments and stood in their ill-fitting aircrew underwear, those long pants of film comedy vintage which most of us were only too grateful to wear in cold weather. The stores had them in three sizes but only seemed to issue the very largest. Still, they were warm and shrank if persistently laundered.

K for King had burst two oil pipes. This kept us at St Mawgan along with several other crews who were in trouble. While the pipes were being fitted the weather over East Anglia settled down in its intention of being thoroughly bad. We slipped into an easy routine of living. We were shaved by the barber, enjoyed substantial meals in view of the American connection and spent our time as we wished. It was a luxury to get baths, when the pipes at Chedburgh had been frozen for a long time. Our hosts provided towels and soap as none of us had been prepared for diversions, although subsequently I always carried some gear with me on operations, having profited by this lesson.

The climate here was ideal, being crisp and sunny. A party of us found our way on to the sands below the airfield. Like schoolboys we removed our hot, sheepskin-lined boots and paddled in the sea, or explored the caves, or pushed someone into a rock pool.

Up on the field were many American aircraft, guarded by big GIs. Johnnie amused everybody by exchanging his cap with a souvenir-hunting Yank for one of the jockey-like affairs in which they worked. He walked around in this declaring that he could have exchanged a whole Liberator for his flying boots. Neither was Harry behind in this process of barter for he acquired a packet of shot cartridges of a calibre to fit his revolver and swore to poach a few pheasants on getting back to Suffolk. He only succeeded, when he did try later, in hitting an owl and then only after chasing the unfortunate bird down a country lane on a motorcycle.

Several times a day we trudged up to the aircraft and then pestered Control to see if we could take off, but without success.

At night there was a coach to take us into Newquay where the discomfort of walking around in flying gear was more than balanced by the enhanced glamour of our appearance. Bomber crews were commonplace in Suffolk, but Cornwall was different. The ale flowed for some of us in the harbourside inns, while others went to shoot lines and make their conquests of the Cornish lassies.

This pleasant state of affairs could not be expected to last. On the fourth day after landing at St Mawgan we were able to return to our base. Frank did a showy take-off, holding the Lancaster on to the extremely long runway and then pulling steeply away. To show the Americans, he explained.

To our great disgust we found on arrival that we had been transferred to 'C' flight in our absence.

Another day, another target and another cancellation. That was Thursday. Friday was similar, a trip to Stuttgart being washed out by snow falling. Saturday and Sunday were equally disappointing but there could be no question of flying when snow clouds over Europe extended above twenty thousand feet. It was very demoralizing.

On January 22nd after an unsuccessful morning we were airborne in the late afternoon. There had been adequate time to prepare for an attack timed to open soon after nightfall. It was strategic and our personal first blow in the battle of oil. The oil offensive had been the cause of controversy between Sir Arthur Harris and the Chief of Staff and it was favoured by the Americans rather more than by him. But it must be said that Albert Speer had concluded as early as May 1944 that the continued bombing of fuel plants would mean the end of German armaments production. To this extent it seems the proponents of oil bombing were right, although the difficulties of hitting small targets in bad weather had not been solved before the coming of navigational devices such as GH.

Our target was the Thyssen plant situated at Hamborn in the Ruhr. Hamborn adjoins Duisburg. It was a heavily defended area and we might expect trouble.

The meteorological conditions had changed considerably, for the cloud of the past few days had gone, giving place to a neutral pressure system known as a "col" that covered northern France. A col is a region of light and unpredictable winds. It sometimes happened that the forecast, upon which was based the timing of a raid, proved to be entirely wrong in its estimation of wind direction. Such was the case of this day.

Once again the route out was just north of Brighton and I must needs look out of the cabin to say *au revoir*.

It became evident that we should be late. There was a concentration point on the French coast. With no possibility of cutting a corner to make time I had to call for increased airspeed.

Johnnie moaned and groaned but the revs went up nevertheless. He was very proud of his economy in the consumption of fuel and I could hear him mumbling into his microphone in disgust before he switched it off. We could not increase enough to be over the target in time: we were a trifle late but so was the whole attack.

The bombing was visual, in excellent conditions of visibility. Jack, unperturbed, took his time about the run.

I had my usual look out. The night was gloriously clear. Four miles below, the target glittered through the gulf of air and flashed its wicked looking cluster of colour to the stars. The area was ringed by searchlights but so clear was the atmosphere that they faded into nothingness at a few thousand feet and looked ridiculously impotent. Dancing a saraband to slow music. They were like toy candles and the hardness of colour in the scene reminded me of some fairytale pictured by Walt Disney in glorious technicolour.

Since, rightly or wrongly, I regarded Thyssens as having a fair share of responsibility for the war I looked in great admiration at the undoubted accuracy of the bombing, wishing more power to the bombardiers.

Turner, at his wireless sets was engaged in taking counter measures aimed at enemy night fighters. He was sweeping his receiver over an allotted frequency band in search of enemy radio telephone conversations. If he found anything he would set his transmitter to the same frequency. In the nacelle of one of the engines was fitted a microphone. Turner would switch this in and he would send out engine noise on the same wavelength. Since the most sensitive equipment was used, the effect on enemy vectoring procedure can be imagined. Many of the operators in the bombing force were similarly engaged, harassing further an already demoralized enemy.

Let us glance briefly at radio-countermeasures. Mr Alfred Price has written an admirable and exhaustive account of them. Nevertheless, as we were engaged with them from time to time a brief note may not be out of place.

The radio war, the secret war within a war, was waged ceaselessly from the very early days, and it seems with the British usually a jump ahead.

The countermeasures varied enormously and were aimed at the whole gamut of enemy wireless communication and radar, sometimes with such satisfactory results that he was driven to make-shift measures in order to control his fighters at all.

The British jammed his RT from the air in the way I have described coupled with the activities of specialized machines from No. 100 Group that did nothing else but protect the stream in which they flew. False instructions were issued to his crews in fluent German. As was the case back in the Foreness days when he employed women to transmit the RAF were ready with WAAF. They tried sending instructions in Morse, and indeed we were sent orders in Morse but this is a slow procedure in no way fast enough for interceptions. Besides, Morse transmissions which could be sent and received over considerably longer distances than the short-wave radio telephone were upset with no difficulty at all. The enemy went to the length of interrupting the normal civilian broadcast programmes by interpolating instructions to his night fighters and even arranged to play special tunes which were simple codes of instructions; for example the "Blue Danube" might mean "Return to base for re-fuelling and re-arming".

The use of "window" has been well reported. The Germans had a similar system. Both sides apparently delayed using it for fear of what the other might do. When the Germans realized the immediate effects of the use of window after the Hamburg raids they altered the frequency of their radar within the limits of the apparatus but the RAF were ready with window strips of differing lengths.

Very powerful transmitters in Britain were employed to send out jamming signals, exactly as the enemy jammed our own RDF and Gee. In addition, our bombers were equipped with a device that hunted over a pre-set wave band and if radiation fell on the aircraft the machine concerned would lock itself to the frequency used by the enemy and sent out in return bursts of energy much greater than the normal reflections from an aeroplane, with the result that the DP station received a huge smear on the cathode screen that prohibited the operator from pin-pointing the source.

Turner's "tinselling" as it was called has lead us away from our story, but at an appropriate moment, for our return from the Ruhr was untroubled.

A catalogue of cancellations, or briefings completed just in time to be scrubbed, of targets visited and revisited, the very name of the Ruhr even, became as wearisome in the contemplation as in the endurance. Once, at least, we were spared a briefing which was a matter for gratitude. There can be no doubt that at this stage of the war the Supreme Command required the maximum effort from the bomber force and the oft-repeated briefings were a preparation made upon the slightest chance of a sortie. "They also serve who only sit and wait!" Patience is not general among young men; waiting more hardly to be borne than the brisk business of action. To wait upon the weather was to attend upon the caprice of a courtesan.

One comforting piece of information was that Russian troops were in Silesia, only 180 miles from Berlin. The nutcrackers were squeezing and the pattern of the end beginning to take shape.

T.E. Lawrence once wrote that "The blowing up of trains was an exact science when done deliberately."

Sunday saw us laid on for Köln, that much bombed target, to have a shot at the Gremberg marshalling yards. Whenever the pressure of events allowed, the Command tended to come back to its old targets, attacking the bottle-necks of the German transport system and planting bombs where they would cause confusion of the widest order and making the enemy hordes labour at patching up damage and rebuilding. For him it was like waging war against the sea. At least sixteen railways ran into Köln and fourteen first-class roads. There were complicated rings of switch-over lines within the boundaries but the obstacle of the Rhein forced the railways to bottle-neck together for the bridging of the river and at that bottle-neck we struck.

It was a daylight attack, bombing blind, and the load consisted of a cookie, twelve five-hundreds and the usual target marking flares. The Americans had attacked the city earlier in the same day, aiming at the yards also.

Weather was doubtful. Snow was falling as we rolled around the taxi track. A number of aircraft were forced to marshall on either side of the runway's end and wait for permission to go. Flurries cut down visibility to a few yards and the caravan showed red while the pilots cursed at their overheating engines and watched oil pressures fluctuating.

We got away too late to climb to rendezvous height and contact our followers and therefore after a hurried consultation we decided to cut the track that would be flown by the formation leaders. This we did, Frank placing our aircraft in the spearhead of the attack, trusting to the commonsense of our detailed followers to attach themselves to another GH aircraft.

Except for the difficulties of weather it was a very good trip until we reached the target area.

It was the custom in No. 3 Group that each Squadron in turn should provide the leader of an attack. The job came round no more often than once a month. The Squadron Commander detailed his most capable crew for what was a very heavy responsibility and since there was too much work in a leading job for a single navigator a second was detailed. I shall have more to say on this score later when the lot fell on us. Sufficient for the moment that today was 218's turn and the chosen crew were skippered by Warrant Officer Evers, a highly experienced and most capable pilot much respected on the Squadron. His crew had only this one trip to do before finishing their tour. It was, logically, a job for them.

My friend and former classmate Freddie Norton was detailed as second navigator.

Heavy cumulus cloud and uncertain winds were encountered. We were flying a short distance behind Evers machine, with two or three other Lancasters between us. The spearhead was loose in its formation because of the amount of cloud. However, this began to thin out and as Germany was approached it became evident that there would not be complete cloud below. Soon we were listening out for the bombing wind, the run-in started, and I plunged into the mass of calculation before the target.

"Flak opening up ahead."

"I can see the target. The cloud is broken below," Jack reported. "Plenty of stuff coming up today. Everything bar the kitchen sink!"

The German gunners could see the bomber stream and were laying their guns with accuracy.

"Aircraft going down, starboard bow." Roy, very calmly and then suddenly with feverish excitement piercing through his voice "God Almighty, someone's blown clean up!" A sickening sight to see the machine plunging along bravely one minute and the next nothing but a great black ball of smoke and dripping rags and fragments down the sky. And navigators were supposed to log these incidents.

The action was hot. Köln never was healthy and the stirring up delivered by the Americans earlier had put the enemy on their toes. My room-mate Jock Stark was flying as substitute navigator to the Wing Commander. The whole base of an 88 m.m. shell ripped through the front turret, passed between the pilot and engineer taking off the plastic knob of the outer pitch control lever as clean as a whistle and smashed with a sickening thud into the H2S control box which stopped it or Jock might have been decapitated.

"Let 'em go sharp on the dot nav. There's plenty of overshooting." Jack warned. There had been a last-minute wind shift which could not be anticipated. I muttered OK; I was quite oblivious to everything outside by this time for the skipper was gently weaving the machine, more to reassure himself than for any good it would do in this hail of flak, and I was obliged to keep within 200 yards of track or disconnect the marker flare. I was aware of a great pent up excitement that I deliberately subordinated. I could feel sweat under my helmet and around my nose and moustache. When I pressed the bomb release, my eyes glued to the screen, and let my breath go freely as the load went Frank swung away on course out of the target and commenced dodging furiously.

"Worst flak I've seen." Harry in the rear was getting a grandstand view. "I bet several will buy it today."

"Keep your eyes open or we'll be one of them!" Frank snapped sharply.

Air action tends to be sharp and concentrated. In a matter of minutes we had cleared the defence and were in calm flight.

We landed at base. As the crews were ticked off the Intelligence blackboard two were missing. Evers had failed to return. He was last seen circling in the target area as though he was going back but was probably out of control. The other, piloted by Flt. Lt. Hodnett, was reported to have been losing height well below the stream after it had left the target. He had two engines feathered then.

Some time later we heard that Freddie Norton had been taken prisoner. He had a fantastic escape. The aircraft was hit by an absolute broadside of flak and badly damaged. The pilot called "Parachutes!" He snatched up his and clipped it on. At that moment the machine exploded, bursting asunder beneath his feet. He does not know whether he pulled the ripcord himself or whether it caught on some part of the machine as he fell out for as he left the aircraft he lost consciousness and knew no more until he recovered in a cafe where some Germans were giving him a drink to revive him. There were so far as I have been able to make out no other survivors.

Hodnett was properly riddled over the target and suffered engine damage. Worse still the rudder control was shot away on one side so he commenced sweeping round in an arc. He called the bomb aimer to seize the rod that connected down the fusilage with the rudder and, by instruction over the intercom, when to push and when to pull. By these means he regained some sort of control, sufficient he thought to enable them to reach friendly territory. But he lost height too rapidly and when near Bonn was forced to give the order to abandon the aircraft. All the crew got down safely.

He was captured and taken to Dulag Luft. His experiences there provide some insight into German interrogation of aircrew prisoners, for which this place was reserved.

He was taken before an enemy Intelligence Officer, correct, well turned out and perfectly polite, who wanted to know whether he bombed as an individual or in formation on a leader.

Hodnett gave his name, rank and number.

"We know all that!", retorted the other. "Your Squadron letters are X-H, you belong to No. 218 Squadron at Chedburgh in Suffolk where you moved recently. Your Squadron Commander is Wing Commander Smith. You see we know quite a lot about you." He then produced a large dossier on the Squadron and quoted an amazing amount of information, mentioning names and equipment that the startled Englishman found it almost impossible to credit. Nevertheless, he still declined to talk.

"Come now," said the interrogator quite affably, "these few particulars, please."

"I've said all I have to say," the pilot affirmed and added: "The British Government is behind me!"

"Rather a long way behind, don't you think?"

Still adamant Hodnett shut his mouth firmly and refused to say any more. He was in no mood for conciliation after the ordeal of losing his aircraft. So he was marched off to a cell and shut in.

There was a wooden bed and one blanket. The guards had not ill treated him and seemed reasonable. He looked around the bare cell, shrugged his shoulder and sat on the hard bed. At dusk a blackout was put up to the small window that lit the place and he was plunged into pitch darkness. His eyes imagined at first that there were flashes of light but he soon got accustomed to the blackness and laying himself full length he pulled the blanket over him and lapsed into a half drowsy state, idly wondering what would happen next but not caring particularly.

Suddenly the lights came on and the guard pushed in two slices of bread with some nondescript jam. There was just enough time to consume this meagre meal before they went out again.

He noticed the place getting warm. Since it was mid-winter the warmth was grateful. The rise in temperature was of short duration however for after about an hour heating was turned off and the cold air began to gust into the cell. He pulled the blanket around him as closely as he could and tried to go to sleep but soon it was much too cold and he lay shivering on his hard board, or jumping up and stamping about to revive his circulation, for what seemed to him to be hours.

In the morning he was coughing and sneezing and beginning to feel pretty groggy. Finally his cell door opened and he was taken off to the interrogator of the previous interview.

This gentleman, urbane as ever, repeated his former questions.

"Under the Geneva Convention I am entitled to medical treatment. I wish to see a doctor," replied Hodnett.

"Certainly. That can be arranged as soon as this interview is finished."

The pilot coughed. "And when will that be?"

"When you tell me whether you bombed in formation or individually!"

So back he went to his cell. The heat came on again once more for a short time during the day. In fairness, it must be said that the enemy were very short of fuel and probably could not keep full heating in operation and the comfort of prisoners could hardly be their first consideration. After two full days of this hot and cold routine the pilot's cough was so bad that the enemy removed him to hospital, from whence he was sent to prison camp.

But for the Grace of God, such might have been the lot of any of us that day. Yet so indifferent is human nature that we thought little of the matter once we had eaten a meal and returned to our billet. Only Jock Stark was loud in his lamentations because the Intelligence Officer at debriefing had confiscated his shell base. Jock had expected to retain it as an ashtray but the experts needed anything that might provide evidence of enemy shell filling or fusing, of the type of artillery being deployed, and the quality of metal in use.

We reminded him he was lucky. He might have lost his ashtray but he still had his head.

Now it seemed that our impatience would be satisfied for we continued our railway attacks with another the next day on the yards at Krefeld, where the track line from the heart of the Ruhr divides north and south to feed the front line between Nijmegan and Aachen. We had been there before. It may be thought unnecessary that we should have to go again. In fact, the speed with which the Germans repaired railway damage was equalled only by what our own engineers did here in England during the Blitz. The litter of smashed-up rolling stock pushed aside and remained derelict months after the war had finished as a monument to destruction. Craters were filled in and tracks hastily replaced. Filled-in craters are quite conspicuous from the air; the damage that has been done can be seen even when it has been put right.

This attack of January 29th was routine. We marked the target with a flare and dropped eleven thousand pounds of bombs, on my instruments, over a complete canopy of cloud. One can imagine the sensations of those below in these circumstances as the tornado of bombs comes hurtling through the overcast.

A great weariness accumulated from two days of strain sent me to bed as soon as I could get into it.

During the night snow fell heavily. There was no option but that everybody must get a shovel and clear it away. Crews were detailed to work on the dispersal of their own aircraft and Blenkin's crew were detailed to dig out KH-F for Fox, the kite that had taken us to Krefeld the day before.

"You know," said Frank between puffs and gasps as he slung clods of packed snow from his shovel, "I think I'll ask Allardyce for this kite. No one seems to own it." Squadron Leader Allardyce was the "C" Flight commander.

There was a chorus of approval.

"Suits me. I want to get some guns I can take an interest in," Roy nodded agreement with Harry's remark.

"Well, it's time we had another kite of our own and if we do we shall know it's OK. I'm fed up with flying any ropey old job that comes along - and some of these "C" flight kites are pretty ropey!"

"Nobody owns this one," volunteered the corporal of the maintenance crew, who had contrived a snow plough out of an old door and was doing great execution with it. "I should think you'll get it for the asking!"

"Good enough!" Frank went to work with renewed vigour. "I'll see Allardyce in the morning."

"Considering this snow is only frozen water it's damned heavy." I said rather irrelevently.

So it was settled and we came to be responsible for PD 288 F for Fox, as trusty an aircraft as Avro ever turned out, with ten ops to her credit so far and destined to carry us faithfully for the remainder of our tour and to earn her keep as well as any.

Two days afterwards we went on leave once more. It hardly seemed possible that six weeks could have elapsed, even though time passes very quickly if one is occupied. When there are no days off to mark the conclusion of a week there is little need for the convention of a calendar. The Air Almanac fills all one's need. The sorties we had flown had not been altogether without their teething troubles but they had given us experience that would allow us to consider the elements of the game mastered. No one ever lived long enough to know it all!

Just before leaving the Station we received the news that the operational tour had been put up to forty trips, instead of the present thirty. It seemed that the demands on the heavies were outpacing the supply of trained crews.

"I never thought that when I'd done twelve I should just be starting," was Frank's comment.

"Bet you we never have to do forty", I replied "They alter their minds more often than they change their pants."

"Anyway, we don't have to worry for a long time yet - but I'm damned sorry for chaps like Klenner and Carlton and old Morris." These were all practically up to thirty and would be surprised at the very least to know that their screening was as far away as ever.

"It's hard lines, but I'm certain they'll bring it down. Forty trips is too much in one lump. You start getting itchy and wondering when you're going to buy it, and they'll find that the crews with thirty-plus are getting the chop far too frequently!"

"Maybe. Let's hope you're right." The conversation shifted to the more welcome and immediate subject of leave. "By George, it's good to be going home again."

In our absence the Squadron made several raids. The most noteworthy was directed against the Hansa coking plant at Dortmund and it was a night attack. It was hot, for enemy searchlights were very active and night fighters were up in force. They employed a qualified form of tactics that had been tried and discarded by Fighter Command in 1942, codenamed "Turbinlite". The nightfighter was equipped with a small searchlight. The British method had been to close the fighter right up behind the quarry under ground control and then expose the light when attendant fighters were supposed to close in and despatch the enemy. The snag was that the enemy rear gunner promptly shot out the searchlight and its crew went down. Enemy tactics now were to bring the light to bear from the beam and while the bomber's gunners were swinging their turrets round to bear an attendant nightfighter would pounce from the opposite beam hoping to get in a burst that would do the trick. It was a failure as a tactic.

They were also using fighter flares, which turn night into day almost, and these were observed all the way back to the English coast.

Leslie Harlow and his crew got into trouble again. He was caught by a master searchlight, one provided with interconnected radar detection so that it could be laid on to an aircraft by the detector before being switched on and when the beam exposed the aeroplane would be caught like a butterfly on a pin. Immediately the beam fastened on its prey satellites grouped around it illuminated, forming a cone at the apex of which the aircraft was trapped with little chance of escape from fighters or flak, whichever was operating. The master beam usually appeared of a distinctly blue colour for purposes of discrimination.

Leslie was at twenty thousand feet when he was coned. He did the only possible thing, putting his nose down in a screaming dive and not pulling out until he was down to eight thousand. Even there he was not out of it. In a few minutes the gunners had registered seven attacks by fighters and were in furious action. They managed to avoid the beams of all but a single searchlight which still clung to them however they dodged. Leslie decided to shoot it out. He slid down the beam while Riley stood up in the front turret with both thumbs hard on the firing buttons of the guns. When they were down to very low altitude indeed the light went out. Leslie climbed back as high as he could and bombed the target - "I think we were lower than the Master Bomber", and came home.

Wally, another of my old classmates at Dumfries, was lost with his crew. He was with a squadron based only five miles from us at Stradishall.

The redoubtable Nixon, an Australian pilot of our Squadron, had an experience worthy of Rabelais.

The Air Ministry, in their wisdom, had provided in all bombers a small convenience, placed right back by the tail because the remainder of the fuselage was full of much more important things. The Elsan! This was impossibly inaccessible during an operation when everybody simply must stay at his post for the safety of the bomber. Most crews therefore took with them an old oilcan for the purposes of nature. Nixon then was going merrily along with his engineer sitting beside him and the engineer had just slid back the side window with the intention of emptying the can when a Ju 88 night fighter swung a bright light on to their aircraft.

Nixon corkscrewed violently. The can left the engineer's hand and sailed to the roof, turned over and poured its contents all over the pilot.

He was just beginning to live the incident down when we returned from leave.

Sammy was sitting on the edge of his bed, clad in pyjamas and slippers.

"Any gen, Sammy?" I inquired.

"No, nothing fresh, except old Nixon who keeps taking showers!", and he related the sad tale.

"Tour still forty I suppose?"

"Still forty. We're almost half way. We've been pressing on while you types have been on leave."

"God," I said looking round the hut, "this place is dismal after home! Funny how you get used to it when you live in it. Wonder when the war will end and we'll get out of it!"

"Bags of time yet. I want to get my tour in first. Anyway, have a cup of cocoa."

"Thank the Lord we've got some coke left," I said, wandering over to the ammunition boxes in which we kept the reserve hoard of misappropriated fuel. Then I burst into a sudden fit of almost hysterical laughter at the thought of Sammy's good mother sending him cocoa when he was really at the wars. Who ever heard of a man receiving tins of cocoa in the middle of a campaign. He put the kettle on the iron stove and busied himself preparing the beverage.

Presently the door opened and Blenkin came in.

"Well, if it isn't old Frankie. Good leave, Frankie?"

"Fair enough," he said and was quiet a moment and then he added: "There was a damned nasty accident just now. A chap jumped off the liberty van at the Guard house just as the driver was reversing. I felt the truck go right over him."

We were shocked. "Was he hurt badly?"

"Dead. Quite immediately," was the answer. "There were twenty people in the truck."

"It was one of the bomb aimers," he continued, mentioning the name. "You know, it's strange. There's a chap who goes through half a tour, does a ditching and gets away with it, dodges flak and fighters and then gets knocked off like that. It's queer ..."

"Things like that bear out the old saying," I said. When your number's up you get it and not before and if you're due for it you get it anyway. Poor devil - it does seem hard luck." But we had already developed a cynical attitude to fate.

He shook his head. "We're on tomorrow's battle order," he said slowly. "Let's go to bed."

After a few days of absence from dividers and charts there is a noticeable falling off in the speed and accuracy of plotting. A conscientious man would probably attempt to rectify this by performing an exercise. However, since practice maketh perfect Command itself provided adequately against the hiatus of leave without more ado.

The morning briefing was scrubbed, the afternoon briefing was scrubbed and we were warned to get to bed early as we might be required about midnight.

Not being at all inclined for sleep, Blenkin and I turned in around nine o'clock. I had hardly touched the pillow, it seemed, when I was shaken by the batman and rudely awakened at about ten minutes to midnight. Breakfast was served by sleepy-eyed cooks in the early hours: we pedalled through pitch-blackness to the airfield and while all law-abiding folk were sound asleep made our preparations for a dawn bombing.

Jack was looking casually at the map. "I see there are some unlighted obstructions at Hohenbudberg."

"There ought to be a few more by tonight," I remarked.

It was another rail-junction effort. These bombings were part of the current tactical "Transport Plan" designed to assist the army by disrupting communications in the areas behind the enemy lines. The policy had borne fruit in the Normandy battles. Hohenbudberg is on the same line that feeds into Krefeld, being some half way between the latter place and Duisburg. As was customary when we were attacking rail targets we were armed with a cookie and twelve five-hundred pounders. No incendiaries. Usual target, usual load.

Difficult weather confronted our route and distributed heavy snowclouds about us. The turbulent updraughts played tricks with the wind direction. The upper air was trecherously full of static electricity which flickered around the propellers and jumped between the gun barrels. They that go down to the sea in ships, these men see the works of the Lord. Harry looked at the static with a certain awe, like some old seaman watching the witch-fires in his shrouds. He swore he could feel it running through him when he touched the guns: but this was imagination. Myself, I was worried for the compasses and laid-off vectors on the chart to check their performance.

I had to watch position constantly. As we climbed higher it became certain there was nothing we might do to get to the target at our scheduled time, for we were running in strong, fickle winds and getting later in spite of extra engine power.

As we were coming up to the battle line Harry suddenly blurted: "Fighter - starboard go!" He had no time to give the pilot preliminary warning or even give the full drill patter, for he had spied a Ju 88 closing in from the starboard quarter at about 500 yards range.

"Diving starboard." Frank started to corkscrew the machine which seemed to stand on its nose and fall away from under me. My rulers and dividers fell off the table. I felt light as though I were leaving my seat, everything on the chart table was shifting and in my mind the sudden freezing from fear and feeling like a rat in a trap, for all I could do was sit tight and hope. At least the gunners had the surge of adrenalin. I spread my arms across the charts.

"Rolling - down port."

A great hand pressed me down, pulling at my belly as the pilot pulled up again. Both Harry and Roy had opened fire at the commencement of the dive. I was vaguely aware of the guns. The smell of the cartridges gusted down the aircraft. Again ...

"Rolling, - down starboard."

As we commenced to dive again the enemy decided to seek easier prey and broke off the action. Harry said:

"OK skipper. Level out. We've lost him."

"Resuming course, navigator."

"Nice work, Harry. You saw him just in time." Roy, who was always sparing in conversation was undoubtedly relieved. So was I and now that it was over I had time to realize how scared I had been. It was still dark but the eastern part of the sky was greying with a dangerous half-light which gave an advantage to a fighter coming in from behind. The gunners redoubled their watch, calling now and then for a banking search to enable them to cover the blind area underneath the aircraft. We ploughed on, getting later and later until we were a good ten minutes behind time. The only consolation was that everybody would be in the same boat.

In the first light of a stormy-looking morning we reached the target. I set up the blind bombing equipment and down went the load and our marker flare.

"Holding steady for photo!" said Frank. "I can see bags of TIs."

The road home was blocked with thunderheads. Half way across Europe we ran into a great wall, stretching to the horizon and writhing across our path. The skipper reported that he was going off course to try to find a gap between the cumulonimbus; he decided against going down and risking the machine in the ice and turbulence. Fortunately, we were light having burned off half our fuel and shed our bombs. He was able to get to 23,000 feet before he found a gap through which he thrust the Lancaster. One of our crews took their aircraft to above 25,000 feet before clearing the barrier. The ceiling of the aircraft, unloaded, was supposed to be higher than this but at twenty-five thousand she was slopping and wallowing all over the sky, practically out of control and uncomfortable to handle.

When our particular photograph was developed it showed a very neat and compact cluster of target indicators. In spite of this the whole attack was unsuccessful, possibly through error in calculating the mathematical co-ordinates of release or in the phasing of the ground transmitters. Ground detail showing here and there on the prints was enough to enable Intelligence staff to determine where the bombs had fallen and on the average it was about three miles from the chosen target.

A most disappointing result, even if it were the fortune of war. As well take the golden sovereigns of the British taxpayer and throw them in the sea.

We sat back and did nothing for three days. As Montgomery and his men were pushing forward in the Nijmegen area, getting closer to the Rhein, we smelt some close-support work. The news was certainly greatly improved with progress on both the Western Front and in the East where the Russians were advancing in a series of thrusts all along their extended line. Speculation began to be rife in the Mess on the probable duration of the war and whether or not the "Ruskies" would be first in Berlin. Not in our wildest dreams did we think of where we were going to be sent and of the terrible onslaught that Air Chief Marshall Harris was preparing for Dresden.

Chapter 15

THUNDERCLAP

Volumes have been written about the destruction of Dresden and it may ill become a mere front-line navigator to try to add anything to the highly researched works of such authors as Mr David Irving and Mr Alexander McKee. Be it so, but at least, to employ a cliché I was there and I still retain my logs and chart of the operation, legal documents acceptable as evidence in courts martial, so such data as I may quote concerning the tactics is factual. Moreover, I am amazed when I now look at them at the accuracy and neatness of work I was able to produce under the conditions of the time.

It is not for the fighting man to try to make moral judgments. "Theirs not to reason why!" It probably interferes with his efficiency if he starts to question. Any responsibility for causes and effects must rest on higher shoulders. When, with natural concern, I afterwards pondered over the raid when its horrors became evident, I was forced to the conclusion that it was an act of war. As such it was as clinical as any other.

Dresden, a city normally of half a million inhabitants, beautiful, medieval, the capital of old Saxony, a place noted for centuries of culture, was gripped by fear in the early days of February. On the Eastern front Marshall Konev pushed his forces steadily forward. The Russian flood engulfed the plain and lapped along the mountains to the south-east. Before it swept the refugees, similar pitiful debris of war to that which had so often fled before the Wehrmacht. Apprehension, fearful suspense, must have filled every mind. Those who could flee made preparation. Those who had anything to hide dug holes in the earth for their treasures. The city, threatened with siege, looked to its supplies. The population was grossly swollen by the influx of terrified humanity and the congestion could hardly be relieved for the roads and railways were under military jurisdiction. There was no accommodation; the battalions of the army, reinforcing the front, were using the city as a last depot and railhead.

Dresden at this time probably contained a million souls.

From the East came the danger and few could hazard how long it would be before the Red Army marched in. Here lay the fear, of the possible sack of the city by enemy troops. Dresden had known battles and defeat in the past but no one within it could have imagined the shocking blows that were to fall on the city from the air.

After all, Dresden is nearly 14 degrees East longitude. It could reasonably and legitimately be considered integral with the eastern front. The Russians had only a few bombers. It was as far from the airfields of

Bomber Command as Stettin or the tip of Sweden. Generally untroubled throughout the war, the city was ill provided with shelters or air-raid precautions, even for its normal population.

On the night of February 13th at 22.00 hours the first markers went down, heralding what was probably the most murderous bombing of the war, even including the atom bombings that happened afterwards. The crucifixion of Dresden began.

But, before proceeding, let us glance at that publication so well beloved by Air Reich Marshall Göring in 1942 - *Bädecker*.

Dresden, it says, was first mentioned in history in 1206 and had been the residence of kings from 1485. It was greatly extended and embellished by the splendour-loving August II "the Strong" and rapidly increased in size during the 19th century.

The city lies on both banks of the Elbe which separates the Aldstadt and Frederichstadt with their suburbs, from the Neustadt and Antonstadt which are north of the river and were re-erected after a fire in 1685. The beautiful environs and the magnificent picture gallery attracted numerous visitors, and a considerable English community (according to *Bädecker*) lived there, though these doubtless had gone into internment or elsewhere.

The garrison is quoted at 1,100 men, so presumably it might have justifiably been called a garrison town!

Dresden was the cradle of rococo art. Its beauties, its palaces, its works of art and its royal library of 400,000 volumes occupy thirty pages of the travel guide. There is comment on the manufacture of fine porcelain which is synonymous with the name of the town, but not much other industry, which however must exist in a community of that size, particularly in wartime.

There were four railway stations, three south of the river and one north, the biggest being the Hauptbahnhof, feeding a wide range of railways to Leipzig, Berlin, Chemnitz, Prague and so on. It is a pity that strategical railways must needs run into centres of culture and that porcelain factories can be turned over to the making of ceramics for the electrical industry. It is even more of a pity that the place had not been declared an open city, although that did not save Rotterdam from Göring's Luftwaffe.

By the middle of February Dresden had become a place of the utmost tactical importance to the enemy in view of its relation to the Russian front. Its rail communications, its junction with the autobahn and its telephones, indeed its links with the interior of Germany made it a key position.

Sir Arthur Harris mentions that in previous years the weather, the size of the force and the limitations of H2S had prevented attacks on targets as far away, but with the German army rolled back to the frontiers of the Reich, GH and Oboe ground transmitters were quickly set up behind the front line and these ensured the success of attacks on distant targets. In

February 1945 he was instructed by "people much more important than myself" to attack the city.

The British attack was divided into two parts. The first aircraft were over the target in the early evening, with some cloud below although meteorological conditions on the way out from England had been reasonably good. The cloud did not hinder the markers, in Mosquitoes of No. 5 Group.

Bomb loads were predominantly of incendiaries. The city was old and very soon it was shrouded in flame.

When I came into briefing and learned where the night's target was I experienced a moment of apprehension. It was a long haul, the longest we had yet been called upon to do. I prepared the outward journey on one log form and the return on a second, knowing full well I should need them both for the amount of work there would be before dawn.

We were told we should be in the first wave of the second attack, consisting of some 400 Lancasters and Halifaxes. It was a full scale operation. H hour was 01.30 next morning. Our time on target 01.33 hours.

I measured the route at 803 statute miles to Dresden and 793 back - a total of 1,596 miles. We had full tanks, twenty-two hundred gallons of fuel. The aircraft were armed with one 4,000 lb cookie and all the rest incendiary bombs, six clusters of four-pound incendiary bombs, a total of nine hundred of these wicked little bombs on each aircraft. These incendiaries were hexagonal in section, packed close together in a big canister and locked with a release bar. They were safe when loaded in this way, the fuse being a press-button which was kept in by the neighbouring bomb, but they became live on being dropped.

The perimeter bus delivered me to the aircraft just before nine o'clock at night. The others were all inside, checking and making their preparations. I laid out my table, read the barometric pressure on the pilot's altimeter, logged it and checked the "Z" equipment which I switched on to tell the cathode tube gunners we were friendly. It had got to that stage!

Johnnie wired my curtain and saw no chink of light could show when it was in place. We synchronized the compasses.

At 21.37 we were airborne, climbing and making a great circuit of the airfield. Everyone was relieved when we had attained some sort of height. The whole machine would have burned like a torch with the load there was aboard had anything happened at take-off. Frank got the heavy bomber off the runway within two minutes of our scheduled take-off time, having rolled out of dispersal with excellent judgment. We had forty minutes in which to get to height and settle down. The Squadron was putting out a strong effort and control were having no hasty, last-minute rushes. Once we had reached the circuit height there was leisure to arrange the paraphernalia of navigation in the confined space of the cabin, to put the spare pencils and dividers in the pilot's hat which I always used for this purpose because it did not slip on the table. It was so weather-beaten.

I found three wind velocities that checked pretty well with Met. The airstream was westerly. A calm, orderly, state of mind fortified me to face the long night watch.

At 22 hours 19 minutes 30 seconds, Greenwich time we set course of 244 degrees true, which was 255 degrees by magnetic compass. The aircraft flew at 3,000 feet and true airspeed of 181 mph. The raid that preceded us had already fired the target.

Our first turning pilot point was Reading which we were due to reach at 22.52 hours. When the flight was planned a number of concentration points were detailed together with the times at which we should be on them. By adhering to these times navigators kept the bomber stream together, with mutual protection for all.

At 22.35 hours after taking several fixes and finding a slightly increased windspeed I called for ten miles an hour extra airspeed.

We turned southeast at Reading, within a half-minute of time, and commenced to climb, having 155 mph on the clock and estimating the English coast at 23.13.30 hours. The coast was crossed just north of Beachy Head, a minute late for the wind had backed and slackened. The bomber was now at 9,000 feet, in level flight, crew not yet on oxygen except for gunners and pilot who were using it as an aid to their night vision. Our true airspeed was now 195 mph. At 23.15 hours over the sea Jack tested the bomb doors by opening and closing them, and also fused the load.

The French coast must be made by 23.29.

In point of fact the wind fell off even more over the Channel. When the bombardier pinpointed me three miles to starboard on the track line on the French coast we were two minutes behind. I was not unduly disturbed. In a few more minutes we were going to turn east on an enormously long leg straight for over three hundred miles, with every opportunity for making up time. Johnnie would not consent to more engine now when a few extra revolutions on the long leg would enable us to make up.

At 23.37 hours we altered course eastward, to 103 degrees true, and started to climb at 300 feet a minute. The tactics required the bomber stream to level out at 17,000 feet. I estimated a mean average wind velocity for the climb of 260 degrees 50 mph. The area in which we were flying could no longer be considered to be covered by Eastern Chain Gee. I unscrewed Radio Frequency Unit No. 25, took the No. 27 tin can from the rack and fitted it to the set and then tuned the Rheims Chain.

The rest of the crew buckled their masks across their faces and went on to oxygen.

At 23.49 I took a fix, getting the B and D pulses strongly. I found the aircraft had drifted to starboard and could be considered off track - that is five miles from the ink line on the chart. The fringes of the stream were dangerous; outside the window cover of preceding aircraft. I ordered a sixty-degree alteration to port and working like fury calculating the wind and new course in time to turn within three minutes.

At 23.56 we levelled out; 17,000 feet, and increased airspeed to 216 mph true. This was giving the Lancaster the quite respectable ground speed of 258 mph. Travelling at such a rate we should soon enter a weather front that spread its snares across our route. Sure enough, ten minutes later I found the wind was backing - there had been an alteration of 30 degrees in its direction with greatly increased speed. We were now swinging off to port.

I took another fix to make sure, calculated a DR position three minutes ahead and laid off an alteration of course. The wind had risen to what would have been a howling typhoon on the ground, of 105 mph. In the silence of the upper air it bore us on wings half as fast as our own and pushed us along at 290 mph relative to the surface of the earth.

Twenty minutes past midnight and the bomber crossed the battle line of the Western front. The menacing drone of the airfleet that filled all space for half an hour must have laid cold fingers of fear on the enemy troops in their foxholes below until the sound faded into the distance.

I signalled Turner to switch on our automatic radar jamming apparatus. There had been H2S silence up till now, the reason being that it was considered the enemy could home on to the transmissions. I switched on and tuned the set and started the scanner rotating. There was intercom silence throughout the machine. In one's ears was the faint chatter of mush and the almost inaudible drone of the motors that one felt rather than heard. The pilot sat rigidly at the controls staring into the blackness, hands strong on the wheel. Beside him, sharing his watch, the engineer alternately peered ahead or cast an expert eye over his dozen of dials, making notes by the red light of a shaded torch of his temperatures and fuel consumption. The bombardier laboured at the monotonous job of opening the bales of window foil and pushing them regularly down the chute. The wireless operator listened assiduously as he tuned his dials. The navigator made his endless calculations. While in the isolation, the cold draughty turrets, the gunners swung hither and thither, stiff hands ready on the gun controls, systematically dividing the sky between them and trying not to be caught unawares by the phantoms of their strained imagination or by the prowling night fighters. Thus each man performed his task in harmony, his very life a common stake with his fellows as the deadly efficient black shape of the Lancaster sped eastwards towards the holocaust.

By this time enemy jamming had made Gee practically useless. I took a fix at 00.29 hours from pulses that were obtained with the utmost difficulty against the background of enemy interference.

At 00.41. Position "D", four minutes ahead of time now, altered course

Rivers, Manitoba. Course members in RCAF flying gear. Melville Parry is end right.

Blenkin's crew

Flt. Lieut. R. L. Austin

Blenkin's crew at a dispersal

Lancasters of 218 Squadron showing the banded tact fins indicating Gee-H equipment carried

Navigator and Pilot

A recent nostalgic visit. Two elderly gentlemen, pilot (left) and rear gunner standing in front of the hut in which we were accomodated at Chedburgh. Now used as a farm building!

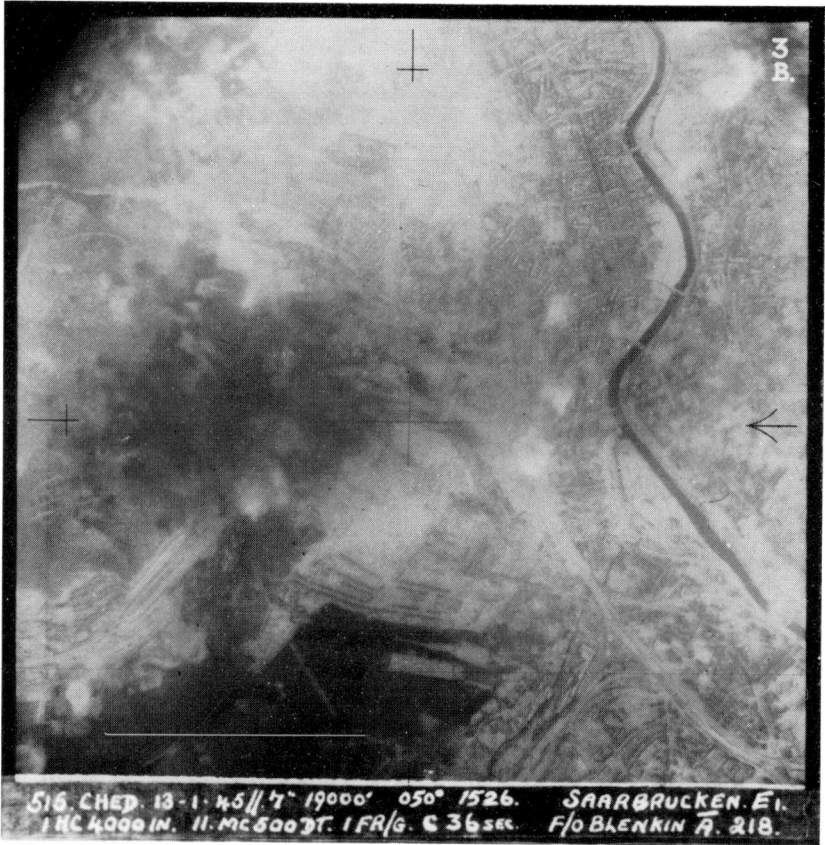

A typical aiming point photograph taken by photo-flash over the target and required to establish where the bombs had fallen.

The Dresden bomb plot - the target entirely obscured by the halations of the fires below.

A daylight target photograph of our last raid on Regensburg.

in accordance with the tactics. Course 079 true, 084 by compass, airspeed 216 mph true, giving a ground speed of just over three hundred, for now the wind was dead on our tail. At five miles a minute a navigator cannot afford to make mistakes. I tried the Gee box again but succeeded in getting nothing better than a position line from the "D" pulse. This provided a good track check however.

As was usual on a full-scale operation Command was broadcasting winds. By providing uniform navigational data for everyone to use they kept the stream intact and compact. The winds were found by experienced crews using H2S, transmitted back to Command, co-ordinated by expert meteorologists and re-broadcast. Turner, who had the times of these transmissions and was listening on the Command frequency, presently passed me a piece of paper. The winds sent were:

Average for the last half-hour   ...   248 degrees 85 mph
Average for the next half hour   ...   255 degrees 80 mph

at our height. Using these, with air positions from the API matching course very closely, I commenced navigating by Dead Reckoning.

00.55.30 hours. Position "E" altered course 036 true 040 compass. The magnetic variation in this area 11 degrees East longitude was only half of that in East Anglia. Half way between the charted isogonals I turned the variation control of the compass back a degree.

We now had to climb to bombing height and had the option of going anywhere from eighteen to twenty thousand feet according to the condition of the aircraft and its climbing powers. Blenkin had already decided that Fox would go to maximum height, which gave the opportunity I was waiting for to loose three minutes that I was ahead of time. I told the pilot to climb at 200 feet a minute with the airspeed back to 150 indicated.

The bomber climbed for 13 mintues 30 seconds before we levelled out and increased speed to 160 indicated, equivalent to 220 true at this height of 20,000 feet. The outside temperature was minus 26 degrees Centigrade. We were just right for time.

More winds came through. They provided a comfortable link with England, where hundreds of men and women were standing watch throughout the tiring hours waiting for our return.

01.16 hours. Position "F", 12 degrees East longitude. We turned for the final leg into the target, now only 76 miles away.

"Navigator to pilot; you can listen out for the Master Bomber any time now. Call sign, "King Cole". Mainforce call sign "Strongman" Target ETA 01.33".

"Thanks, nav."

A short interval, then he called almost with relief, "You're all right nav. I can see the target already. Good show!"

"There's another quarter of an hour to run", I warned.

"Yes - OK - Quiet everybody", as he switched over to RT.

I made all my preparations for leaving the target, set the variation of only 3 degrees west on the control and at 01.20 hours worked out a final position and ETA target, then I extinguished my light, gathered up my oxygen hosing and telephone wire and crawled under the curtain.

Before us, glittering against the velvet black of the night the stricken, blazing city glowed like a great opal. In awful Olympian detachment separated by the gulf of thin, clear air the oncoming aircrews looked down on the work that their fellows had started so well that only a Dante could describe it. The whole area was a great mass of flame. An incredible, fantastic sight. As I watched the yellow flame was shot with pinpoints and splashes of coloured light as the target indicators landed and burst. Blossoming orchids of destruction. Outside the general blurr of the great fires the streets could be picked out as lines of flame like a row of bright bands on a string. Above the city was a corona of glare; as we drew close the black silhouettes of aircraft shot at enormous speed across the picture. We ourselves were bearing down at 300 mph.

The voice of the master bomber came through very cool and clear, giving directions to the bombardiers as he circled away low down where the rain of bombs was already falling.

Now I could see a great pall of smoke rising from the target, changing direction in the upper layers of the air and loosing itself in the night. There must have been huge convection. I stood fascinated, photographing on my mind every detail, straining all my powers of observation to take in every detail for I realized that never again would I see the like of this. Unlike the others I had no need to worry about loss of night-vision arising from staring at the brightness.

Searchlights had either been swamped by the previous attack or there were none. At least, I have no impression of seeing any. Nor did my awe-struck gaze take in any gun fire, although the night was shot with flashes as the attack opened and the sky began to flicker with the unnatural aurora of the bomb bursts, like summer lightning, over the target.

The city was given to the flames. It seemed unnecessary to fling down further destruction. Yet the weight of the second attack had not begun to be felt.

Jack commenced directing the bombing run. I knew I had to get back to my table. I gave a long last look at the inferno and went back.

Our bombs fell at 01.33 hours, exactly on time. The bombardier had the centre of the target indicators well in his sight and was extremely satisfied. It says much for the level of efficiency that Bomber Command had reached by now that a crew could arrive at a target hundreds of miles from home and deliver an attack timed to the minute.

Immediately the camera flashed we turned starboard on to 154 degrees true, increasing airspeed to 180 mph indicated - 248 true.

The aircraft lurched violently as Frank swerved to avoid another aircraft. Even before my heart had time to get back to its normal position we were on an even keel.

"It almost took my turret off," Roy exclaimed. "If he had put his wheels down he would have run along the top of us".

We turned on to a south-easterly course and started to descend. We were now at 13 degrees 55 minutes East and I was working on the extreme edge of the chart, our air position being even farther eastwards than the city ... At this point some of the gunners claimed to have seen the flicker of the Russian artillery on the skyline. The atmosphere was clear and this was quite possible.

Obviously the target had provided a sound fix. From this I derived a wind velocity of 260/71 mph. The windspeed was slackening. The broadcast wind on the next chit handed me by the wireless operators confirmed this, with figures in agreement.

We descended at 500 feet a minute and increased airspeed: then levelled out at 16,000 feet and cruised for half-an-hour at 175 mph indicated, 255 true. In spite of this the wind, now in our teeth, cut our groundspeed down to 150, which was very dangerous.

The crew settled down to the remaining hours of flight. In order to avoid any relaxation of vigilance after the target the gunners maintained their turret swinging and searching. Turner busied himself with "Fishpond"; his radar screen worked from the H2S which could give a blip on a closing aircraft so that the operator could give directional warning to the gunners. From time to time Jack called to the engineer and myself to push forward fresh bundles of "window" from the stock along the fuselage.

At 02.18 hours the glare from the target one hundred and twenty miles away was still visible in the sky. The second wave had all cleared the target by this time leaving behind unquenchable fires.

We commenced to descend at breakneck speed, 254 mph indicated, which was 298 mph true. Five minutes later we levelled out, dropping airspeed to 180. All in accordance with orders. I altered course 10 degrees to port, to allow for decreased wind strength and our lower airspeed.

02.36 hours. Position "J", altered course to 246 degrees true in accordance with the route. At this point the rear gunner passed me a turret bearing on some heavy flak to starboard. This could only be from Nürnberg and the bearing provided a very useful position line. Some luckless crew were having trouble with their navigation and stirring up the defences.

H2S was of little use tonight. Those sets were certainly temperamental.

Fifteen minutes later we were edging to starboard and altered course six degrees to correct this. By the time our next turning point was reached we were right on the ink line but beginning to lag timewise.

03.13.30 hours. Position "K" altered course 265 degrees true making good a due westerly track. Here we were ordered to climb to 14,000 feet maintaining the same airspeed. These changes of height were all part of the tactical scheme for giving the enemy as much difficulty as possible with interceptions. We were now in the thick of the night-fighter belt.

I took a fresh packet of Horlick's tablets from the skipper's upturned hat and asked if anyone wanted a couple. Frank asked for a benzedrine tablet. Harry, who was undoubtedly feeling the strain of continuous tension, called me for an ETA at the battle line. I calculated it at 03.44 hours and told him. Truth to tell I was beginning to feel very tired; there was a vague ache in my head and I relished the Horlick's greatly. Presently Johnnie also asked for benzedrine.

At 03.35 I recorded my last series of broadcast wind, for the blips were beginning to tremble on the turned-up Gee screen. I took and plotted my first fix from the box and a load of trouble fell from my mind as I found the aircraft on track, with everything under control.

"Gee's back, skipper", I reported, expecting my own satisfaction to be shared by everyone, for the reappearance of the blips to me engendered feelings rather similar to those experienced by Columbus when he saw a fresh green log.

"OK. How much longer before we're back home?"

"Two-and-a-half hours yet".

"Fair enough - everybody OK?"

We were over the Rhein. Position "L" was reached at 03.55 hours and the new course set. We were running behind time, constantly losing minutes in the face of a strong wind. We kept to the briefing airspeeds for there was no use in straining to keep time at this stage of the return, with most of the bomber stream behind us and fuel none too plentiful.

04.43.45 hours. We changed course at Position "M". 49 degrees north 05 degrees east for Orfordness on the English coast. A long straight leg of 261 miles and infinite weariness. I asked the pilot for 190 indicated for we were beginning to get well behind time. The Lancaster commenced a gentle descent, not before time for the oxygen was getting low. We had been using it for five hours. At length I was able to uncouple the mask and wipe the sweat and moisture from my face.

Jack, who had his maps out, passed the time of crossing the Aisne. I made a small alteration of course to starboard and then, finding that the sky was clear and we were flying level at 7,000 feet, I decided to take an Astro fix for practice. I therefore went through the labour of shooting Jupiter, which was unmistakably brilliant, then the much more difficult Pole Star. This gave me a good cut but the fix, compared with Gee positions taken before and after, was nine miles too far to port. It would have been better than nothing in an emergency, but more could not be said of it.

We crossed the French and English coasts. Oh welcome England! We came down to two thousand feet and reached base. The aircraft landed at 07.09 on February 14th, having been flying for 9 hours, 32 minutes.

Tired out, so that we sat in the perimeter bus staring vacantly ahead;

dirty, the outline of helmet and mask drawn in grime on each face; hungry, we gulped down the coffee and the grateful shot of rum, we dragged .through the formality of debriefing and fell into bed like men drugged.

While we slept a great force of Americans formed up and went flying over Germany. Four hundred and fifty of them turned towards Dresden which they reached just after mid-day. The ill-fated city still burnt furiously and was covered by a thick pall of smoke, into which the Fortresses unloaded their bombs. A force of similar size split away to plaster the industrial town of Chemnitz, which is thirty-five miles south-west of Dresden and is a large manufacturing centre besides being a railway junction.

As the reports came in it was more and more apparent that Dresden was the scene of the most frightful havoc. In the first place, photographs taken by the crews gave ample evidence both of the marking and the subsequent conflagration. Our own photograph was a mass of halations from fire glare, streaked with the brilliant zig-zags of burning incendiary clusters.

Then the German radio. According to *The Times* of February 15th: "The German wireless announced last night that the Dresden Opera House where most of Richard Strauss's operas were first produced, was totally destroyed by air attacks". It continued: "Other buildings laid in ruins are the famous Zwinger, built in the reign of August the Strong, a jewel of European baroque; the Royal Palace, the picture gallery which before the war housed the Sistine Madonna; the Academy of Arts; the Japanese Palace and the old and new town halls".

All the British newspapers next day carried stories of this triple bombing when 650,000 incendiaries had gone down, besides 4,000 and 8,000 lb cookies in the RAF raid alone. Yet another quote from *The Times:* "The RAF made two night attacks on Dresden. In the second the master bomber watched the bombing throughout and as soon as part of the industrial area (sic) was well alight, switched the attack to another. There was only a small amount of flak and crews were able to make careful and straight runs". (The parenthesis are mine).

One report suggested that the heat of the fires acted like a gigantic Fido and cleared the clouds away from the area after the first attack got under way. However this may be, there is no doubt that atmospheric conditions for bombing were excellent, so far as I myself saw them.

Accounts came from various sources that proved beyond doubt that a mortal blow had been dealt to the city. Stung to fury by the raids Hitler threatened to shoot a number of British and American airmen prisoners of way as a reprisal. He was dissuaded from this by his advisers.

Some time afterwards I met a Frenchman, a DuClos, who was a prisoner of war on forced labour in Silesia. He passed through Dresden, and also Chemnitz which was bombed next night, within a week of the bombings. He told a terrible tale.

The night bombings, he said, were very destructive, causing the bulk of the casualties, about 113,000 out of an estimated nearly two hundred thousand. These figures have since been discounted. An enormous number of the dead were trapped in the railway stations waiting to get away from the advancing Russians. For weeks the dead lay around the streets in great heaps - he claimed to have seen piles of corpses so high he could not look over them. Many died of sheer suffocation because the fantastic intensity of the flames sucked up all the oxygen from the air. The terrific heat caused trees to explode and light up like torches without being touched by nearby flame. Faced with this tremendous temperature doomed citizens were unable to leave their cellars while the houses fell about them. It was a fire typhoon, similar to that at Hamburg.

He further added that when the Russian army took the city on May 8th they had to use flame-throwers to clear up the remains of a horrifying mess.

This is no figment of the imagination of a Gustave Doré. DuClos, who when I met him was employed in Joint Air Traffic Control in Paris at the same time as myself, was a man of phlegmatic temperament, unlikely to exaggerate. There were other tales. For instance, an RAF officer friend of mine met a German woman in the Rheinland who had been in Dresden at the time. Two days before the bombing she gave birth to a child. She was driven from her bed by the raid and the new-born infant killed. Terror struck, escaping for her life, she managed to flee from the city and dragged herself westward for weeks until she reached the Rhein.

Months later the occupying Russians allowed some American correspondents to visit the ruined city. The Associated Press reported that the Russians expressed "amazement at the results which Western Air power had accomplished in less than a single day". Major General Dimitry Dubrovsky, the Governor, said that bodies were still being taken out of the rubble.

I am able to quote from an article published in retrospect in the *New York Herald Tribune* of January 11, 1946 by their correspondent Mr Russell Hill. I quote with their permission the following extracts which closely tie up with the words of DuClos. Russell Hill wrote:

"The ruins of Dresden are more depressing to behold than those of any other German city I have seen. There is a completeness to the destruction in the heart of this town, which was counted among the most beautiful in Germany, that is not matched in Berlin ... One cannot help feeling unhappy as one views the pile of ruins picturesquely set along the winding Elbe ... Dresden's historically famous buildings were concentrated in the old city ... All are gutted except the Frauenkirche which can be accurately described as levelled".

His next paragraph questions the necessity of the bombing. He goes on to say:

"Against whatever dubious military advantages may have been gained must be set the destruction of irreplaceable artistic and cultural monuments and a death toll estimated by the Germans at up to 300,000". (A grossly exaggerated figure).

It will never be known exactly how many died. But it may be said confidently that from the point of view of the civilian population, the bombings that were concentrated into the two days from February 13th to 15th were the most horrible that occurred anywhere, at any time, in Europe ..."

"The population was taken by surprise when at 10 o'clock on the night of February 13th the first wave of RAF bombers came over. They literally set fire to the city. The second wave came at 1.30. The houses crumbled, caving in the cellars where the terrified people huddled for safety. If the cellars held up the people suffocated inside them. When they tried to come out they were thrown back by the heat in the streets.

"The next morning many of the survivors fled to the "gros garten" to get away from the burning houses. They were caught by the 8th Air Force's noon raid by 500 bombers. The Americans were supposed to attack the marshalling yards but could not see them because of the clouds, so the bombs were dropped on the general area of the city.

"In the main railway station three trains full of refugees were caught and destroyed ... When the Red Army arrived on May 8th it ordered the thousands of corpses that were still being taken out of the debris to be piled up in the Altmarkt, or Old Market. The streets leading to the square were roped off and flame throwers were turned on the putrid bodies."

Mr. Russell Hill's vivid and factual report crystallizes the horror of the whole business. If one subsequently spoke to any German and mentioned the name of Dresden he would shake his head numbly and turn away his face. Whenever I think of bombing and what it has come to mean as a means of war there rises in my mind a picture of that doomed city blazing five miles below. A picture that only time perhaps will dim. Let us hope that men will not have to see the like again.

* * * * *

Hardly, it seemed had my head touched the pillow when I was conscious of a rough shaking.

"Wake up, sir", said a voice, "briefing is at 15.30."

I struggled into wakefulness, still heavy with the fatigue of the previous night. I was furious. My watch told me the time was half past two. Precious little time in which to get ready and have a meal.

Frank rubbed his eye and sat up in bed. The extra hour between navigation and main briefings gave him plenty of time.

"Curse it, Frankie ... I had no idea there was a battle order today. Why the devil don't they put these things up!"

"Hope it's a Ruhr trip. Another like last night will just about kill me!"

Zip - zip went my flying boots. I hastily stuffed my pockets with diversion kit, checking as I went ... "Identity card - yes - flask - yes - pen and pencil - O.K." I thrust a torch down the side of my boot.

"See you later!" and I slammed the door of the hut behind me.

Hopes of a short trip were doomed to disappointment as soon as the Navigation Officer came into the briefing room. "After last night's very successful effort you are going to do another job in support of the Russians. The target is Chemnitz."

An audible groan went up as the navigators hastily scanned their charts to see where the place was situated.

"The Yanks have been there today with 450 Forts. We don't expect you'll see anything though, for Met. expect cloud over the area." The briefing officer droned on while I tried to concentrate on drawing lines and measuring angles and forcing the tiredness from my mind.

"Broadcast winds again tonight. You are in force B and you'll get your winds at fifteen and forty-five minutes past the hour. H hour is 00.30. You are on at H plus eight to H plus twelve", and so on with all the repetition of detail that had to be recorded. The tactics in the target area are more complicated than usual, I thought, as I inked my planned route on the chart and marked the points of descent and level out as a guide. Possibly Command expect fighter opposition. Nice thought! Not helped when Intelligence came in with a lot of small British flags having an identifying message printed in Russian. "If you're shot up over the target, better press on into Russian-held territory - you should easily make it", adding, "for God's sake wave these when the guerillas come up!"

"As long as last night - damn all difference. I make it 1,567 miles in all". The man behind leaned over my shoulder anxious to check the route with me. I passed the involved Flight Plan back to him and went out for a cup of coffee.

We went out on to the dishpan, waiting for the trolley accumulators to start up our engines. There was time to look around the machine while the last cigarette was puffed by the smokers. The bomb doors were open, long black shapes below the length of the body, and as the bombardier flashed his torch along the load I saw it was almost entirely incendiaries. "What have we got, Jack?" "Fourteen hundred incendiaries and one five-hundred pounder to stir up the fires!" he replied, rather pleased at the thought of getting his eye on a bombsight and dropping the load himself. Last night had whetted his appetite after all the instrument bombing we had been doing.

The quiet night, accentuating the senses, was full of the pungent, oily smell of the aircraft, not unpleasant to those who were the creatures of these machines as we all were from pilot to fitter's mate. The mind emptied itself, the body relaxed, drawing all its energies into itself against the strain of the next ten hours. Waiting to go, the very fact of having to go, was anathema, although once the routine of flight commenced one would respond automatically.

The outward journey was uneventful, a repetition of a dozen others, or, perhaps, it would be better to say that it was quite successful, with good track and time-keeping and nothing untoward to hinder us as we climbed to 20,000 feet.

At 00.30 hours the engineer went down into the bomb hatch to continue the pushing out of "Window" while Jack was engaged on the bombing run. Excitement started. The attack was opening and the voice of the master bomber crackled in the telephones.

"Bombardier. There go the flares. Ten degrees left - left!" the run up had started.

"Seven minutes to go!"

"Yes, O.K. nav. We can see the target."

Time for me to get under the curtain. I slipped up beside the skipper and was leaning half left, very intent, looking down to port. As my sight began to be adjusted to the darkness, without saying anything, I commenced to search on the starboard bow as well as my eyes would let me.

The area was covered with cloud that entirely obscured the ground. Over the aiming point hung the great candles of the sky-manner flares, slowly burning as they settled down turning night into day. Now and then I caught a glimpse of a bomber, minute and black, as it sped away. The clouds illuminated from below by the fires from the rain of bombs were luminous to a remarkable extent, a sea of mother o'pearl shot here and there with red and orange, and flickering constantly as they diffused the flashes from beneath. I formed the impression that the attack would be scattered, a difficult enough matter to judge from the short reconnaissance I had time to make, yet the lit-up areas seemed too dispersed for a really concentrated effort. There was no moon and if searchlights were active they were unable to penetrate the cloud but the amount of light below the overcast was enough to give one an uncomfortable naked feeling when the thought of high-flying nightfighters entered the mind. In these circumstances, plainly silhouetted, it was necessary for the gunners to exercise even more than usual vigilance, if that was possible.

When we were on top of the markers I went back to work.

About ten minutes out of the target Turner passed me a message chit and in doing so must have knocked his elbow against the switch panel on his starboard side. In an alarmed, urgent voice Jack shouted ...

"The nose light's on."

"Christ! Get that light out ... quickly!"

I waved my hand frantically in front of Turner.

"Wop speaking."

"Get that nose light off, Turner. The nose light's on!" The skipper's orders came before I had time to speak. Turner leaned over and in the dimness I saw him flick over the switch.

"O.K. skipper." Jack reported.

"I must have knocked it with my elbow", from Turner. Relief settled over the aircraft for a few minutes. "We'll have those fuses out in future Turner" said Frank.

The sight of an aircraft showing any lights would be greeted with perverse satisfaction by other members of the bomber stream, who immediately took steps to get away as far as possible from the culprit. We learned our lesson from this scare. In future the fuses of the light circuits were removed before we crossed the English coast and I took care to ascertain where the switches were that governed the lights, just in case.

I went on systematically plotting position with the broadcast winds. I plotted a DR every ten minutes, automatically. We were all weary and in such conditions habit takes the place of positive thought. Now I discovered that we were off track to port by about ten miles.

"Navigator to skipper. Alter course thirty starboard - snap alteration".

"Thirty starboard it is!"

I intended to regain track by running on this roughly amended course, using the time this would take to make fresh calculations.

Frank began to see flak bursts above. He didn't take much notice of them but saw them in a detached fashion as though they were of no concern. He said, in an undisinterested tone: "There's flak bursting up above."

At this time we were cruising with altitude eleven thousand feet, doing a steady 220 mph over the ground.

"Funny, there's some bursting below!" Jack called as if in answer.

Suddenly - whoosh, whoosh! The flak was bursting all around us and we were caught in searchlights.

The nose went down; the pilot acted instinctively. My charts began to rise from the table and I spread my arms over them. The needle of the airspeed indicator in front of me was going right round the clock, 220-240-260 and it commenced a second revolution. The altimeter fell back like the seconds hand of a watch. We must have been approaching 400 mph.

Harry, with great presence of mind called out: "You all right, skipper?"

"Yes, - O.K."

"Pull out!"

In fact, Harry told me afterwards that he thought we had had it and rotated his turret on the beam and grabbed his parachute.

"Yes, right."

Frank, recovering from the temporary blindness of the searchlight glare, pulled back on the stick but strong as he was it was not enough to pull the plunging bomber out. We were in the most deadly danger. The elevator design of the Lancaster was such that there might come a moment when it would be impossible to pull out. It was a matter of seconds.

"Trim back, - trim back!" he ordered, his voice tense. The engineer needed no bidding. He was winding the elevator trim as hard as he could go. Frank braced desperately, pulling the column with all his might and after seconds that seemed ages the tail started to come down and she eased out of the headlong descent and started to climb.

As soon as the machine was thoroughly under control "Good thing you called, Harry," the skipper said.

"I was getting pretty windy, stuck up in the air like that!"

"Christopher - that was near." But perhaps the saint was indeed fulfilling his function as far as we were concerned.

When I considered the position on the ground later I came to the conclusion that in all probability we were tracking perfectly satisfactorily before I decided to alter course and either my DR wind velocity was at fault or I misread the API. Or there is the possibility of a sudden shear in the wind on a restricted front that might have tossed us like a cork in a stream off our predetermined heading. In any case I had done the very thing I was laughing at last night, at the expense of someone else. I had got over Nürnberg, where the exclusive benefit of all the defences was ours.

I resumed course on this assumption, recklessly entering the name of the town as a pinpoint in the log, and when we finally came within the range of the radar stations, found that I was where I expected to be. The incident was a practical demonstration of the maxim "Stay on track if you want to get back". I subsequently replotted the chart to see if I had been in error but nothing conclusive came to light. Things happen in the upper air for which there is no reasonable explanation on the ground, particularly in the nature of sudden, unexpected and often freakish wind shifts, especially in winter time. Moreover we were all tired with a weariness that drugged all sense of danger and lulled alertness into a stupid half-security. The back ached, the eyes burned around their rims, the brain was a dull sensation behind the forehead. We had had little sleep, perhaps five hours, since the long trip of the night before and once past the target experienced the dangerous relaxation that is apt to come when the outward part of the operation is safely accomplished. When the aircraft landed at base at 06.30 in the morning we had spent seventeen-and-a-half out of the last thirty-six hours in the air, plus another eight in the briefing room ...!

All were literally exhausted. We didn't even trouble to count the holes in the fabric of the aircraft but climbed into the waiting transport and, utterly subdued, made our way to report.

Chemnitz received the fantastic total of seven hundred and thirty thousand incendiaries, besides HEs. Coming on top of the deadly blows at Dresden the night before, these raids paralysed German communications in the whole south-eastern front. When the last British aircraft turned for home it could be said of those two cities, as of two others of old, that their smoke went up as the smoke of a furnace. Reconnaissance made during the attack on Chemnitz showed that Dresden was still alight.

Chemnitz had been a great industrial centre, making textiles and machinery, serving the rail system and acting as an army depot. It might well have been a more satisfactory target than Dresden, but it did not experience such awful devastation. Strangely enough three statues survived the bombing and stood intact in the square outside the smashed cathedral. One was of Frederick the Great, one of Bismark, and the other of von Moltke!

These two forays into the Russian zone of operations had provided us with extremely valuable experience, besides being an entire change from our stock-in-trade runs to the Ruhr. I found a confidence in my own navigation which I considered, on the whole, to have been amply justified by both trips, for I was not likely to have to do any of longer duration, or involving greater difficulty. Also, there was the test of endurance of body and mind against exceptional strain. The quickness of the gunners and the steady, accurate flying of the skipper were further grounds for the mutual trust we felt. It was not that we were in any way giving ourselves airs or even considering ourselves "gen.men". But when we had gone on our last leave I was fairly sure that we had mastered the job. Now I knew we had and had reached that state where one just would not fly with any other crew whatever, for no other crew could possibly be just the same; could possibly engender the same confidence. These sentiments were general and common to all crews that succeeded in working together harmoniously. Yet they came as a revelation to the individual on first experience and gave a great deal of satisfaction.

Our work as a crew had not gone unnoticed in higher quarters as it happened.

Chapter 16

LEADERS

We spent a lazy evening drinking quietly in the Mess, after having been in bed all day, and we retired with the prospect of a daylight raid on the 16th. The British armies were pushing into the Siegfried Line west of the Rhein and the Squadron was prepared to join in a close-support attack. We, Blenkin's crew, were given the job of leading the strength of our Base, a wave of some fifty bombers. As it happened, the raid was cancelled at the very last moment for we, as first aircraft to be airborne, had taxied to the end of the runway before we got the red from the caravan and were intercepted by the Flying Control van. Even in these circumstances Radio Telephone silence was observed.

A Base, in passing, is the first sub-division of a Group. It consisted then of a parent station - "full of thick rings" - and two satellites. Each station had one, possibly two Squadrons and the aircraft of the Squadrons were divided, in war, into two or three flights of approximately fifteen bombers each. The effort that a Base would put out, considering the limitations of serviceability was around sixty aircraft but this number could be increased if Command called for a major effort, when the CTO and his staff exercised more than ingenuity, even imagination, in putting as serviceable the maximum number of machines.

The individual aircraft had to be inspected every seventy-five hours - a hanger inspection by the engineer staff quite thorough by comparison with the daily inspections - and after three hundred hours of flying all engines were changed, those removed being returned to Rolls Royce for complete overhaul. At the end of each six hundred hours, if it lasted that long, the machine went in for a major inspection at the Base workshops and was practically taken to pieces and rebuilt.

Which has taken us from the thread of our story.

In the early evening of that same day a Dakota circled the aerodrome and slipped in. When Blenkin and I came up from the Mess after dinner we found a fair-haired, khaki-clad Yank sitting on the edge of Sammy's bed. Sammy was on leave.

"Hello. You from the Dakota?"

"Sure!" he said. "Say, that weather was closing in so fast when I saw this field I just put down straight away."

He was from Texas. He had been put into Transport, much to his disgust, and was itching to do what he called some "combat flying."

"Gee," he remarked, "if only I could fly one of those Mosquitoes. Now there is sure some ship."

This, of course, won us completely. We told him how we ourselves hoped to get into Mosquitoes when we had done our first tour. We discussed the merits of British and American aircraft. We opened our trunks and provided him with towel and soap and razor. But he wouldn't have any pyjamas.

"Pie-jammers - never use 'em."

"How do you boys find your way around the country?" I queried, seeing no navigator with him.

"Aw - map read. Fly the beam. We get by!" and added: "Say, have you fellows seen that Gee box? That is something!"

I laughed. "I was weaned on it."

Frank and he fell into a long debate on the flying habits of Harvards, of which they had mutual experience. Meanwhile, I stoked up the stove and dipping into Sammy's stores, produced three cups of a doubtful beverage made from cocoa and powdered milk, on the strength of which we turned into bed. With no battle order hanging over our heads the talk went on well into the night.

Strange trick of fate which threw a Texan into a miserable hut in East Anglia. I wonder if he remembered us and what luck the rest of the war brought him. I shall never know. At least we were glad to provide even rough hospitality and none were more welcome among us than American flyers, who were sometimes diverted to our field.

Now comes a name of which we shall hear a deal. Wesel, a small township on the Eastern side of the Rhein.

Anyone who has followed the progress of the British armies through Holland up to the natural barrier of the historic river will recall that at this stage Montgomery turned south down the Siegfried Line following the attempt at Arnheim which ended unsuccessfully in September of 1944. He was once more in a position to try to cross the Rhein.

Below the Dutch frontier it is true, minor railways cross the river from Cleve on the eastern side, but the manifold nature of the communications at Wesel made it the obvious place. Here were good roads branching in all directions, railways to the four cardinal points and the junction of the Lippe with the Rhein. Over the latter river had been good bridges but the American 8th Air Force bombed the six-span road bridge on February 14th.

The terrain, moreover, is satisfactory. The countryside thereabouts is gently undulating at the most, well-wooded but not so as to hinder military operations. Zig-zag entrenchments were to be seen and the concrete work of fortifications, but these signs of war soon lost themselves in the park-like German countryside.

Such considerations were emphasized at our briefing on February 18th. Intelligence sketched the strategy behind our projected operation, showing our part in relation to the whole and pointing out how much successful attacks could mean at this time. Wesel, he declared, was chock-full of

German troops and transport and must be smashed.

Today we, as a crew, practised the art of leading a large formation for the first time.

During the months we had been operating the business of forming up the bomber stream had developed to a very great extent. In the early days, as I have said before, an aircraft detailed to lead three or four others because it was fitted with special equipment, would pick up the followers either over their own aerodrome or a nearby town and then converge on a point at the coast at a specified time, joining the general stream in whatever position the pilot decided was convenient. Night tactics translated today. The RAF had tried daylight formation flying in the early days of the war with little success. Now a much more systematic and decided technique developed, until the raid was assembled according to a very definite plan.

The whole attack would be constituted in three waves, each wave consisting of the aircraft of a single Base, stacked down in height from front to rear and arranged so that the leaders of the second wave were just behind the aircraft of the first. This stacking reduced the nuisance and fatigue, even danger, of flying in slipstream from earlier machines and ensured that if formation were properly maintained the bombs of higher aircraft would not fall on machines flying lower.

The three waves would form up separately in the area of their particular aerodromes and converge to the Group rendezvous. It was the responsibility of the navigator of Base Leader to see that his wave arrived at the rendezvous exactly on time and of the pilot to ensure that he positioned himself behind the others at correct height well closed up. Were the middle wave in particular to arrive late there would be universal confusion. One aircraft - a Squadron even - can be manoeuvred fairly readily; but a wave of fifty or sixty is a juggernaut which goes relentlessly on, only turning with wide dignity and altering its relative position by the use of miles of sky.

The fighter cover, provided from airfields in France usually would join the bombers over the Continent at a given time and longitude.

In order to form up the aircraft of a Base a cross-country flight of specified route about sixty miles long was adopted. At either side of the track of this route, allowing room for a side orbit were a series of rendezvous points, quoted as Gee co-ordinates, alloted to aircraft at briefing. To these, the leaders of Vics proceeded and circling with wheels down for identification waited to be picked up by their three followers, all the time keeping at a thousand feet above formation height of the cross-country and flashing from the astrodome an identifying letter.

The Base Leader took off and went to the point of commencement where he orbited until his deputies had joined him and it was time to set course. He then ran the gauntlet around the forming route, firing a succession of signal cartridges to identify him to the others. They, with the help of their extra height, were easily able to drop into place in the procession.

From the point of view of the leader, the successful forming up depended on his being in such a position that he could start over the appointed place at the exact instant. This is not so easy as it sounds. Not only is it impossible to turn a loaded bomber like a fighter, but also all the time the machine is circling it is being blown down-wind, a fact that has to be impressed on the navigator's mind. Since, in these winter days, rendezvous was invariably made over cloud, the only guide to location was the relative positions of the pulses set on the Gee box and the orbit had to be controlled by the navigator, who told the pilot to turn at so many degrees a minute, while keeping watch over the radar.

On this day, then, we made sure to get away to a good start, and anticipating the turns in the route with care to prevent overshooting our track. Turner's sturdy figure stood by the spar, head in the dome, as he fired away a veritable Brock's Benefit of Verey cartridges.

"What's the forming up like, Turner?"

"Eh, it's a grand sight!" he replied. Like myself, he usually saw so little of what was going on that he enjoyed this opportunity of looking out.

Soon we were crossing the Thames estuary, feeling rather important, and as we converged on Tonbridge were able to pick out the first and second waves coming in ahead. We fell into position.

So we went to Wesel. We carried a load of all HE bombs including some with special long-delay fuses, calculated to give the enemy trouble. The upper air was almost calm, the outward journey uneventful.

We bombed in the late afternoon. The run was not easy. The radar pulse that was being used for tracking kept blinking and disappearing. Both pulses were wobbling and as more and more aircraft switched on their transmitters both became difficult to pick out from the cluttered-up trace. Finally I had them strong enough to enable positive bombing - the ground stations may have pepped them up at the last minute - which was a good thing as there was complete cloud cover below.

"This cloud shows up the flak bursts!" someone remarked.

As our load dropped, Jack's voice came over the intercom. "The skymarker's hung up."

"Don't let it drop. Bomb doors closing," from the skipper. Obviously if a marker is being dropped it must go on the instant, for these smoke puffs hung over the target in the air as a guide to anyone who might have to bomb visually.

We were carrying a second pilot, a new driver sent to get his first taste of powder in more experienced company. While we were in the target area he had been looking round with eyes as big as organ stops. Now the aircraft was well on the way home Frank suggested he might like to take over. Putting George, the automatic pilot into engagement, the skipper climbed stiffly from his seat. A moment later I was mildly surprised to see his grinning face appear under the curtain.

"Hello, like to do a bit of navigating?" I laughed.

"Not bloody likely," he quoted Shaw. "I'm going back to have a look at Roy and Harry," and he struggled past me in the confined space, catching the hooks of his parachute harness into my own and pushing me forward over the table.

Fresh, and in good humour, we came home from what had been a pretty easy trip.

One of the wonders of the war was the remarkable way in which the enemy stood up to heavy bombing and contrived to patch up damage, at least enough to carry on the struggle. With the persistence of despair, and in spite of the 700 tons of bombs which we had poured on the town, he rushed in large reinforcements during the night.

As soon as this became known the bombers were whistled up and there was a hurried briefing in the morning, with instructions to go and repeat the dose.

Satisfied with our performance of the previous day, the Wing Commander gave us the leading of the Base again.

The outward journey calls for little comment, except that the stream was not as compact as it might have been. Bombing pulses were good when we turned in and the run was readily controlled. Although we bombed on my instruments, this time the target could be seen quite plainly.

Harry followed our bombs down the sky, keeping his eyes glued on to our cookie in order to distinguish it in the general rain of destruction. He saw the stick hit and dissolve some large buildings.

Enemy opposition was very light. Yet, as so often happened, the leader of the stream went, and a sad and heavy loss it was. There are some men who are possessed of a quiet form of courage that is partly determination to go forward steadily in whatever enterprise that may engage them and partly from possession of an untroubled spirit. It is not fanatical, it possesses no flash of outstanding brilliance. Rather it is built on the foundation of their own self knowledge and the confidence of their ability to trust themselves in any situation.

This courage Pete Dunham had.

He was, until shortly before, a Flight Commander with us at No. 218 Squadron and had left to become Wing Commander of No. 138 stationed at Tuddenham. It was his third tour of operations. He had done his first as a gunner, his second as a navigator. Not content, as many others would have been, he took a course of training as a pilot. In which capacity he was flying on the fatal day. He had done seventy trips.

The aircraft was hit by flak before the bomb load went, so that it blew to pieces in mid air.

When the news became known even the cynical and hard-bitten among us could not but feel badly about it, for Pete with his ready smile and bristling whiskers had been so popular with everyone. So heavy was the price that Bomber Command required of its men and so it went on till the end.

I heard two other pieces of bad news on the same day. The first that a crew from our course at Conversion Unit, good friends of ours, had crashed in a most peculiar manner returning from an operation. The machine suddenly went nose down and flew straight into the ground killing most of the crew. It was rumoured that the pilot went to sleep at the controls. There was the personal loss to me of the dead bomb-aimer, a New Zealander who had spent many drinking hours in the "Oak" with me.

I also learned that another of my ill-starred AFU course had gone on the last Dortmund attack. The Air Ministry's formal announcement "... from these operations six of our aircraft failed to return", cannot convey that it is Bill or Charlie who has bought it. And the Committee of Adjustments have to pounce on their gear and parcel it up for their relatives with the formal letter of regret from the CO.

* * * * *

Since there was nothing on in the morning the Squadron was forced to parade on the perimeter and after the usual dose of PT exercises I made my way to the Navigation Office.

"Ha - Dicky - just the man I want to see", was the greeting I had from Frank Glover, the Navigation Leader.

"What have I done now?" I queried suspiciously, wondering what might have been found out and deciding it could be nothing more serious than my repeated raids on the coke dump.

"Squadron Leader Dixon and I have decided to put a senior navigator in charge of each Flight. You get the job for "C" Flight.

"Oh!" I said, taken aback.

Jock Stark, standing by, burst into unholy laughter.

"Don't laugh so fast, Stark. You get it for "A" Flight."

"Your first job", he continued, "will be to gather up some bodies from your Flight to sweep out the briefing room. You don't have to do it yourself", he added quickly, "just supervise."

"I'll be bloody lucky if I don't have to do the lot!" I said, making for the door.

"Come back when you've finished. I've another little surprise for you."

When I returned, smothered in dust, the Navigation Leader outlined his scheme.

"I want to get you chaps, Harrison and Jock and you Dicky, lined up so that you can take a briefing at any time and also be responsible for all the navigators in your Flight, the new ones particularly. Make sure they know the aircraft thoroughly when they come to the Squadron and see they are acquainted with our methods of working. The experience will do you a lot of good. After all", he smiled broadly, "you may be navigation leaders yourselves some day".

"Heaven forbid!" said Jock.

"The artful old devil wants to work some days off" Harrison added, "He's getting us to do his work."

"I'm always taking sprogs over aircraft now", I protested, and then, as my favourite grouse occurred to me I added: "How about some second rings for it? The pilots get 'em without any trouble."

"My lad," he replied, "you'll get no second ring. You'll just get yourself into a nice mess this afternoon. You are in charge of tonight's briefing."

So I found myself, feeling very self conscious, standing on the rostrum giving the crews all the details of a trip to Dortmund and experiencing the strange feeling of sending other fellows when not going oneself. There was a lot of behind-the-scenes work co-ordinating the navigators' times with those of Group, issuing flimsies, running backwards and forwards between the telephone and the planning room. What a villainous looking lot they were too, as they assembled before going out. Clad in all sorts of adjustments to the normal uniform, some with hats battered beyond description, with white or yellow sweaters and wearing every variety of neckchiefs the sartorial world could devise. Their heavy sheepskin flying boots were finished with dagger-like knives thrust down the leg. Here and there a mascot dangled from a collar. Their clothing too made their bulk larger than normal, giving them a strong outline. Could this serious, purposeful lot of men be the light-hearted fellows of the Mess and billet?

We got them off and then took a car to the caravan to watch the departures and then I had to report to the office to prepare the reports against their return. I had rather flown too, I fancied, than do the office work. I settled down for the long wait until de-briefing.

Chapter 17

NEVER A DULL MOMENT

On the 21st of February our crew was detailed to take part in a raid against Gelsenkirchen, flying XH - A Able, the same aircraft we had used for Wesel. This was as a result of Command coming back to the oil plan, which had been on and off.

Things were bad from the start, for when I arrived at the dispersal armourers were still working on the rear turret. Although I had come to regard such setbacks with as much philosophy as I could muster, I cannot claim to be over patient and I viewed the perspiring mechanics with annoyance. The rear gunner was doing himself no good by endeavouring to assist while dressed in full flying clothing. Frank, his forehead thunderous, stood looking on and was not pleased when I started pinpricking him by talking about take-off time.

"Hell", Harry panted, "I'm cheesed off with this turret!" His hair was sticking out on either side of his head and rivulets of sweat ran down his face and lost themselves in the neck of his shirt.

"If it were only the mid-upper I'd take off with it unserviceable."

"Can't he rotate it manually?"

"If I were you Harry, I'd take that Sidcot off."

"Why not let Johnnie have a go?"

"We should be off the deck now, skipper."

"What's the last time of take-off?"

"Hang on!", I said, "I'll give you the alternatives," and going into the aircraft I worked out a time on the assumption that we took off directly and joined the stream at Tonbridge. This proved to be the only alternative. We were away too late to do anything more than climb on track to make junction with the force below the Estuary.

The French coast had barely been left behind when we ran into more trouble. An oil pipe burst and we promptly lost the use of all hydraulic services. The undercarriage red lights came on and I heard the skipper asking the engineer if the wheel had dropped on his side.

"Yeah! - starboard undercart half down - seems stuck."

"Try the bomb doors!"

"No - they won't open".

"Get the Wop to check the hydraulic tank!", and when Turner had answered the call-light that the skipper flashed: "Check level of hydraulic fluid, Wop."

The Scotsman came back with a curt: "Empty."

Meanwhile Johnnie had checked the undercarriage lever, which was in the "Up" position. Hindered by the drag of the wheels we were slipping back in the stream.

"I'll go back skipper, and if I can fix up some emergency air we might open the bomb doors."

"Yes - try to lock the undercarriage. We'll press on."

Johnnie went back along the fuselage. He went to the mid-upper turret and drained off sufficient of the oil from its working system to enable the main hydraulics to function temporarily. He transferred this, employing a spare can, to the tank. When he had poured it in he asked the skipper to reselect the undercarriage, hoping it would retract, but it refused to do so.

The skipper tried the "Down" position. The warning lights showed green and from his seat Frank could see the port wheel right down, but in order to make absolutely certain he operated the M-S supercharge gear switch.

"O.K. Johnnie - undercart locked down. Now if you can fix the bomb doors we'll be all right."

The Lancaster was now over Belgium, rather below the rest but still not at the end of the stream entirely. Even with the additional drag of the wheels it would be possible to make the Ruhr and back.

Johnnie's idea was to take a bottle of compressed air from the undercarriage emergency system and connect it to the bomb-door control, so that he might literally blow open the rams that forced the doors apart. He therefore nipped the pipe between the two air bottles and disconnected one of them.

The bottle contained air at a pressure of 1,200 lbs per square inch. This was too much for the pipe as soon as it had been disconnected and suddenly it gave, whipping through the air like a snake and tearing a nasty gash across Johnnie's forehead. As the air escaped frost covered the iron bottle and froze his gloves, which were covered with oil from the turret, quite solid. His hands escaped injury.

Now, less than a hundred miles from the target, we were reluctantly forced to turn back. Frank asked: "Give me a course for the best jettison area, nav!".

"Damned shame. Hard luck Johnnie!", I replied, giving the vector.

We were not yet out of the wood. Overweight to make a safe landing and with the cookie aboard it was imperative that the engineer got the bomb doors open somehow at the jettison area. This he did by making Frank select "open" while he poured into the main reservoir all the remaining oil from Roy's turret. Even then the doors would open only partially although enough for the purpose. We had five tons of bomb load and I suppose had we been forced to it we could have let the lot drop on the doors which would not have stood such weight. Anyway, such a desperate expedient was not necessary.

"There goes some more Income Tax!" commented the bombardier as they fell into the sea and a geyser sprung up from the exploding cookie.

It was impossible to pursuade the doors to close so we made the remainder of the journey with an infernal draught blowing about our ears. When we joined circuit they managed to get about 20 degrees of flap out for the landing and no more. Frank did a careful approach and touched down with all the runway he could allow considering the high landing speed.

By the time we lobbed down some of the Squadron had already returned. They reported heavy flak at the target, which had been no picnic. The Squadron lost an aircraft navigated by an old classmate of mine in Canada, Bill Porter. Doing their first trip. Four parachutes were seen, so all hope was not abandoned for the crew, and as a matter of fact Bill turned up safe and sound at the end of the war.

I obtained access to the engineering leader's report on the actions taken by Johnnie. He had already had a commendation for something he had done on a previous operation. This report now read:

"Sergeant Wortley had two further opportunities to practice his knowledge and initiative in two later sorties but was prevented from completing his next repair due to a bursting air pipeline. After 1½ hours flying a failure occured in the hydraulic system and the undercarriage dropped to about half way down. The undercarriage red lights came on and the bomb doors would not open. The captain then decided to lock the undercarriage down and if possible to continue the operation using the undercarriage emergency air system to open the bomb doors.

"The undercarriage selector lever was checked and found in the up position. The main hydraulic system was found to be empty. Hydraulic fluid was drained from the mid-upper turret and used to replenish the main hydraulic system. The undercarriage still could not be retracted so a down selection was made and the undercarriage locked in the down position. To make absolutely certain that the undercarriage was locked down although the warning lights showed green, the M-S supercharger switch was operated.

"The pipe line between the two emergency undercarriage air bottles was then sealed with the intention of disconnecting the pipe line at the non-return valve and to disconnect the emergency air control. During the attempt to connect one of the bottles to the emergency bomb door control the pipe line between the bottle and the valve burst and all the air was lost.

"The operation was now abandoned but the all-up weight was still too high. It was decided to jettison the bombs. The bomb doors were opened sufficiently for this purpose by selecting open and by pouring more hydraulic fluid into the main reservoir, which had been drained again from the mid-upper turret system. After jettisoning the bomb doors would not close and on landing only 20 degrees of flap could be obtained but a safe landing was made."

We had similar trouble at a later date as will emerge, but there can be no doubt that Johnnie's resourcefulness had saved us from a very tricky situation, which indeed had done nothing to help the skipper's flying.

This Gelsenkirchen raid was directed against the ever dwindling oil supplies of the Reich and ushered in another period of blows against the synthetic oil plants, liberally scattered around this area in close proximity to the coal mines.

Life for all of us on the Squadron was becoming extremely circumscribed. We flew. Then we ate and drank and slept for the sole business of flying again. Endowed with strong constitutions as a condition of our calling, yet we had to keep constant watch on our bodies in order to be masters of our work. Were we out in the evening? We dared not be late for fear of a sudden early call and the uninviting prospect of a trip with dulled faculties. Were we drinking? Better cut it down and keep sober. Our social life was restricted to evenings when there was definitely no possibility of an operation on the following day, and then we let go with a vengeance.

Harlow and his crew now became second string to us on Fox and flew her on such days as we were non-operational. This had one distinct advantage in that the daily inspections were shared, though we would have been disinclined to trust our aircraft to anyone we knew less intimately. But it meant the machine got constant wear, and workshop inspections came along much sooner.

One day following our last attempt, we took part in another attack in the Gelsenkirchen area. This time we reached the target without trouble, but for some time before the run-in we were flying in cirrus cloud with the vapour, or more exactly the filaments of ice crystallites, closing us in so completely that we could hardly see another aircraft. The effect was so weird that the pilot called me out to look. In what seemed a spirit world, with cloud whipping back along the wings at tremendous speed, we would see the black shapes of other aircraft loom out of the irridescent vapour and vanish again. We were G-H leaders. I do not know how our followers managed to keep up with us - the strain on the pilots must have been very great since there was strong risk of collision, a thing we all feared.

In this solitude we dropped our bombs and although it did not make the slightest difference to the accuracy of our aim whether we could see the target or not, it was strange to be up there shut in a tiny seclusion cut off from our fellows.There is no icing risk in cirrus cloud, fortunately, and it relieved us of the sight of any flak; even this false sense of security was comforting.

There was cloud all the way back. Frank found lanes wherever he could and flew between the layers. Finally it became necessary to break through for we were over the English coast. We were at 7,000 feet.

"O.K. to break cloud, navigator?"

"Base is eight minutes flying ahead. Safety height one thousand feet."

"Right. Going down!"

It was at these lower altitudes that the critical icing temperatures prevailed. He descended as quickly as he could while I swallowed hard to equalize the pressure on my ear-drums. At a thousand feet we were still in cloud.

"Almost over base!" I said, adjusting the markers on the cathode tube to the values of our field.

"Quiet, everybody. I'll call up. Going to eight hundred navigator." Frank edged the machine lower, pressing the Chedburgh button on his RT control. "Wastage Fox to Roughedge - over!"

"Wastage Fox, you are diverted to airfield number ... is this understood? ... over!"

"Fox wilco. Out!"

By this time we were at 600 feet, only two hundred above the aerodrome and still in cloud.

"Twenty six-fifty, plus six!" Frank called to Johnnie. "Give me a course, navigator!"

I was fumbling in my bag for the diversion schedule to look up the whereabouts of the airfield whose number we had been given. Our position was extremely hazardous climbing in thick cloud over our own airfield with others undoubtedly doing the same thing. There was no time to delay so I answered that he should steer 040 degrees, knowing the ground fell away in that direction.

"Will you give me your spare protractor, nav.?" called the engineer. He had found by experience that the bevelled edge of a plastic protractor was ideal for scraping ice off the windscreen, making a much more satisfactory job than the glycol spray fitted by the makers. He opened the window, put out his arm into the freezing air and got to work to improve Frank's vision.

"The place is Hutton Cranswick, near Hull. Alter course 355 degrees skipper."

"Near my home. I know it well," he replied and added: "Going round 355."

A little later we replaced oxygen masks. Still in cloud we did not get clear until we were up to 14,000 feet. But as the aircraft winged north breaks began to appear until finally the Humber estuary appeared, green and silver in the evening light. After all the excitement we were not sorry to land; the prospect of a square meal was about the most alluring thing in the world.

Hutton Cranswick seemed to me to be the cleanest airfield I had ever seen. It was almost as though the runways had been swept and the grass ironed. There were a number of Vultee Vengeance aircraft arranged in picket lines, all very spick and span and very different from the East

Anglian bases where the squatting bombers were dispersed as much as possible.

"Hun hasn't been hereabouts lately", Jack remarked, nodding at the line of fighters.

"Blimy, tons of bull here!" was Harry's comment.

It was a reserve Fighter field and as always when we were guests of other Commands nothing could be too good for us. After we had deposited camera, magazines and secret material in the tower we all went, Squadron Leaders and Sergeants, to the Airman's Mess which was the only one big enough to hold us all, for most of 3 Group had landed here it seemed. I had three eggs, baked beans and some excellent hot tea.

The party in the Mess that night went on into the early hours. Much ale flowed and many songs were sung from that vast store of Service folk lore that some daring soul subsequently published privately as the Fleet Air Arm song book! No doubt these songs were sung by the Roman legions as they marched to the Wall. They are passed from mouth to mouth over the generations like the Icelandic sagas. There is a great deal of wit in them in spite of their bawdy nature; they are the unfailing corollary of a really good session with the ale pots, the only other necessity being a piano and someone who can knock up a good tune. And since the singing of these anthems outrages the taboos that hedge our lives they let off a great deal of steam without much harm to anybody.

The last recollection I have is of seeing a wild youth on his back on top of an inclined table while someone else held a glass of beer for him to drink in this topsy-turvy position. A third party was busily emptying another tankard down the victim's trouser leg!

Since the weather cleared overnight we were able to return to Suffolk next day and we came in over our aerodrome in tight formation, doing a classical break-away and firing Verey cartridges just to show the Wing Commander that we could do it if we tried!

Our next sortie was on Sunday. They had changed our worthy George for a batwoman and this poor girl came along at four in the morning to wake us. A bed in a Nissen hut is sheer luxury by comparison with the outside world at this hour and no place on earth is as dark as the black expanse of an airfield. Of course the briefing was postponed for reasons known only to Group so that the morning was well advanced before we were airborne. The attack was another oil raid aimed at a plant in Kamen in the Dortmund area and we carried a typical bomb load for such a job, one cookie, a dozen five-hundred pound HEs and a sky marker smoke puff weighing a couple of hundredweights.

The swarm of aircraft set course in clear sunlight over England. When fairly under way I spared myself a few moments to put my head into the astrodome and look at the French coastline for invasion damage. But all I saw was a sandy beach and trim looking peaceful fields stretching inland; and the exhilarating sight of the Lancasters undulating gently all around.

Once in the air the Lancaster assumed a grace that no bomber can have on the ground as she breasts forward like a seal meeting the waves, her untidy undercarriage hidden in the wings and the propellers forming a faint nimbus around the engines.

There was not much time for reflection, but work in my compartment, for it was time to climb to height. We began running over broken strato-cumulus cloud. It persisted all the way to the Ruhr but was not enough to provide complete cover being no more than five-tenths in the target area; our following Vic had no difficulty in keeping close on our tail as I commenced vectoring the pilot to the target. There was the usual jockeying, the usual anxieties and the usual feeling of relief as we were running out of the target.

The route for return lay between Düsseldorf and Köln, and before we set off I had selected the co-efficient of a Gee line that almost paralleled the track. Our best plan would be to home along this until we were clear of the Rhein before resuming normal navigation, so avoiding the heavy flak awaiting the unwary. I had calculated the time it should take us from the target before striking this line and therefore immediately Jack called out that the camera had turned over I gave the pilot the course and pressed the button of my stopwatch. I set to work as quickly as possible to change over from G-H to Gee, tune the Ruhr chain and set up the strobe marker on the chosen value.

We commenced tracking on this line but our efforts did not save us. Port and starboard flak was coming up in a dense barrage and the stream of bombers that had scattered on a broad front on leaving Kamen was closing together like a school of startled fishes, the black puffs all around them.

Suddenly we were in it. "Flak!", said someone and then - whoof and the machine bucked violently. I actually heard the explosion through my helmet, which shut out nearly all the engine noise even. It was much too close.

"Bloody close - that one. Burst right under us." Harry's voice sounded scared.

"Kites going down behind, navigator!" he reported.

"O.K. chaps. Any damage anywhere?" came the skipper.

No one could see anything amiss though. Indeed the old kite - it was Fox - flew back remarkably well and Frank remarked that she was handling as good as he had known her fly.

We put down at base and when we scrambled out of the machine we went quizzing round in an half-amused way counting the holes. They were plentiful but no essential damage had been done, nothing that could not be repaired in a few hours with some rivets and aluminium sheeting. We had been lucky.

A nice, comfortable way of spending a Sunday!

The Squadron was out again next day. I did the briefing and part of the interrogation on return and busied myself with odd jobs. I had accumulated sufficient Astro shots and operational hours to apply for my Navigator's Warrant and I went to see the Station Navigation Officer about it. The mills of God grind slowly. I got it a year later! It is a rare distinction. Mine is No. 352.

Since the afternoon was our own Frank and I cycled into Bury St Edmunds for exercise. The hedges and trees were just commencing to push out green shoots and the industrious farmers were busy at their ditches and fields. The ride was extremely pleasant for the day might have contained more than a hint of spring.

We were packed off to Stradishall, our Base station to collect a brand new bomber and do an acceptance test. It was wonderfully clean, smelling of dope and fresh paint. We took it over the Wash, fired the guns and tested the turrets. Then we climbed to 22,000 feet checking the performance on climb. We dropped practice bombs and put her through stiff corkscrews to see how she handled. There were, perhaps, a dozen minor faults for adjustment and these were logged. Then, finished with the serious business we beat up the clouds and rushed down the valleys of air without any thought of where we were going. How I loved this, the real flying - the only time I had any pleasure from it as I stood in the warm sunshine of the pilot's cockpit watching the clouds race by.

Johnnie flew the aircraft home for a change.

That night we saw our names on the battle order carrying with us a second navigator.

Blenkin and I looked at the Battle Order on the board with very mixed feelings. Against our name was that of Flying Officer Lillis, which could only mean that we were booked to lead the morning's attack. Secretly, I think we were both rather pleased for although there was a very good chance of being shot up as leaders of the spearhead there was a certain amount of honour to it, being first into the target. For myself there was the additional satisfaction of providing the pattern of navigation for the whole bomber stream. But since we had been with the Squadron, Evers and Pete Dunham had both done the job and both had been shot down. Moreover, I could not help casting my mind back to the old night-fighting days at Foreness and recalling Mawhood's determined instruction: "Get the Hauptmann!". With our present "window" protection it was the leader of the stream who stood out like a sore thumb, the rest being submerged in the cover.

I commenced to turn over in my mind a suitable plan of co-operation for Lillis and myself in order to obtain the greatest benefit from his help. In the end I decided to draw a set of charts for him and get him to spend his time taking fixes at intervals of five minutes, which would virtually enable me to track crawl. I would be free to perform the general navigation and whenever I wanted a position check could transfer a fix from his chart to my Mercator by eye. While I found the bombing wind he would set up the G-H apparatus and when I was controlling the bombing run he could be working out the courses immediately out of the target, thus allowing the bombing to be deliberate through ample time. I discussed this proposition with Frank, who agreed. There was no laid-down Command procedure. The RAF still left that sort of detail to individuals.

Since there was some prospect of leaving the land of the living I sat down and wrote a special letter to my wife, intending to give it to Sammy for delivery in this event. Then I thought the whole business too morbid and tore it up, writing instead a quick, matter-of-fact note that I dropped in the post. I turned into bed in a state of subdued excitement and took some time to go to sleep.

The attacking force consisted of 157 Lancasters. The target was the Nordstern Benzole plant near Gelsenkirchen.

Lillis and I worked through the briefing with meticulous exactitude but the others had time for wisecracking which mostly resolved itself around Harry ... "If you've never had the twitch before you'll get it today, Harry!"

"I don't mind," said Harry emphatically, "I don't mind how far in front we are. All I object to is seeing a dirty great Lancaster up above us with his damn great bomb doors open. And", he added, "listening to the navigator niggling about five degrees port when he can't see the other kites all around us!"

"You'll be all right today, Harry!" Jack's chuckle was not too amusing on this tender subject. "All we'll get is the predicted flak!"

The formation diagram showed that Harlow in HA-L for Love was flying on our port beam and the redoubtable Nixon, XH-L on our starboard, as first and second deputies and assistant windfinders. In addition to Gussie Gordon and Bremner, their navigators, two other crews were detailed as windfinders. These had navigators, Flight Sergeants Noy and Camkin, who were among the most proficient on the Squadron and it would have been difficult for any Group to have put up a more efficient spearhead than the Wing Commander had chosen that day.

At position "D" a dog-leg was inserted into the route, a denticular portion forty miles in length. Here lost time might be regained by cutting off as much of the triangle as necessary.

The route took us north-east to 51.45N, 05.55E. Our fighter escort of Spitfires and Mustangs from No. 11 Group would join us at Eindhoven. Another small leg would bring us to the commencement of the run and the approach to the Ruhr from the north-east. To get out we must run the gauntlet between Essen and Bochum as far down as Wuppertal, where a right-hand turn would take us between Düsseldorf and Köln to safety across the battle line.

The formulated plan worked remarkably well. Lillis sat beside me on the long seat "box-bashing" as hard as he could. In other words, he took a constant stream of radar fixes. Relieved of this work I was able to give particular care to everything else with the result that we were never more than two miles from the track line inked on the chart.

Blenkin was flying very steadily. At first I was like a cat on hot bricks but when I saw the turning points coming up to time and the fixes dropping along the track as though they were printed on it I could not suppress my satisfaction by nudging Lillis and grinning, seeing his eyes grin back above his mask.

Presently Frank decided to give the RT an air test and asked for intercom silence and if radio silence could be broken. On receiving confirmation he pressed his button and called Harlow.

"Caesar to Caesar two - over!"

"Caesar two answering - go ahead."

"Testing. How are you receiving? - over."

And the reply came, "Strength five."

Frank told him to stand by, and switching to intercom called me: "Hello nav, will it make any difference to you if Harlow sends out the bombing wind? I think this RT is too weak to reach the end of the stream."

"No. OK by me."

So he called Harlow and asked him to broadcast the instructions. I then thought it would relieve my pressure of work at a critical time if Gussie averaged out the bombing wind, so at the appropriate moment I passed him my calculation and asked him to strike the mean between mine, his and the results of the other three windfinders. I spoke to him over RT and was amused to hear him come back from the other aircraft, for usually the pilots did the talking.

Lillis was setting up the cathode tube while I took the warning period from the tables. Then he moved to the end of the seat and I took over for the run in.

Now as I looked at the tube with its pulses and standing out like signposts to the target the uncomfortable thought of my own position came to me. "Here we go. We'll get the predicted!" I thought. With sudden surprise I heard Harlow's voice cut in, clear as a bell.

"Caesar to Brutus. Bombing wind two five zero degrees, forty miles per hour," repeating it several times.

I called to Jack: "window, bombardier!" Down in the hatch he commenced to push it out at five bundles a minute and a dense cloud of silver strips must have fluttered away from the spearhead as the other aircraft followed suit.

The enemy opened up. There were bursts all round, a certain amount being accurate. Harlow, who was always in trouble, had his windscreen blown in, letting the icy upper air into the machine and blowing Gussie's charts all over the place. We were peppered but not badly, although our bomb doors were holed and the load was still on. Of course, weaving was out of the question for us under the circumstances. Frank just had to hold tight and follow my instructions and corrections, for it was essential to put the first lot down accurately. The tracking pulse clung nicely to its counterpart on the strobe. The release pulse crept in slowly until I changed to the expanded time base, when it started to move into line with obvious speed.

The bomb doors opened; the bombs were fused and ready. The skipper knew his course and speed and held them grimly. Back at the flare chute the wireless operator waited to see the dangerous marker flare fall safely away. The bomb aimer stood by to let them go manually if anything failed.

And all around the exploding shells of the enemy thumped and whoofed.

My thumb was on the button. Now - now! and I dug deeply, calling at the same time,

"Release pressed. Steady on course!"

A moment's suspense. The bombs were falling away. Lillis pushed a slip of paper over to me with the course, waving his thumbs up in glee and relief. He was really thrilled.

I gave the course to the pilot, while Turner sat down at his sets and hammered out a message to tell the Group Captain and the staff waiting at home on our aerodrome that the target had been bombed. As I logged the bombing details I saw that the load had gone down half a minute off H hour. Most satisfactory.

"What's it like Harry?" I asked as soon as we were clear.

"Pretty good, I think. There's cloud below but the bombs are falling very close together". And Roy chimed in: "Yes, the smoke puffs are very concentrated. Looks OK to me."

So we came home delighted and beat up the aerodrome for sheer exuberance and tried to look modest when people congratulated us on a good piece of work.

Reports of following crews stated that the marker puffs had fallen in a very compact cluster, particularly the first eleven of them. The tail end of the force had seen black smoke billowing up through the cloud layer. There was every indication of a good attack.

Cloudy skies over Germany prevented the planes of Photographic Reconnaissance from getting pictures for a couple of days and I haunted the Intelligence Library incessantly, impatient for the damage plot to come in. Here, in the words of the official report, is the havoc we wreaked at the Nordstern plant. It said:

"Very severe damage to this plant can be seen. All four coke oven batteries are affected, three with direct hits on the ovens, and pipe lines about them are disrupted. Both sulphate houses are damaged, both exhauster houses have the roofing stripped, gas scrubbers have been damaged and the tar loading area and one gasholder have exploded.

"The Gelsenkirchen Nordstern 1/2 colliery was moderately damaged; one wing of a cooling tower was destroyed; three wings have roof damage and the railway lines serving the mines to the coke ovens cut in several places. A pipe line from the coke ovens to the mines is severed.

"A new installation 500 feet north-west of the sulphate house was heavily damaged, four large buildings, several sheds and a bridge connecting with coke ovens are destroyed. Many craters are visible just north of the plant."

Then follow fourteen detailed damage catalogues too long and wearisome for inclusion in this narrative. However, one may perhaps quote Albert Speer with some relevance. Reporting to Hitler at the start of the oil offensive in 1944 he said: "The enemy has struck us at one of our weakest points. If they persist at it this time we will soon no longer have any fuel production worth mentioning," and again later, he commented: "Surveying a bombed hydrogenation plant from the air I was struck by the accurate carpet bombing of the Allied bomber fleets."

Our Nordstern raid was done on instruments, entirely blind through complete cloud cover and is, I consider a reasonable confirmation of his opinions.

Chapter 18

MAINLY OIL

By this time the Germans were pulling back to the Rhein really quickly
and the Allied armies were forcing their way into the Köln area to such an
extent that on the Friday morning the line of the advance was reported to
have engulfed München Gladbach and Rheydt and also Krefeld. These
were all more than names to us; they were the battle-honours of the
Command and with the Ruhr area threatened it was obvious that there
were many familiar places that soon would be visited no more. Whether
from a sense of nostalgia, or with the view of harassing the retreating
enemy, a large force of 700 heavies was sent to much-bombed Köln that
morning and we were part of another 150 due to arrive at the same target
in the early afternoon.

So fluid was the state of affairs on the ground that we were given the
strictest instructions forbidding us to bomb except on GH pulses of
undoubted accuracy and were allowed a maximum tracking error of 200
yards. Otherwise the bombs were to be brought back. There was a very
present fear of hitting our own troops in forward positions.

We were airborne around mid-day and reached the Rheinland with the
comforting thought of flying over friendly territory all the time. Winds
were high, above the 80 mph mark and we were tracking into the target at
a fairly high ground speed but with satisfactory pulses appearing on the
screen. Suddenly the release pulse disappeared from its trace.

I warned the pilot at once and said that if it did not reappear we should
be forced to bring the load away. I could imagine the awful consternation
in the minds of the leaders of the stream had their radar behaved
similarly.

In fact, one of the ground stations had gone off the air just before H
hour, probably acting on information from the front line.

Then passed minutes during which we could only play follow-my-
leader. Obviously, uncertain that the pulse might reappear the leader held
steadily on course till beyond ETA target and the airfleet swept over Köln
without a bomb falling away.

Jack saw the city through breaks in the cloud - one could not fail to
recognize such a landmark as the Cathedral - and reported as we went
over. There was no alternative target allotted but a few aircraft dropped
bombs some miles down the river.

Pressed on by high winds, we were down to Bonn before we began to
turn. Then we described a great sweep and, near Koblenz started back to

cut our original track. For a moment it appeared that the leader might make another attempt but in a few minutes it became evident from our direction that the sortie had been abandoned and we had turned for home.

"Going up into Holland, skipper," I reported, and added: "Thank goodness this didn't happen to us on Wednesday."

"Where's the jettison area? We shall have to get rid of the cookie."

"Off the Dutch coast. I'll let you know when we get there!"

"Well, the fish are in for a good time!"

As I have previously commented, it was imprudently dangerous to try landing with a cookie aboard. A heavy landing might tear it away from the release hooks and explode it, for its thin case would not stand a severe blow. Therefore orders were to jettison off the coast of Holland and the force of bombers threw their four-thousand pounders into the sea.

That evening we stood in the Mess with cans of beer in our hands discussing the possibilities of confusion at the battlefront and considering that Authority would not have sanctioned the loss and expense of an abortive raid unless our troops were inside Köln, so that the city might now be ours. There was dissatisfaction because there had been no alternative target, but this was partially allayed when we were told we would be credited with an Op.

Bombing attained a crescendo that could hardly have been reached at any other period of the war and now the aircraft of the Squadron were being flown to death. By the 4th of March our own aircraft, Fox, had been out on ten consecutive raids in the same number of days, either with ourselves or some other crew flying it. I had no time to record anything like the full activities of the Squadron; not even the targets it attacked, or its losses. If I were not down to fly I was either doing briefing or spending my time analysing the logs of less experienced navigators with a view to passing on any knowledge that might be useful or to correct any faults. The crew did their inspection of the machine at any time they could. This was one of those frantic periods which give the lie to the famous dictum of T.E. Lawrence that war is mostly waiting. It sometimes forces activity at such a pace that there is no time to think.

"This is no good", Frank complained to me. "They're flying the guts out of the aircraft. No sooner does she come out of the hangar after one inspection than she's back again for the next."

"We're certainly piling up the score. We'll be finished soon at this rate. The next leave we get will probably be the last one we'll get on Ops."

"No damn fear it won't. You'll see. They'll put the tour up to forty."

"They won't get forty out of me on one tour," I said. "I'll go batty first."

"It doesn't give the ground crews a dog's chance to do anything. There's all sorts of little things that want doing - nothing important but they just don't get to doing them."

Which was perfectly true. The maintenance crews worked at the highest pitch, and not only men but a certain number of women who had jobs to do about the machine, such as radar maintenance and oxygen wagon driving. These girls, dressed in dirty trousers and overalls, their hands and faces red with exposure to the open air throughout the winter, deserved as much praise as any of the men. I would speak to them with as much kindness as I could muster for the war bore hard on them in many little ways that a man would not notice and it is impossible for a woman not to lose femininity in these circumstances. The constant familiarity with coarseness provided every opportunity for a girl to become rough and ready. Many of them had been robbed of their adolescence having been hardly more than schoolgirls at the beginning of the war.

About this time a modification was being fitted to the aircraft that would automatically calculate ground speed on the bombing run, eliminating still another chance of error. We were prohibited from using the device until we had adequate training with it. Consequently, it was necessary to alter our procedure on the run into the target to this extent, that the navigator counted out to the bombardier the number of seconds, delay between the warning point and the release point and on the zero the bombardier released the load. Thus he had the satisfaction, so long denied to him on a GH squadron, of pressing the fatal bomb-release button himself.

This procedure was put into effect on our next raid and was directed against another coking plant in the Gelsenkirchen area. Once more our crew led the wave of aircraft of the entire Base. The forming up and outward journey went as planned and although strong winds were encountered at height that blew the stream off track the bombing run was good and the raid, so far as we could judge, satisfactory. We bombed from a height of 21,000 feet entirely in ice-crystal cloud, so even if there were any opposition from the enemy we were not worried by seeing it.

Next day the Squadron flew a sortie in the morning with an average battle-order and was called upon to supply two aircraft for a special night attack. Even two aircraft have to be briefed and interrogated. The pressure of events, which were piling up to a climax, was being felt by everyone.

On the Tuesday news came through that the German army was in full retreat across the Rhein, and driven by Allied forces was packing into the town of Wesel, or what was left of it after our raids of last month. In the haste of the retreat, Wesel with its bridge and railhead, was a constricted bottle-neck crammed with troops and transport; an ideal air force target. Three attacks were made on it in the early hours of Wednesday morning. This made the fourth target visited by our Squadron in 36 hours.

The raid was timed for that period of the night, just before dawn, when sudden terror and destruction have a more overpowering effect on the human spirit than at any other time; when the blood runs sluggishly and the urge to sleep presses heavily on the eyelids; when the very wish for life that keeps the soldier on the ground sane amid frightful hazards, must be at its ebb. The raid came into the target at half-past four.

We took off at 02.30 hours carrying a second pilot, a freshman who had come to see what it was like before starting on his own. Blenkin, feeling rather superior, had given him a lot of fatherly advice. Once we were off the deck the engineer gave up his seat and came and sat at the end of my form but on the other side of the curtain. That curtain was Johnnie's special care. Before we took off on a night sortie he would carefully examine all round its edges for any little chink of light and fix me in with bits of wire here and there, lest any gleam should give us away. Now I could see the bulge of him outlined in the dim light of the cabin as his back indented the material. On the other side was Turner, with a ray of light striking across his strong face as he sat before the black bank of his sets. I felt enormously glad and happy and cocked a thumb at him around the corner before I set the skipper the course.

Our journey was an easy one. We bombed from the south, heading into a strong northerly airstream so that our bombing run, usually only a matter of about six minutes, was as long as fourteen. The target was within easy reach of the ground transmitters that sent strong, readable pulses and the low ground speed gave ample time for leisurely calculation and careful bombing. It was an excellent attack.

We went home in fine spirits and finally descended at early dawn. We had our coffee with a shot of rum in it and a huge breakfast with bacon and eggs, and a relaxed half-hour in which the raid was fought over again. We finally turned into bed as everyone else was going to work, feeling thoroughly satisfied.

The battle against Germany's rapidly dwindling oil targets continued, with an air attack at night aimed against Dessau in the Leipzig area. The raid was routed so that a spoof was made on Berlin, the bombers turning south at the last moment and striking a track to the real target. Enemy nightfighters were persistent however and there were plenty of combat reports; Warwick's gunners, for example, saw a Ju. 88 stooging along against the bright part of the sky. They let him have it before he spotted the bomber and saw him break away downwards, apparently damaged. No tracer ammunition was being used as by this time it had been decided that tracer gave away the position of the bomber, but they had the new gyro gunsight which corrected deflection automatically from speed figures supplied by the navigator. They claimed the enemy as a probable. The PFF markers were late in putting down their flares and several of our aircraft had to orbit in the target area before they could drop their loads. Nineteen bombers were lost of the four hundred that took part, among them being a machine that carried one of the Squadron's best navigators.

One of our crews, doing its first night trip, was still unaccounted for an hour after the rest had landed. The operation had lasted about eight hours but, as was usual, the Lancasters carried fuel for approximately eleven hours to provide enough margin for a diversion anywhere in Britain should the necessity arise due to weather clamp. The navigator of the aircraft in question must have been suffering from oxygen lack on leaving the target for he commenced plotting the fixes on the wrong lattice chart. Although such a mistake would normally have been obvious he blissfully gave his pilot courses based on this false information. At one period his log and chart showed he had sat still doing nothing absolutely for an hour - an unforgiveable thing in normal circumstances. The aircraft flew on, all alone, over southern France for an hour after its Estimated Time of Arrival at Base before he realized there must be something wrong. Then Flying Control at Chedburgh heard that the aircraft had been picked up asking for homing bearings and fortunately the pilot had the good sense to turn on the course sent from England, although he must have doubted it. After he had been flying north for another hour he was intercepted by a British nightfighter and led into Manston where he landed with only thirty gallons in his tanks.

Next day the experienced leaders of the Navigation section took the log and chart and replotted and analysed it to see what they could find. Seeing the very neat work fade out and become meaningless over the return journey they were forced to the only possible conclusion that something must have gone wrong with his oxygen economiser. He was watched very carefully over his next few trips but never had any more trouble and his crew stoutly refused any extra navigational exercises for him. They had lost no confidence and were allowed to press on.

Fox had to go into the maintenance hanger after the Dessau trip. The starboard inner engine had been driven to death. It had been leaking oil copiously and continuously for days, smothering the nacelle and running down the oleo leg on to the wheel until finally the motor had given in and now it had to be changed. Frank and I caught the harassed CTO in the mess that evening.

"Have a drink, sir?" said Frank.

"Small beer," the engineer replied. We let him sink his first one in silence.

"Have another, sir!" It was my turn.

"Ah!", beamed the CTO, feeling a little better, "I think I could manage one more!"

"Cheers," we said.

Frank now felt it opportune to begin. "Our kite went in for an engine change today," he mentioned casually.

"Which one is that?" queried the Squadron Leader.

"F-Fox. "C" flight. When do you think we can have it out again?"

"My boys", he said with a wicked air of finality and the frustrated look that engineer officers bore in those days, "I've got kites in every hanger and kites on every apron around the hangers. Half of them ought to go to an MU. I've tyre changes, engine changes, turret changes, modifications, majors, minors and no spare parts. And you ask me when you can have a kite out that's only been put in today."

"But this is different. This is an emergency!" I could not help laughing.

Seeing the CTO about to be seized by a sudden spasm. Frank hastily ordered up more beer. He queried: "Shall we say the day after tomorrow?"

The old man gulped. "You young bastards", he said with easy familiarity, "you'll be lucky if you get it in a month". Then, noticing how our faces fell, "We'll see what we can do."

We did not get the machine back until the beginning of April.

On March 10th another benzole plant was laid on. Four miles from Gelsenkirchen at a place called Buer, it was only just inside the battle line now deploying along the Rhein. Jock Stark, near the end of his tour, had the job of leading the Base with ourselves as deputies. It was a trip without much incident, by day with the inevitable cloud undercast shutting out the ground and the necessity of bombing on radar. The squadron maintained a tight formation all the way to the target and back. Jock's Gee set packed up halfway home and Johnnie O'Brien called Blenkin to take over the formation for the rest of the way. In the hut that night I good-humouredly told Jock he was a lazy devil for not finishing the trip on DR or H2S.

"Eh man, I just knew ye were waiting to do some work", he laughed.

Bomber Command put out one of its big efforts. Over a thousand - 1,044 - Lancasters and Halifaxes pasted Essen putting paid to the last remnants of the Krupp concern. Our battle order detailed seventeen aircraft, of which only fourteen took off; three skippers being unable to go because of unserviceabilities discovered at the last moment. One other of our machines had to force land at the emergency airfield at Juvincourt, near Rheims - a graveyard of derelict RAF and American machines, but a place worth its weight in gold to crews in distress over the battlefields. This was the same machine, A-Able, that had given us trouble with the hydraulics and now it finally gave up the ghost.

The Squadron had operated fifteen times in the past fourteen days. Crews were adequate but the aircraft were feeling the strain.

A second effort, also of over a thousand bombers, was directed against Dortmund. The stricken Ruhr was receiving some of the last and heaviest blows from its destroyer.

The Wing Commander left Blenkin's name out of these main force efforts preferring to send newer crews. He was conserving his experienced GH markers for blind bombing. The tempo of operations had upset training; crews had to go to Feltwell for it and there were delays.

Gussie remarked to me: "Dickie, my boy, he's saving us for the long night stooges."

Nevertheless, our next was a daylight attack on Datteln, again in the coal mining district of the north Ruhr, where a benzole plant needed a little attention. The German oil industry must have reached enormous size in its heyday; in spite of the prognostications of the experts it had been keeping the war machine going for over five years of hostilities. In the past month we ourselves had visited six different plants, all in the northern part of the Ruhr, and there were others to come. It is impossible not to admire the tenacity of the enemy, whose oil supplies were so confidently predicted at the beginning of the war to be enough for six months!

It would have been quite possible to choose a route to Datteln that should offer practical immunity from flak defences. In order to confuse the enemy and simplify the work of the fighter top cover we were routed in with another body of machines that had to turn off at the last moment for another target. The track lay right through the remains of the Ruhr and as I drew it on my chart I pointed out to Blenkin, with evident disgust, that we would be certain to draw plenty of enemy fire, and wondered why such a route should be chosen.

Meteorological conditions promised well for bombing. West winds of almost negligible strength were not expected to exceed 30 mph. There was the likelihood of uncertain weather on return for Abingdon was given as a diversion field.

Johnnie's undoubted experience, deriving from his earlier days as a fitter, enabled him to distinguish himself again on this operation. On the outward journey, without warning, the undercarriage doors opened and the undercarriage dropped about a quarter of its normal travel. Fox was still in dock - this was a spare aircraft XH - K King, and it seemed that dropping undercarriages were a habit with these loveless spare machines.

The undercarriage lever was checked and also the reservoir, which was quite full. Johnnie came to the conclusion that emergency air was leaking past the control valve into the undercarriage hydraulic system.

He therefore disconnected the pipe lines to the undercarriage and allowed the compressed air to escape. Frank selected wheels "down" and then "up" and to everybody's satisfaction up they came.

The official report said: "Sergeant Wortley's third repair also concerned the hydraulic system. During this operation the undercarriage doors opened in flight and the undercarriage dropped to about a quarter of the way down. The undercarriage lever was checked and found to be in the down position and the hydraulic reservoir was found to be seven-eighths full. Subsequent investigation revealed that the emergency air supply was leaking past the control valve into the hydraulic undercarriage system. The air pipe lines to the undercarriage were disconnected and the air in the pipe lines allowed to escape to the atmosphere. The undercarriage was then selected "down" followed by a selection "up". The undercarriage and all other hydraulics services were then found to be serviceable. This repair was 100 per cent successful and enabled the crew to bomb their objective."

By any road you steer you need an engineer!

We met the expected anti-aircraft fire going into the target. Every battery in the Ruhr that could get a gun to bear was firing. Our individual luck held - we were missed but as happened on another occasion ours was the only aircraft in the spearhead of our attack that was not holed. The bombing run was good in spite of opposition, the attack sharp and concentrated, delivered with real efficiency and on time. As the Lancasters swept away north and I switched off my GH equipment I felt somewhat hot around the collar but distinctly pleased.

When we came back over East Anglia the ground was obscured by a thick ground haze. From a thousand feet it was quite invisible. The industrial murk of London, trapped under a layer of warm air through which it could not rise and spread by a light westerly wind, had drawn a curtain over the Suffolk aerodromes. The London haze often extended over the North Sea. To make matters worse it was late afternoon; the flat rays of the setting sun shone redly into the haze, diffused and decreased the lateral visibility and were directed into the pilot's eyes on the approach to the runway.

I homed the skipper over our field and called that we were there. The radio was full of the noise of other aircraft calling control.

"Wastage King, join circuit," ordered the ground.

"This is no good. We shall have to go down", muttered Frank. "Everybody keep a look out for other aircraft."

"Wastage King, prepare to land!" The cold, efficient, disembodied voice crackled its instructions over the radio.

I left my seat and came out into the space behind the engineer. Visibility was shocking. Every now and then I could glimpse another aircraft ahead. We were going round the circuit on the skipper's blind-flying panel, losing height slowly. Fortunately, Chedburgh is as high as anywhere in that area and one could let down to 300 feet above the field in reasonable safety.

Looking downwards one's eyes took in nothing but grey obscurity.

Control, knowing the conditions of visibility, had turned on the night lighting. At about 400 feet we caught sight of the lamps, that are set on the tops of wooden poles and form a large circle around the field. The lights are a matter of four hundred yards apart. We could see no more than two at a time.

Someone in the funnels called out that he was going round again. Frank said: "We'll follow the outer circle Johnnie, and I'll do a steep turn in."

"Fair enough. I'm ready."

Roy, whose position in the mid-upper turret allowed him the best view of the lights, was calmly giving corrections to the skipper. I slipped back into the cabin in order to call out the airspeed on approach, which was my job.

We received permission to land and skidded into the turn. I commenced to call regularly as the airspeed indicator fell back.

Suddenly: "Overshoot ...!" from Frank in a voice full of tension, and "Overshooting!", from the engineer as the throttles went forward and the wheels and flaps commenced retreating. We had missed the runway. The engines gave out a fiercer note under the extra power as the machine started to climb. I came forward to see what was afoot.

We were in the murk. The clear voice of the WAAF operator at Control ordered us to circuit height. Someone else had a try.

"There goes Harlow!", said Frank "He's done one overshoot already. Wonder if he'll make it this time."

Harlow slipped his machine in and we heard him call clear of the runway. Then it was our turn again.

We were going down. I called: "160 ... 150 ... 145 ... 145 ... 150." Keeping it high to be on the safe side. Suddenly, with a horrible lurch, the wheels touched down. We were on the runway with 150 on the clock.

I thought: "God ... we'll prang!"

No brakes would stop her at that speed on two thousand yards or less of runway. Before I had time to think any more, or do anything, Blenkin was pulling the machine off again. We were all scared. He flew well clear of the field, getting his heart back into place, and I had to home the machine back again before the third attempt.

"Well," I thought, "I'll be ready for this". I drew on my leather gauntlets, pulled my goggles over my eyes and as we began losing height sat along the seat with my feet braced as well as possible against an upright. That was all I could do except check the nearest axe and extinguisher out of the corner of my eye - and hope!

Frank was too shaken to take any risks and did a third overshoot without getting anywhere near the runway.

"Why the hell don't they give us the diversion!", I said, trying to speak as calmly as possible. No one had got down since Harlow and the sound of pilots calling overshooting was getting monotonous. I pulled the pink diversion book out and plotted Abingdon on the chart.

We made another attempt. Once again the wheels touched but we were badly aligned and swinging and had to take off again. We had been over the field at a quarter past six and now it was nearly seven.

The sun's disc went below the horizon. Finally we got down.

I stepped out of the aircraft into an evening full of light. Aircraft were still in the circuit, probably a dozen of them, as plainly visible as could be wished. So extraordinary is the freakish business of downward visibility in haze, of which that evening was the worst example I ever met.

"When you ran along the runway, Blenkin," a controller remarked afterwards, "the C.O. nearly had a baby!"

"I think I *did*," Frank smiled.

There followed a couple of comparatively easy days; most welcome particularly as the peace was disturbed by only one briefing. We were dismissed from this with instructions to maintain strict security about the target as it would probably be the subject of the next sortie. The weather had turned bad.

The overworked Murray Jones, tour expired navigation leader, pounced on me to help him clear up the analyses, promising me a cup of tea in mid-afternoon as a reward for my labours. Another bait that the wily Murray used was the plentiful cigarette supply he received from New Zealand. He did not smoke, but distributed them amongst the navigators. When one of these dropped into the office to borrow a cigarette Murray would confront him with his last chart, grimly annotated in red ink. Murray was, and is, a farmer in civil life yet he had a business man's gift for organization, was extremely methodical and his painstaking work on the logs and charts of the Squadron pushed up the standards of navigation considerably. Any deviation from the systematic drill of regular fixes and air positions would rouse in him a mild indignation. Gussie and I used to make extra efforts to get his comment: "Very good trip", that was given sparingly and appreciated accordingly.

On the 17th the objective that had been expected since the last briefing was detailed again. A coking plant and the coal mine that supplied it, in the Ruhr, at a place called Huls.

Huls is north of the mass of the Ruhr, about five miles from the nearest town of Recklinghausen and so unimportant except for the oil plant that it was not even marked on the half-million maps. The target was not considered enough to merit the full weight of the Group's daylight attack, so the stream was briefed to divide in the Ruhr and strike two blows. Blenkin was to lead the Base in. We considered we had struck an easy one.

Wind strengths were greater than forecast and everyone became progressively late. At 16,000 feet the aircraft began to form condensation trails that persisted and spread so that all but the few machines right at the front were flying in cirrus cloud of their own making. It became difficult, and then impossible, to see the top cover of fighters. On the bombing run, as the stream packed together we were almost rammed by some Lancasters that appeared out of cloud at our level. As Frank lurched the aircraft away, my tracking pulse danced off the strobe. There was no question of going round again on a daylight such as this. The stream went through the target and away, not loitering as an invitation to enemy fighters. Also, the ground transmitters were active only for a short period, enough to cover the raid, so that their frequencies might not be jammed. We laboured to regain track and heading as far as possible before the bombs went away. The best we could do was to get back just within the tolerance of track permitted, and then away they went, with our followers' bombs too. Apart from the purely natural difficulties though, it was an easy trip.

There was a comparative lull and for three whole days the only flying we did was to go to Down Ampney and pick up a crew that had been flown in by Transport Command after a forced landing in Belgium. Down Ampney, where we landed in the sunlight of a beautiful afternoon, was only about ten miles from my sister's home in the Cotswolds and I had visions of a civilized evening, but I was doomed to disappointment. The grinning passengers were waiting outside control; we merely taxied round, piled them in and took off again. How easy it was to fly around England on a pleasant day. I just stood behind Frank with a map, enjoying the clearness of the air and the white clouds and the warmth of the spring sun striking through the perspex of the cupola, picking out an occasional landmark to steer by.

This break was a bad thing in some ways, however, for there is nothing like going on when the nerves are overstrung. I was not aware of this at the time but retrospection convinces me that I had built up a certain amount of tension which showed itself in such petty ways as a burst of indignation when Allardyce, the Flight Commander, insisted that we do an H2S cross-country exercise. Here I was, the acknowledged senior navigator of the Squadron with twenty-five trips in my log and fancying I knew all the answers, being detailed for some practice. Still, the Squadron was compelled to log up training hours and orders are orders, and we had to go.

The Squadron was put on a state of stand-by, being almost in the nature of close-support bombers for the Army. The policy at this junction was to hold No. 3 Group, with its blind-bombing capability, in readiness to answer any request from the battlefield for heavy co-operation. From this fact, and probably because the army was making such excellent progress, they were out on only one occasion and when I was away. This was by night when they went to Wesel, eight GH markers of No. 3 Group each bombing on his own radar while the appreciative infantry lay in their foxholes on the other bank of the river only 1,500 yards away. So good was the attack that only one stick of bombs fell outside the target area. In the early hours of the morning the soldiers crossed the river and took the oft-bombed remnants of the town with only minor casualties. In a congratulating message from the Army that was displayed on the Squadron's notice board it was stated that there were only thirty-five of these casualties for the crossing of the Rhein at such a place! Compare this with the fracas at Arnhem.

This last attack was classic. We have heard the name of Wesel before and it will appear finally when I describe how the town looked when I saw it after the war. Some credit for its obliteration must go to the Tactical Air Force and the Americans but it is safe to say that the attacks on Wesel represented the highlights of GH bombing and a tribute to the navigational skills of crews who could, and did, obliterate the town without even seeing it.

Conditions were possibly helpful, for the town, situated outside the generally considered area of the Ruhr, probably never had the permanent defences of some of the targets lower down the Rhein. Also it was not a distant target which meant that petrol loads were light and bomb loads heavy when we visited it; besides its geographical position in relation to the south of England, where were sited the main GH transmitters, meant the pulses were received strong and steady. Nevertheless, Group Captain

Brotherhood, our CO, with whom I was discussing the matter one day, affirmed that bombplots showed a concentration of bombs could be expected within 300 yards if a GH attack went according to plan. This was much more accurate than visual bombing could hope to be except under ideal conditions, considering the bombsights in general use. There were bombsights coming along to replace the Mark XIV but they were few in service.

That conditions were not always ideal was instanced when on Thursday March 20th our machines went to a target over 10 degrees East longitude by daylight. An indication of the way the battlefront was moving and of the decaying power of the Luftwaffe. The place concerned was Hallendorf. Reports indicated a haphazard attack for many navigators could not pick up a release pulse and they were flying in cloud of a density sufficient to make it almost impossible to bomb in formation with anyone else, and in any case extremely hazardous. Icing conditions were encountered adding an overriding risk to all other difficulties.

The Ruhr was now practically surrounded by the army. Aircrew were jubilant. With the easy enthusiasm of the young some were saying: "We've had it. We might as well go home."

"Might as well get your tropical kit ready!" the older hands would reply in the superior manner of men who see others involved in some unpleasant thing that does not concern themselves.

Even Tee Emm, mirroring the official view, was publishing instructional articles on how P/O Prune could take to life in the jungles of Burma.

April Fool's Day and the whole of Bomber Command changed over its navigational procedures from statute miles per hour to nautical miles and knots. This little joke meant all-night work for the instrument mechanics who had to fit or alter on each machine. Airspeed indicators of pilots, navigators and bombardiers. Bombsights, and Range screens on H2S sets, and, I believe, the gyro gunsight where fitted. The pilots and engineers had immediately to learn the aircraft performance in terms of the new units, new approach speeds and so forth; the navigators had to undo all the habits of their Squadron days and revert to those of training. Hordes of conversion tables were issued, showing that if you bombed from X feet at Y mph before you must now do it at Z knots.

I convinced Harry, keeping a perfectly straight face, that in future altitude would be recorded in fathoms!

All these tables and all the instrument modifications were prepared and ready so that it would have been possible to go on an early morning raid on April 1st, navigating in the new units.

* * * * *

Blenkin, shaving his stiff bristles at his portable wash basin, was alternatively screwing up his eyes as he took a scrape and singing in snatches a mournful, tuneless air,

"There was Guy, Guy
Having another try
In the valley of the Ruhr..."

referring to Guinane, another of the pilots of the Squadron.

"Do you know," I remarked, "what day this is?"

"April Fool's day."

"To be exact it is Easter Sunday," I replied.

"Good. Should get an egg for breakfast. Makes me nostalgic for a pre-war Easter egg of real milk chocolate."

I said suddenly: "If we're not on I think I'll cycle into Bury St Edmunds tonight and go to church at the Abbey."

His razor stopped in mid-air. He paused, and looking round at me in surprised exclaimed simply: "Oh!"

Bury St Edmunds, at least at that time, was a sleepy provincial Assize town with little extraordinary claim to fame. But it has the ruins of what was once an abbey of unsurpassed beauty. Today, there remain foundations and walls and two of the old gateways. One is a most excellent example of Norman work, a square stone tower decorated with bizarre and leering reliefs that remind one of the carvings of the Mexican Indians, magnificently proportioned and in a state of preservation hard to believe after going on for a thousand years. The other gateway, built two or three hundred years later, is insignificant by comparison. Also remaining are two of the abbey churches; one of them has a carved wooden roof of the Perpendicular period claimed to be the finest of its kind in England.

Whenever I could get to Bury this ancient abbey was a never failing source of pleasure partly because the town itself held so little attraction and its inhabitants, grown blasé through continual association, had long since come to ignore the existence of British and American airmen who might have found some relaxation in the place had such been provided. There were the usual pubs, but even aircrew cannot drink for ever, and sometimes beer was in short supply.

Soon after tea I mounted my bicycle for the journey.

Spring was in the air. The Suffolk countryside was beginning to burst into leaf and the freshness of the day took all the work out of pedalling. Sticky buds were beginning to open on the chestnuts, thrusting their decoration against the bare filigree of twigs. In Horringer, that model village that houses the workers on the local estate, people were standing at their gates, gossiping as country folk would do, probably for lack of any other amusement. There was one cottage in particular, a perfect gem, whose owner must have been a topiary expert for the gate was flanked by trees cut into the shapes of pheasants. Dominion lads would whoop with delight on seeing it and unload their cameras to take a picture of what they imagined an English cottage should be like.

So to the church with its stately pillars bearing old masons' marks and with the evening fading outside the stained glass the clean-cut voices of the choir boys rose to lose their notes in the darkness of the roof. Yesterday was war and tomorrow will be war but today was a link with the centuries of peaceful England. And yet the stones of this abbey have known their strife, and many have tumbled down.

* * * * *

The Wing Commander invariably had us on parade in the morning when there was no battle order. He was an old Cranwell man! On one of these mornings that was no exception to the rule we were lined up on the perimeter track, each crew in file behind its skipper, with the Flight Commanders out in front and the Adjutant fidgetting in an uncertain way in charge of the parade. A perfect spring sky was flecked with cirro-cumulus cloud at terrific height, and the Fortresses were forming up for a mission. We cast idle glances upward, where their leader was ranging round the sky trailing a smoke candle that left a long plume behind it. As they fell into formation they shot off Verey lights, red or green; it didn't seem to matter which; in fact the Yanks probably banged away for the sheer joy of it.

Every now and then someone would murmur appreciation at the excellent formation of the Americans; passing professional judgment. Occasionally, a machine would strike a patch of atmosphere where incipient condensation trails could form and then the bomber would appear as a four-tailed comet, white streamers running away for a short distance behind it and then fading out.

Presently there came a Squadron Leader. "I want you all to listen carefully to this dispatch from Group," he said and went on to read. It was a warning of the dangers of not maintaining compact formation in the daylight attacks. On a recent operation a complete wave of our bombers had lagged behind and were some minutes late by the time they reached the point where they should have joined the fighter escort. The Mustangs had gone on with the preceding wave. Enemy radar, doubtless, had plotted the conjunction of fighters and bombers and detected the delayed wave. By a combination of quick thinking and the presence of fighters in the locality his controllers were able to orbit a detachment of his own machines at the rendezvous.

One can imagine the crews of the wave of bombers. As they approached the fatal spot the navigators would say:

"Fighter rendezvous coming up. Any signs of the escort?" and the gunners would strain their eyes up and pick out the little motes flying above, flashing now and then as the sunlight caught a wing, and say:

"Yes - there they are. OK, port bow up!"

Everyone would feel relieved and perhaps a little relaxed. Next minute the enemy was among them with guns flickering.

Sixteen went down.

Somehow a lot of the sunlight had gone out of the morning as we left the parade.

Chapter 19

NAVAL OCCASION

On April 4th we were in action again. Oil was the objective; to keep pounding and pulverizing the last supplies of the Reich; to leave the German trucks on the roads and the tanks stranded on the battlefields for lack of fuel; to put the refineries out of commission faster than they could be repaired, and starve the Reichswehr into immobility.

We were deployed against the Leuna oil plant, the biggest synthetic producer of them all and claimed to be Germany's most heavily defended target. I was not pleased to sit in briefing looking at the flak map and hearing that there were 400 anti-aircraft guns and 50 searchlights waiting at the refinery.

As part of the tactics No. 100 Group were put in to do a feint attack and operate the usual mandrel screen against enemy radar. Also, besides the four hundred odd thrown against Leuna, another six hundred bombers were out that night against other oil targets in Germany. It was hoped that sheer pressure of work would paralyse the efforts of the nightfighters.

We were due into the target at H hour and No. 8 Group were supposed to open the attack four minutes earlier with their markers.

It was one of those nights when Met. had been deceived by the weather. It was obvious almost from the start of the journey that we should have to push the aircraft if we were to be at the target as the schedule required. Fortunately, we had Fox again having tested her thoroughly two nights previously on an exercise. We put up the airspeed and used every time-saving dodge we knew in order to be punctual.

Beyond eight degrees East I turned on the H2S in line with the orders, hastily tuned it and left the scanner running. About ten minutes before the time of bombing I called the bombardier, for it was to be a visual attack. "Commence running up. H hour in eight or nine minutes", and with four minutes to go I said "You should see the markers going down now!" The Pathfinders markers were to fall at H minus four minutes.

"Not a sign yet. Not a thing."

"Three minutes to H hour!"

"No, nothing!"

I looked at the H2S screen. On the edge of the ten-mile scale luminous and well defined, was the smudge that could be nothing else but the town of Leipzig, moving from ahead to astern on the port side.

"We're OK," I said, emphatically. "I've got Leipzig on the H2S as clear a a bell, skipper."

"OK, nav."

At that moment the voice of the master bomber came over the intercom, quite audible in spite of the crackle, frantically calling for markers.

"H hour", I said. Nothing could be seen below. PFF were already four minutes late.

At H plus one Roy exclaimed: "Flares going down under the starboard wing."

"Yes, there they go," called Jack, "Can't bomb on this run - we shall have to go round again."

"Shall I orbit port or starboard, navigator?"

I replied immediately: "Orbit starboard. If we go port we may go over Leipzig. Do a wide orbit or we may run into the stream coming in."

"Don't worry!", Frank replied.

I thought: "Here's my opportunity." With the markers now going down plentifully there would be no need for me. Jack would take the Lancaster in for the bombing run. I worked out my next courses, jotted them on my pad, turned out the light and slipped under the curtain.

We were already halfway through the turn and under the starboard wing bright febrile clusters of skymarkers were grouped in the darkness. The attack was opening, flashes of bursting bombs following each other so quickly that they merged into a long flicker. The hard-pressed enemy who had concentrated into this area all the devices he could muster, had lit up any number of spoofs; clusters of green electric lights and dummy fires, but the colours were wrong and in any case the real attack was unmistakeable. A remarkable number of isolated lights burned on the ground. Some of the fifty searchlights had come into action and there was some cloud below that provided isolated cover.

Suddenly an explosion much greater than had happened before lit up the sky and lingered for perhaps a full quarter of a minute. This time may sound short, but it can cover a tumult of experience lived at the tempo of the target area. The low cloud banks were pearled and turned into an orange-yellow counterpane, translucent and pulsing like the Northern Lights. Plainly seen were the black silhouettes of other bombers, sharp in the glare and seeming to be going in all possible directions, emphasizing the frightful danger of collision over the target. In the stream most people kept station through the necessity of being at the concentration points on time. But over the target ...!

Harry saw a fighter standing off near us. Then in quick succession the gunners reported two others. They made no attack on us, however, and we were relieved of the necessity of corkscrewing. I saw none of them although I was looking out for my eyes were not really sensitive enough after the light of the cabin. The turrets were swinging continuously from side to side.

As we were edging on to the correct heading for bombing the skymarkers extinguished. "Damn it, the skymarkers are finished. I shall have to bomb on target indicators," Jack called.

"Pick 'em out," ordered the skipper. "Make sure of them."

"Cloud's a nuisance but I think I'll be OK."

Reluctantly, for I was fascinated by the sight, I went back into my cubbyhole to record the bombing details. I set up the range and bearing of Leipzig from the target, on the H2S screen in order to have a rough check as the load went.

We bombed twelve minutes late on our briefed time, although this was in no way our fault. Most of our Squadron, it proved, had lagged behind on the journey in and were able to bomb on the skymarkers first time. So the concentration plot of returning aircraft subsequently prepared by Group Navigation did not show us at all - we must have been among the last away from the refinery.

On the way home we ran into a sudden wind shift, a minor front, and the nose was covered with static electricity, St Elmo's fire.

I became aware that my pants were feeling uncomfortably damp. I had not noticed anything untoward until about half way home, when we were still at 10,000 feet. Instinctively, I worked my hand around behind my back, with some difficulty, and down through my clothing, expecting to bring blood out on my fingers. I thought I might have been hit by a splinter in the excitement and not noticed it.

There was no bloodstain to be seen, although my fingers were obviously damp. Suspiciously, I pushed my mask aside and sniffed ... brandy! I struggled the flask out of my hip pocket. It was smeared with the spirit but seemed intact. When later I examined it I found that a seam had cracked to the slightest extent. On the ground it was airtight but the relaxed pressure at height had allowed the contents to ooze away until it was half empty. That night Blenkin and I finished it off before going to bed.

We reached home and landed last. "First to the target, last to land," complained Harry. "That's us, always the same."

Two of the Squadron's aircraft collided on the ground at the end of the runway, which held up landings. The outer propeller of one chewed the wing off the other down to the starboard outer nacelle, and both machines were badly knocked about. The crews escaped injury.

Otherwise, the Squadron suffered no casualties. A lucky thing when the target was Leuna.

Now the weather turned unfavourable for a couple of days. A Hamburg briefing that was prepared on the Saturday was scrubbed after all the work had been done. With such major targets as this coming up one was almost ready for anything and therefore very little surprise was expressed when on the April 9th an Operations form came through giving the night's target as Kiel.

At this time the harbour was sheltering a pretty hornet's nest of trouble. The *Admiral Scheer*, last of Hitler's pocket battleships; the cruisers *Hipper, Köln* and *Emden*, some forty submarines, as well as destroyers and merchantmen. Two separate aiming points were detailed in the dock area. This was one time when a few overshoots would do no harm - as the briefing officer dryly remarked.

To attack a naval base was a definite change and the idea was rather exhilarating. There was bound to be opposition of a certain warmth. When No. 617 and 9 Squadrons had made one of their earlier attacks on the *Tirpitz* the flak from the battleship had been heavy. We could expect to run into that. Still an attack on enemy shipping in harbour is part of a long British tradition. Other days, other ways, but the strategy remains.

Another change was making the journey almost entirely over the sea. As we were struggling into our equipment in the locker room I overheard Jack say to Harry: "Better test your Mae West tonight Harry. You may have to use it!"

"If we have to make one of Blenkin's special landings on the sea, no one will need a Mae West", the gunner said gloomily.

Nevertheless, life jackets were blown up and deflated and torches checked for the second time, just in case.

Over England and the North Sea a large anti-cyclone was settled, giving pleasant spring weather and light, unpredictable winds. Urged by the necessity of providing data for the planning of the operation Group Met. postulated a westerly airflow. "Group are going in for light south-westerlies," said the forecaster at briefing, "but I'm not so sure."

We set off into a beautiful evening, flying low across the sea which was hardly ruffled with only tiny waves. Waves always look small from the air and wandering currents mark the surface with lace-like tracery.

The attack was scheduled to open soon after dusk, at 22.30 hours. We were in the first wave.

I started finding winds that were almost reciprocals of those briefed.

"Navigator to pilot, can I have more speed?" adding, "Sorry, Johnnie."

"All right" growled the latter.

"Twenty-three hundred, plus seven, Johnnie", Frank ordered. "Maximum economical cruising, nav." This gave us a true airspeed of 200 knots at 2,000 feet, which was very good engine handling and enabled me to get through the concentration points punctually. There were very few troubles on the way out. At low height, unhampered by oxygen equipment, one can plot with great rapidity and turn out a chart that is a relative work of art compared with some of the efforts, marred and smudged by the drippings from the mask and furnished with the barest details that are produced at altitude. The navigation was done on the North-Eastern Gee chain and we began climbing before the pulses weakened with the curvature of the earth.

We also amused ourselves by plotting a series of loop bearings on English stations and Turner's readings were very accurate. Our track took us to 55 degrees North latitude where there was enemy WT jamming, although as we passed 7 degrees East Gee became unusable through this heavy railing-like interference.

Twenty minutes before the Danish coast I motioned Turner to go back and switch on the main voltage of the H2S and I tuned the set. It was most useful. As the coastline came near I picked it up on the long-range scan without any difficulty and on the short range the picture was perfect.

At 22.19 hours, at the top of our climb, we crossed the Danish coast going in. Kiel is on the eastern side. It was dark by this time and the farmers below, indoors at an early hour as is the custom with farm folk, must have heard the swelling roar as the great fleet of some 500 bombers went over. Some probably rushed to their doors with a mixture of curiosity and apprehension. But to the German outposts the noise must have meant fear and frantic telephoning and the manning of guns and stand-to for the searchlights from Flensburg down to Bremen.

A feint attack was being made towards Hamburg by No. 100 Squadron whose energetic window-scattering so often drew the nightfighters on a false scent.

Suddenly: "Bombardier to skipper. Target sighted!"

"No, no!", I cried emphatically. "We've ten minutes more to go".

"There's red and green target indicators on the ground. Those are tonight's indicators."

"No. Press on. I'm certain of position!" as indeed I was for H2S could not have been better if it was a map.

"Must be a spoof. Come and have a look, nav." from the skipper.

Curiosity conquered my vague annoyance at the interruption of work. I slipped under the curtain and looked down.

It was the most perfect imitation of a target one could wish to see, with well-simulated ground markers and even skymarkers bursting above it. These were being fired up from the ground and were of poor colour. I do not doubt it drew a few salvos that night because one of our own Squadron's crews were trapped into bombing a dummy further to the south. Sure enough, punctually on time, the British markers went down ahead.

"Buzzbomb to Firepump - bomb the reds - bomb the reds!", called the master bomber. Which we proceeded to do.

So quickly does a major attack develop that in the minutes between the opening and our arrival over the target the area had turned into a scintilla of coloured lights and flame, shot with the twinkle of flak. Not only the heavy stuff but the long streaks of tracer ammunition from the light anti-aircraft of the ships which exploded harmlessly below and served little purpose apart from relieving the feelings of the gunners in the German fleet.

We bombed in workmanlike fashion and got away.

Once the aircraft was clear of the target the bombardier came up from the hatch and settled beside me, fussing with the controls of the radar set. There was a most satisfactory picture, enabling the most exact navigation.

Nothing gave a crew more confidence than enthusiastic assurance from the navigator that all was going well.

Our route lay between the islands of Sylt and Bornholm. I was able to direct the pilot by map-reading the radar screen, while the crew had the satisfaction of seeing the flak pouring up to port and starboard as we passed through unscathed. Even so, the losses were remarkably light for only four bombers failed to come back. We returned steadily; it was just routine flying across sea where one could relax in the knowledge that the only shooting likely would come from some unit of the British navy, a very trigger-happy organization, that had been known to fire on any aircraft that happened to be in their vicinity.

The photograph plotted well. It was a picture of bright streaks and dots that meant a lot to Intelligence and very little to the uninitiated.

Next day the news came through that the pocket battleship *Admiral Scheer* had been sunk in the raid and was lying over on the bottom of Kiel harbour. Everyone was delighted that Bomber Command had finished off yet another large unit of the German navy. Not content with this success, our fellows went out the next day and sunk the *Lützow*.

News came that the total of operations required for a tour had been reduced from the resented forty to thirty-five. In fact, one of our crews, an Australian, had already done a tour of forty and his bomb aimer wrote a book about it subsequently, (Miles Tripp: *The Eighth Passenger*). Neither Blenkin nor I was particularly moved, having become accustomed to our business and having ceased to regard ourselves as likely candidates for an interview with St Peter. It is curious that having become keyed up to an entirely different mode of life man will proceed quite philosophically about an occupation that would fill others, and possibly themselves, under different circumstances, with dread and apprehension. Myself, I had always held a conviction that we should not have to do a tour of forty as there were spare crews about, so I regarded the reduction as a vindication of my theory. In any case, by now we felt ourselves completely competent and if we ever thought about it at all felt that with normal luck we should be finished very soon. We had already been out 29 times and one acquires experience very quickly at the bombing game, or not at all.

The war was rapidly becoming a rout. Optimistic people were predicting dates for the end. The old hands were looking superior before the newcomers, saying condescendingly, "You'll never get a tour in now!" Crews were coming in fast, fresh from Conversion Units and wondering how soon it would be before they were posted to Burma. We had almost enough crews to allot two per aircraft, there were now sixty crews in the Squadron. Almost every day some new face would appear in the navigation office and I led a constant stream of newcomers, it seemed, to Fox's dispersal where I explained the functions of the multitude of knobs, buttons and dials.

Jock Stark and Johnnie O'Brien finished their tour at Mildenhall, and by some peculiar circumstance were posted straight off to the Far East without any rest period. "Ye'll rest on the wee boatie, ye ken!", I said unsympathetically when Jock had phoned his adieu. Also at Mildenhall, Maxie Hill had practically finished and Melville Parry was still struggling gamely along in spite of his constant airsickness.

The order came through that we were to commence practising low-level bombing and the bomb bays were fitted with a peculiar wooden box that opened to release a bag of sand when the button was pressed. A white target was marked out on the airfield and everyone spent hours of the bright April weather running in and dropping on this. Often the sandbag refused to budge. Since the exercise involved making wide circles with the airfield constantly in sight I had an easy time and was able to sun myself in the cupola and watch the dolls-house landscape go by. Jack was trying to cope with a special low-level bombsight that was held in the hand and squinted through as if it were a camera. There was no great difficulty in dropping within the target although we found we could dispense with the bombsight and do as well by relying on Frank to direct the aircraft and releasing when the target was just under the nose, for there was no consistency in the fall of the sandbags.

In the grass area formed by the triangle of the runways the white target looked insignificant enough. What was more prominent was the wreck of a Stirling, partially dismantled but with fuselage intact that had been there since the days of Conversion Unit when we were flying these monstrous aircraft. It was "Herepath's prang". It had been swung off the runway by that same pilot who had the bad luck at Witten. Now, an empty shell, it was a mute reminder of what seemed to be years ago.

Another thing that we did in the free days after Kiel was to swing the loop ariel of Fox. Since loop-swinging was optional and most navigators were content to come and go by radar it was probably a fact that Fox was the only machine of the Squadron with a properly swung loop. Harry, who came along with his gun cleaning gear and perspex polisher to work on his turret was intrigued by the whole business and gave a great deal of advice of dubious value as we hauled the Lancaster round the various headings with the tractor.

Although a few days with no battle order were welcome, they were usually occupied in catching up arrears of necessary work. The engineering staffs and ground crews had no respite but were able to push forward their maintenance schedules. The bombing up teams had time to put a load on to the machine and the long trains of flat steel trolleys with their sinister cargoes might be seen making the rounds of the dispersals, the quaint Donald Duck winches standing on the tarmac by the aircraft.

On very rare occasions the CO would order a stand-down.

We learned that our sandbag dropping was in preparation for the possibility of dropping food sacks in liberated Europe.

Chapter 20

BERLIN

"God - the Big City. We're on the Big City."

"Potsdam!", said some literal individual.

"So what. Look at the map."

"Yes, but it's on the outskirts!"

"Well, it's good enough for me. The suburbs are part of a town, aren't they?"

When Blenkin came in just before main briefing, Jack looked up from the maps he was preparing and said: "You've got your wish, skipper. We're on the Big City at last."

The pilot pushed his battered hat over the back of his head and smiled.

"It's Potsdam," I said. "I'm going to log it as Berlin in big letters with a little Potsdam in brackets afterwards."

"Well, at least we'll pay it one visit before Uncle Joe gets there."

"The way Blenkin turns", chimed in Harry, "we'll go right over the centre of Berlin anyway."

Berlin was the nightly target for a regular small force of Mosquitoes at this period and they harassed the capital with such regularity that the crews almost regarded the trip as a milk run. In duration of time, with the much greater cruising speed of their machines, the journey took no more than one of our runs to the Ruhr. They each carried a cookie, 4,000 lbs, and besides forcing the population to spend their nights in bunkers they constantly did material damage. Air Marshal Harris had waged large scale war on Berlin around the end of 1943 but the city had been spared the attention of the heavies for some time. However, I do not think that the C-in-C ever really forgot the capital for his expressed opinion had been that if he could reduce Berlin to ashes he would have won the war.

Our briefing room was packed, crammed to the back with crews for we had put out a big battle order. As usual, I had taken my meal immediately the dining room was opened so that I could secure my favourite table in the briefing room two rows from the front. The late afternoon sun struck the closed and painted-out windows of the room, casting a solid blue haze through the tobacco smoke where a shaft of light struck through a ventilator. I worked, Jack folded and refolded half a dozen maps and diagrams. Harry and Roy, both of whom had on long thick underwear, fidgeted and sweated until their hair was damp and little trickles crept from their temples, fringed with grime as they went. By contrast the burly form of Turner looked as spruce as if he had just come from his civil office, for he was well brushed about the hair, had just shaved, and was wearing at his neck a silk scarf of RAF colours. As if he were going to a cricket match.

The Wing Commander droned on, repeating all the details the others had given more explicitly.

At last it was over and the great surge to the door left the navigators in reasonable quiet to receive the final details of tactics and concentration. WAAFs came in with cups of tea, an incongruous, domestic thing on the eve of battle, if a chipped mug hastily snatched can be called domestic.

It was a relief to get out into the cool air and wait for the truck. I looked for the driver with whom I always rode. I never knew her name but she always wished me luck so pleasantly that I valued it and I had reached that stage of a tour when one begins to think of luck, however lacking in superstition one may be. I used to wonder how these drivers ever found the right aircraft, which they always seemed to do, until I happened to ride in her cab and found the dispersal numbers chalked on the dashboard.

"The capital", says Clauswitz, "must in every case be capable of making some resistance." We, therefore, had the prospect of some certain degree of opposition as well as a long night haul.

At first it was just another night trip. Harry, in rare good humour, kept amusing himself by lining his gunsight on ground objects and passing me a string of drift estimates. We were airborne at 18.29 hours so the ground was still visible. Even the warm front predicted by Met. was encountered where it ought to be and gave no more weather than a certain amount of cloud and a fifty degree shift of wind direction. Then Johnnie changed tanks and a temporary vacuum set up somewhere in the system caused a petrol leak. The gunners reported petrol streaming away from both outer motors. This overflow stopped itself before any serious loss of fuel could give rise to alarm but the sickly fumes filled the bomber with an unpleasant stench so that the mouth felt full of petrol and the stomach retched vaguely. I looked at my watch and logged: "20.49 hours. Petrol leaking. It's only overflow from the tanks," I heard Johnnie say, and then had to dismiss it from my mind for the more urgent drill of taking a fix.

We were on the German frontier and I set about finding our ETA at the last main focal point of eight degrees East. The Lancaster was on time.

Almost an hour later the Rheims radar began to fade out and I tuned the receiver to the frequency of the new Metz chain getting one very reasonable fix from the B and C pulses. Metz failed me after ten minutes. The C pulse had gone completely in the enemy jamming. The other new chain, Munster, came in as we started to climb steadily upwards. Track keeping was excellent. The light winds of the last ninety minutes began to blow stronger, with increasing altitude, but they were still manageable.

22.15 hours. At a position on the ten degree meridian we turned on to the final leg into the target. Here it was possible to break radar silence and as a matter of course I turned on the H2S set which had the low-tension on only, pressed the HT button and set the scanner rotating. I found a return from a small town to port of track, took a fix that agreed with my Gee position and then went back to my chart.

The next bearing and distance was from the town of Magdeburg which had just come up on the edge of the screen on the ten-mile scan. The aircraft was seventy nautical miles from Berlin, levelling out at twenty thousand feet. Then:

"I can smell smoke. Can anyone else smell smoke? Tell the Wop!", Blenkin's voice over the intercom was full of anxiety. Although we had been on oxygen for some time, with the mask over the nose and face, the outer air could and did enter through a valve and one did not breathe pure oxygen.

I tapped Turner to come on intercom. Before anyone could reply to his question the skipper ordered: "Lights out. Everyone look for traces of fire."

Torn from navigating at this crucial stage by that dread word I snapped off my light. I bent to look under the table and as I did so my eye passed the H2S screen at the instant the trace collapsed and vanished, leaving a ghostly smear that faded on the instant. I looked at the Gee indicator. The tube was dark. Instinctively I whipped off the main switches.

"Gee and H2S gone," I reported.

With great presence of mind Turner disconnected the heavy power cables that ran in from alternators in the motors to connections by his seat. Before I could make a move Johnnie was under the curtain crawling on the floor, an extinguisher in one hand and a torch that he flashed warily in the other. He passed me the jack of his telephones and I plugged him into my spare intercom position as he groped under the table.

"Engineer to skipper. It's a short circuit in the power cables. It's all right now."

With audible relief Frank replied: "I knew we were afire somewhere - the cockpit was full of smoke. It was clouding the instruments ..."

"I disconnected the jennies," Turner reported briefly.

The word "fire" is the most terrible sound an airman can hear. He sits in a machine made from light alloys that will burn like a torch. He has in the wings hundreds of gallons of highly volatile aviation spirit and beneath his feet are canisters full of trapped flame and explosive. Coming in the wake of a petrol leak the signs of fire were enough to sting one into frantic activity or freeze him with horror according to his temperament.

It was not till afterwards I had time to think that luck was with us. At the moment my immediate problems were pressing on me. My last ETA told me we would be early at the target as increased wind was blowing from our port quarter and pushing us along too fast.

"Hello, skipper, ETA target is 22.52. Four minutes early!"

"I'll cut her back," he replied. "Can't do much - about ten knots, we're right down already."

"I know. It's too late to do a dog leg here. Just have to carry on."

We were thirty miles from the target. I laid off a hasty DR position, told Frank to hold course and warned the bombardier of spoof targets on both bows.

"Flares going down ahead", called Johnnie and almost simultaneously Jack replied to me: "OK nav. The target's just coming up. Bags of markers showing now."

Indeed the target was well marked. It was a straightforward job. I came out into the cockpit and made my observations. The smudge of flame had not yet engulfed the flares and the Master Bomber was calling in a thin voice for crews to bomb certain markers. Patches of yellow incendiaries burned together, searchlights danced, and over Berlin's heart lit the sky like torches.

I returned. I had some tricky tactics to follow. Fox must run on for one mile, expressed in seconds, beyond the target which meant the stopwatch marking off eighteen only. Then turn through eighty degrees for a short leg of five nautical miles at 155 knots indicated. This put the groundspeed up to 255 and meant more stopwatch work. Another turn, nose down - airspeed up and altitude reeling off the clock at 1,500 feet per minute down to fourteen thousand feet with the bomber covering the ground at over three hundred knots. Time was the essential factor. To be on track meant keeping one eye on the ticking second hand, the navigator's enemy that itself takes wings in the air and seems to sweep at double speed, deriding his sluggish efforts to complete all the columns in his log.

Herein lies the difference between bombing Berlin in a Lancaster and a Mosquito. The latter, its much smaller load gone, is able to remain at very great height, immune from flak and until the coming of the Messerschmitt Me 262, from fighters, and streak for home, or descending gradually, build up such a speed that the night fighter had no hope of catching it. Its safety lay in its speed. Unable to outstrip the Ju88 the heavy four-engined bomber had to seek immunity by the judicious use of well planned tactics. Keeping in company for the mutual cover of 'window', the stream had to present a compact mass on the radar screens of the opposition, a stream that at any time might change height or direction to the confusion of the interceptors.

Deprived of my radar I knew it would be hard to remain with the stream until we were well clear of Germany. I must rely entirely on orthodox Dead Reckoning, at least until we were over Holland, for I knew the skipper would only consent to hold straight and level for an Astro shot if we were really lost.

I had noted our Air Position as the bombs went down and using the target as a fix calculated a wind to start us on our way. At the same time I reset the Air Position Indicator, that would have to see me through the tactical evasions and allowed me to shorten the wind vector on the chart. I called to Frank:

"I don't want to bind, skipper, but I want you to fly extra carefully to course and speed. We've a lot of variations to cope with and not much to go on."

"Fair enough. Any broadcast winds tonight?"

"No. I'll take a couple of shots when we're on our way a bit."

"Righto nav. Anything you say!"

With the faint crackle of intercom for company I settled down to careful plotting. I compared the winds I had found on the way out with those forecast, and assessed the flow of the airstream as far as possible by interpolation - another name for commonsense. Keeping rigidly to a drill-like system I laid off DR positions every ten minutes. I took the sextant out of its case and made a bubble.

Presently, there was another breakneck descent, welcome because it took the machine down to 9,000 feet and oxygen masks could be undone. Only for half-an-hour when we went up to 14,000 feet again at only 135 knots indicated.

I have said enough to show that it would have been a simple matter to get beautifully lost without some effort to fix position. I asked what the sky was like, and Roy, who had the best view because his turret swung through a complete circle, said it was not too good but one or two stars were visible.

Heaving up from the table I stepped back to the dome, giving Turner a thumbs-up as I passed. His eyes, that were all I could see of his face, grinned as he nodded. I put my head up in the perspex hemisphere and looked around.

Nine-tenths of the sky was obscured by clouds; high veil-like cirrus with here and there a star.

There was an elaborate theory taught in the schools whereby a navigator might use the Astro-compass to identify a star through determination of its Sidereal Hour Angle. Unfortunately, it was almost impossible to get both the Astro-compass and one's head into the dome together, and the bracket provided as a compass mount was so poorly designed that it was a work of art to set up the instrument even on the ground. I looked rather hungrily at the few stars, trying to imagine them into a constellation but had to give up the idea.

I then motioned Turner to come on to intercom, and asked him to try some loop bearings.

He stood up, his head against the ribs of the roof, turning the calibrated drum of the loop and tuning his set, while I watched anxiously in the dimness of the cabin.

Then he shook his head.

"It's no good. I canna get it for jamming", his voice seemed thicker, more Scottish than usual, in his disappointment. He was such a reliable operator that he almost blamed himself for circumstances entirely beyond his control.

He kept trying, and passed me three bearings at intervals but they were all doubtful and I had to reject them.

The only thing to do was wait for a clear patch of sky.

Harry was getting trouble with his oxygen tube. In his position, sitting in a cut-away turret with the freezing air all around him, he was the most exposed man in the aircraft. Whereas inside it was exceptional for anything more than a trace of ice to form, the rear gunner was liable to get his oxygen tube choked from his own exhalations. He was under the obligation of constantly flexing his air tube to prevent its blocking, which would mean unconsciousness, possibly the loss of the aircraft. The temperature was only some minus thirteen degrees centigrade but there must have been a certain amount of humidity.

Every ten minutes or so Frank would check him. "OK, rear gunner?"

"Yes, OK, skipper. I've got a bloody great icicle about a foot long on my mask!" Gunners had a push-to-speak button for intercom mounted on the gun control handles and therefore were not liable to have a microphone switch freeze on them.

"I'll send the Wop to have a look at you. Tell the Wop to come on intercom nav.!"

Turner, who got all the odd jobs, unhooked himself, clipped on his parachute and a portable oxygen bottle and stuffed the cord of his intercom into his pocket. He looked like something from outer space.

I shouted into his ear: "Have a look at the master unit."

He nodded and lumbered off on the uncertain journey to the back of the machine.

Presently they reported that the sky was clear and a sight possible, so I went to the dome and found there was a reasonable chance, although the high cloud dimmed part of the sky. Jupiter, large and clear, shone on the beam. I set the approximate altitude and went to hook the sextant in the dome when to my surprise a large spark jumped across. We must have been heavy with static. No wonder the loop bearings were rough.

When I was ready I called Frank to steady on course. I took four or five deep breaths to fill my lungs with oxygen, unclipped my mask and took the shot. Experience had taught me the futility of attempting to use a sextant with a long tube pulling at one's head.

Back in my seat I asked Frank if we could break wireless silence to ask England for a medium-frequency DF fix. This was obtained from bearings plotted at three ground stations when the aircraft transmitted on their common wavelength. The enemy can plot the aircraft equally well.

While Turner was getting the fix I worked out the Jupiter position line, which put us north of track, over Holland.

The fix, passed as second class, nevertheless fell on the position line. I altered course for the English coast.

All this time, with more alterations of height and speed than I have cared to mention, Frank had been flying the bomber steadily on course and Johnnie had been holding the speeds faithfully. At 01.48 hours Turner

received another fix that put us in the Channel approaches to the North
Sea at 51 degrees 11 minutes North, 01 degrees 43 minutes East. Thirteen
minutes later Jack reported crossing a coastline in, that bore away North-
east to South-west. We were home.

Just after this Roy spotted an occult through the scattered cloud below.
An occult was an aerial lighthouse. This enabled me to locate position
with a high degree of exactitude. On the strength of this occult we made
our Base, listening out from the London area in case we might get the
code word meaning intruders. Enemy night fighters had recently shot
down a number of unsuspecting freshmen at a Lancaster Finishing School
and smarting from this unnecessary loss, Command were still wary.

We made RT contact with Chedburgh at last, being above cloud still.
Even so our troubles were not entirely over, for when we attempted to
descend below 2,500 feet we ran into cloud and commenced icing up,
being forced to climb again. We arrived over Base above cloud that was
down to 800 feet. So we descended in an easterly direction to avoid
Stradishall's circuit and were fortunate enough to come into the clear in
the vicinity of a pundit.

I made a timed run from this beacon that brought us nicely home after
eight-and-a-half hours in the air. We had our shot of rum, our eggs and
bacon and sought the glorious oblivion of bed.

Now the news began to be rumoured that the tour was down to thirty
again. Melville telephoned from Mildenhall to say they had heard officially
and Max Hill and my old pilot "Killer" Arkens, the Australian, had been
screened immediately for they were over the mark. The length of tour of a
crew was usually reckoned from the number the skipper had done, which
included his second-dickie trips at the beginning. By this standard we
should be finished there and then for Blenkin ran into the thirties.
However nothing was said at Chedburgh, and crews that were involved
muttered darkly at the Wing Commander suggesting that he would press
the Squadron on as long as he could. Blenkin and I discussed the future
with the crew and suggested we should try to get into Transport Command
without delay as a long-distance crew. It would mean keeping together all
but the gunners if we could have Jack as load-supervisor.

Therefore we spent many fruitless hours haunting the Orderly Room,
getting vague promises and as afterwards proved, no action whatever.

Then Frank and I filed an application to go as pilot and navigator in
Mosquitoes immediately we had finished with Lancasters, which we knew
must be soon. We were desperately anxious, having come through so many
adventures together not to be separated and given some office job on the
ground. This is a common feeling among tour-expired aircrew; men
become so attached to each other that they will accept the hazards of the
game for the sake of the comradeship they get out of it, and the end of a
tour is looked for as something almost unattainable, so that if it does
arrive it is not altogether wanted.

Chapter 21

LAST OPERATIONS

Tuesday afternoon was a stand-down and a gloriously sunny day. That year, April provided one of those rare spells of settled weather that make England seem the most desirable place on earth and make the farmers start grumbling for rain after a week of sunshine.

"What are you doing, Dicky?" called a voice as I was walking out of Operations to go to the Mess; and Jacobs came out of his so-called snuggery. This was an abandoned office tucked away behind the briefing block and he had found some old furniture, raided the dump for fuel and made the place comfortable. Whenever he had the opportunity he would sit there planning for after the war, studying and writing notes. He was an architect by profession. He always carried his brief case with him like some London business man.

He was of that sprinkling of men one found in Bombers, men who were into the thirties and therefore rather above the age at which most aircrew were flying. Like myself he was married, and settled in life before the war, he had few of the interests that took the younger men into town when chance arose. One would find him with the *Daily Telegraph* in the reading room of the Mess. He was all good humour and easy nature. Tall, thin, fresh-faced and fond of a large pipe. A good and popular man.

"Lunch!" I answered, thinking of food as usual.

"Don't be stupid. I mean this afternoon."

"Oh - nothing. Go for a ride possibly."

"Come to Ickworth Park with me. I want to look at the house. We could go on to Bury for some tea afterwards!"

"What!" I said. "That imitation Greek temple that makes such a good pinpoint from the circuit?"

"That's the place. One is allowed into the park. There are some magnificent trees there and a rather lovely chapel."

"Well, as you wish. I'll even try a stately home once!"

So after lunch we made our way to Ickworth. It was a huge country estate full of the serenity and aloof peace with which the rich of England surrounded themselves in their golden past, now thrown open to the public, but since it is off the beaten track it was quite deserted.

We sat on a fallen tree trunk enjoying the country scene. A large herd of deer scampered across the landscape and presently a keeper made his way slowly into the woods. Jake smoked his pipe and we talked as men will about what we would do after the war. We wandered up to the mansion and satisfied our architectural curiosity and for a time were back to civilian life.

When we got back to the airfield there was a battle order pinned on the board.

Much to my chagrin, particularly when I saw the target was Heligoland, I was detailed to do the navigation briefing. There were to be about a thousand machines on the raid, indeed the numbers were as impressive as any I had seen for a daylight operation. Our squadron were put on well towards the end of the attack and the Wing Commander had wisely left his veteran crews on the ground.

They tried new forming up tactics, designed to get a squadron formation over the airfield, but this was poorly done since the take-off didn't go to schedule. As I stood outside the navigation office I was joined by Blenkin who had cycled up to see them take off. He asked me the time of set-course and after I told him kept glancing at his watch as the Lancasters roared off into the brilliant sky and chased after those already in echelon.

Blenkin shook his head and said: "Poor - dam' poor," when the time came for them to set course. "Two still on the ground!" he growled, nodding towards the marshalling point at the end of the runway.

As it happened, lack of formation made precious little difference. When the first wave of the attack reached the target the German gunners seemed to have lost all stomach for retaliation and some were seen to scuttle for boats and hastily pull away from the island. The fortress, and indeed the whole place, was soon obliterated in a pall of thick smoke as wave after wave of bombers ran up as if on a practice range and unloaded their bombs. Photographs, which were crystal clear, showed nothing but a dense cloud of eddying smoke as though a volcano had opened in the sea.

In fact, it was a milk run! Returning crews were jubilant when they came to de-briefing. They had returned from a picnic.

We were out of bed in the very early hours of Thursday, April 19th, creeping in the dark to go to briefing. We were detailed to bomb an absolute pin-point target, a control house in the railway yards at München. This target, Pasing, had been visited during the previous night by Mosquitoes using Oboe but had failed to achieve success.

There was a Y-shaped junction west of München with a transformer station due north, just on the München side and a switch house controlling all the traffic running down to Italy. The Mosquitoes had tried to knockout this house. It was a nerve centre of importance far beyond its size; if it were paralysed the whole southern front would be affected. In spite of the remarkable accuracy of Oboe the job was not done, probably because of the extreme range at which the Mosquitoes were operating. The whole target was only 300 yards square and if this could be plastered the control house would be bound to suffer.

I fancy a last-minute decision had been taken to smother the place with a carefully selected GH raid. In any case, the briefing bore all the marks of extreme haste. As it went on the OC detailed us to lead in the Squadron. A little later he mentioned that the Squadron would lead in the attack.

I felt a momentary jump of the pulses as it dawned on me that there were implications here. I waited until the customary, "Any questions?", and stood up.

"Do I understand, Sir, that we are to lead the attack?"

"That is so, Austen."

"Thank you Sir." I sat down thinking that I had no second navigator and wondering how I could cope with the work. "I suppose the old man thinks I can cope without a second dickie," I thought. "Well, fair enough, I'll have to chance it."

So at 08.21 we took off and soon found ourselves at the head of a force of 50 Lancasters. Outbound. All marker crews, all experienced.

Over the Channel our No. 3 deputy flashed an Aldis message to say that his Gee had failed. It was a nuisance, but not at this stage a tragedy.

The work was not beyond my powers although I had my hands full. The pilot flew obediently as always in these leading jobs and gave me every co-operation. Apart from the deliberate over-running of a dog-leg to waste a couple of minutes the major part of the outward journey was according to plan.

Presently it was time to open up on the RT and the wind-velocities started coming in from the deputies; clear and unemotional, unreal against the background of noise, far away as if projected from a great distance into the helmet.

I began to be very hard pressed. I vectored out the average of the found wind velocities and as master windfinder decided what to broadcast to the attacking force. I passed this result to Blenkin for him to send out. Then I set myself to taking a last fix before setting up the radar for bombing. Into these last twenty minutes of the raid were crowded almost as much work as a normal hour; the final wind, the courses in and out of the target, the bombing delay calculations and timing, the setting up of GH and the control of the run itself.

I spun the dial of the RF unit to 120 and patting Turner to attract his attention jerked a thumb to the aerial unit above him. He was so used to the game that he selected the stud with a nod of acknowledgement.

The Starting Point was coming up. On a screen shot with elusive echoes there appeared no trace of the tracking pulse.

We turned on ETA and started to run into the target, now only a matter of minutes away. I tuned the set, anxiously examining the enlarged picture on the strobe time base for any ghost that might be a pulse. Nothing showed but the mocking jitter of the noise and atmospherics.

I called to Blenkin. "No pulses, skipper. Have to get a deputy to take over!"

"OK nav. Quiet in the aircraft." The switch clicked. "Steel-grey Leader to Steel-grey Two. - Over."

"Steel-grey Two - over."

"Steel-grey Two - Take over. I repeat, take over."

"Steel-grey Two to leader. No joy. No joy. Cannot take over." Now we were faced with a dilemma and Blenkin with a quick decision. If neither ourselves nor the remaining deputy could tune the pulses it was unlikely that the rest would have more success. One deputy was out anyway. Many crews, having received the bombing wind, would be on intercom only. Some of the navigators might be able to tune. Whatever we, in the spearhead, might do, it was impossible for us to turn aside for the stream would follow without ado. At this moment Jack called:

"I can see the ground, skipper. There's about five-tenths cloud. Can I do a visual run?"

"Grand. Visual run OK!" Frank's voice was charged with relief.

"ETA target six minutes - six minutes!" I called.

This was one of those situations dear to Tolstoy who declared that once a military action has started the actual pre-planning rarely goes into effect; that subordinate commanders act within the framework of circumstances and events shape themselves under the impact of unforeseen circumstances. The whole success of the attack was now dependent on a clear view being obtained through broken cloud as we swept over München. The force of machines that had brought considerably over two hundred tons of bombs halfway across Europe now pressed relentlessly on before raining down destruction, with seven men in the leading aircraft sweating with tension, waiting for the barrage to come up and hoping against hope for a sight of the railway.

Jack, seeming calm enough, said: "I can see the railway. Target coming up."

"Three minutes to go." I gave the last help I could and abandoned the H2S set that I commenced to tune for I should have proposed bombing on this instrument had Jack not picked out the ground, even at the necessity of orbiting the town. I changed back to Gee in the hope of getting a fix at the target for checking.

Without panic, almost indifferently as was Jack's way, the corrections came up. "Left - left - steady". Suddenly there was the accustomed lurch and the bombs were going, doors closing and our immediate followers sending theirs down too.

"There goes the flak!", said Blenkin as he turned away on to the new course. But I was too busy working out the fix I had taken as a position check on the instant of bombing and did not leave the cabin.

"We were short, I should say, judging by the flak."

"I could see the junction." Jack answered. "The photo will tell anyway."

But the photo didn't plot and events moved much too quickly during the next few days for me to obtain access to any intelligence report. Some long time later I came across a bomb-damage plot for the raid that showed the yards were cratered but the fate of the switch house I do not know.

In fact, although the chain stations had been moved forward to new sites as the armies advanced the range was too great for the strength of the ground radar transmissions. Some few aircraft tuned weak pulses and bombed on them but most shared our own miserable luck. For as soon as we were away from this target and the pressure of work eased I felt the keen disappointment at doing a navigational job that satisfied myself, only to fail at the last moment.

We were sent to bomb the oil plant at Regensburg, the refineries of Rhenania-Ossag Mineralölwerke A.G. and Danubia A.G. für Mineralöl Industrie, to give them their grandiose names.

Albert Speer had written on September 16th, 1944: "The idea is spreading that reconstruction of synthetic oil plants and refineries is purposeless, since the enemy always finds a suitable moment soon after resumption of work to destroy these installations again by air attack."

Regensburg, on the Danube in Bavaria, was the only plant supplying the German armies in Austria. The oil was shipped by barge down the river without the usual burden on the enemy's hard pressed transport system. The refineries were not large, having a storage capacity of 45,000 gallons only, but they were important because of their position and that there were hardly any refineries left. It was a normal daylight effort. Our planned position was well back in the stream. I decided it should be a sightseeing trip for me and told Frank I would do only the minimum amount of work necessary and so have time to look at the countryside. There was no possibility of getting lost. He grunted an assent of sorts.

So I made the usual preparations, arranged my table, put the dark shades in my goggles and then, as we were taxiing stuck my head in the astrodome to look out.

How often had I heard them at the marshalling point without taking any notice.

"Trim forward", and the engineer repeating, "Trim forward."

"Flap 15."

"Pitch fine."

"Fuel No 2 tanks on port and starboard."

"Booster pumps on."

"Friction nut OK," (to hold the throttles and prevent them slipping back).

"Supercharger low."

"George out. Bomb doors closed." and then as the machine turned on to the runway at the permission from the caravan, "Radiator shutters closed. Pilot heat on."

I withdrew from the dome in order to log airborne time and to watch Johnnie's red lights on the warning panel of the fuel supply. This was my usual job while we were going down the runway, to see the fuel was pumping properly. The trembling machine rolled forward, gathered speed and under full throttle became a thing of life and left the ground.

It was a glorious day. Summer had lost count of the months and had come in April instead of July. There was scarcely a cloud to be seen. I stood by the starboard frogs-eye and looked critically at the English scene as it passed below, contracted in importance because so much of it could be seen, occasionally smudged by smoke but very fresh and clean.

Every twenty minutes I took a fix and worked out a wind velocity. This was the bare minimum I could do particularly as it was going to be a GH attack.

Now and then, as we passed through France and Western Germany the results of bombing and fighting could be seen. Here a smashed town, there an airfield littered with wrecked machines and well cratered. A crater is surrounded by a pattern of splashed-out earth, like a sunflower against the brown soil. The Rheinland was pocked with them, a lunar landscape. But I was surprised to observe how much of the countryside seemed to remain intact. It seemed impossible that the full flood of war could have passed over some of these areas and villages. On such a day as this even the idea of war seemed remote.

The bomber stream stretched ahead and astern for miles, aircraft making the same speed, rising and falling gently with the upcurrents but otherwise seeming to stand still in the air. It was a thrilling sight.

Much of Germany seemed under the plough. England in April is a green country. Germany a brown one. Well watered too, for often enough the brassy reflections of the sun would be thrown back at us by lakes and streams.

At last it was time to get back to my cubby-hole and prepare for the attack.

Regensburg is 12 degrees East, yet on this occasion the pulses came in good and strong. Possibly enemy jammers had been over-run. We were able to make a first class run. The target was smoking merrily when we went in. Jack reported that every detail of the landscape was as clear as could possibly be and the refineries were being bombed thoroughly.

Our bombs went down precisely. As they were going down and we were holding straight on level for the camera we were predicted and flak started bursting near. One shell exploded below us and peppered the aircraft without hitting anything vital. In fact it was the last salute the German gunners were to give us. Blenkin held on for the camera light and then pulled the aircraft away. The photographs plotted perfectly.

"Eh skipper. Look at that - starboard down," Roy's voice was excited and promised something out of the ordinary.

"God! What an explosion."

"Come out and have a look at this, nav."

I dropped my pencil, pulled out my telephone jack and scrambled out. Johnnie pushed a socket into my hand.

"Where is it - what is it?", I asked.

"Under the starboard wing. I'll put the wing down - just a minute. It must be an ammunition dump going up!" said the pilot.

There had just been a terrific explosion on the ground that caused a dense mushroom of white smoke to billow up above some 5,000 feet. The head was smooth and round and the fringes eddying and swirling and the column was rising still.

"The TAC boys are out," said someone.

I looked around for the smoke of the target but could see little. Johnnie gave a grin at me - at least his eyes twinkled above the edge of his mask - and pointed downwards. I was amused to see a group of some 50 craters arranged in a neat cluster in the open fields well west of the target. In fact, on the other side of the railway. Someone had been before. "Someone seems to have boobed!"

"Allied bombing," said Johnnie dryly.

I finished entering my bombing details. "Think I'll map-read you home," I told the skipper.

"Better give 'em to me. Never knew a navigator who could map-read yet!"

We brought the aircraft lazily back, with George in to do the piloting. We did not worry ourselves about the track of the aircraft. What had been a bomber stream dissolved itself into small elements of four or five, perhaps only two machines. Eloquent testimony to be able to *admire* the Rhein valley. I picked out Koblenz, where the Moselle flows in. The country is spectacular hereabouts, being well wooded, and the river flows in a deep gorge unmistakably flanked by railways on either side.

Later we passed over Brussels. Finally there was the glittering sea, the low East Anglian coast and home.

As we came from the field to the briefing block we were met at the door by the Group Captain whose face was one broad smile as he held out his hand to each member of the crew in turn.

"Congratulations," he said, "you're screened."

So ended our tour. Regensburg had been thoroughly bombed and photographs taken by the aircraft of the Squadron showed the refinery installations well hit. The centre of our picture plotted at less than 300 yards, so we straddled the target without any doubt for we had carried sixteen five-hundred pounders. As for the miserable log and chart that I handed shamefacedly to Murray Jones, he marked it. "Not so bad for a last trip," and sent it up to Group navigation who were doing some sort of investigation at the time.

It is difficult to explain, even to analyse, one's feeling of finishing. At first there is enormous relief, for having lived with the prospect of death for months one is suddenly given a new lease of life. You think: "Won't my wife be glad," or whoever is uppermost in your regards and you send a message giving the news. The relatives of bomber crew lived in a constant state of anxiety. You hurry round preparing for leave, which comes immediately. Then, after the first excitement has worn down, the backslapping and congratulations over and the tankards empty, one begins to think of the crew, the comradeship in danger and the excitement of it; the great satisfaction of leading in the Squadron or getting a good photograph. You think rather bitterly that the crew will be split up and someone else will fly your aircraft, and subconsciously realize that never again will you live this peculiar disciplined, exhilarating life.

For all that I went on leave gladly enough.

During the week I had a letter from Murray. He wrote: "In case you haven't heard I am writing to let you know the bad news about Tubby's crew. They returned from Bremen on three engines, had to do an overshoot and went down out of control. All were killed instantly except the two gunners and one of them died in hospital. The funeral is in Cambridge tomorrow and I hope to go.

"That isn't all the bad news either. As you may have seen in the papers another crew crashed on take-off on the morning of the 24th between the road and the WAAF site. Bombs started exploding immediately and none of the crew had a chance. I doubt whether they even found any bits. It did a lot of damage, unroofing quite a lot of the WAAF site. Luckily none of the girls were killed, although a couple were injured."

This letter was a severe shock. It told me I had lost another friend for poor Jacobs was Tubby's navigator. It didn't seem possible as I thought of him in his little room pushing coke on the fire and planning for the post-war world.

The regrettable thing about Tubby's crew was that most of them were married family men. The bomb aimer had three children who were now, of course, left fatherless at an early age. The pilot was one of those men whose wife would insist on being with him and followed him round from station to station, living in furnished accommodation somewhere outside the perimeter. This was the craziest thing a woman could do since every time the man went on operations she must have endured a frightful suspense, much of which she could have spared herself, since she would always have an exaggerated opinion of the number of times he would be going out and, in fact, as one can only die once there is no point in anticipating the event every day. In fact, when they did crash she must have known instinctively, for the Flight Commander who went to tell her found her half hysterical and had a dreadful job to give his heavy message.

It seems they lost an engine on the operation for they came back with one of their propellers feathered. They received permission to pancake and everything in the way of safety equipment was standing by ready as they made what seemed to be a reasonable approach. However, Tubby must have decided he couldn't make it, for at the last moment they commenced to overshoot and climb. At this point something must have gone wrong for before they had any altitude they were seen to falter, loose height and crash.

A plucky land girl, working in the fields nearby, dashed into the smoking wreckage and brought out four of them before other help came. Navigator and bombardier were both dead; the pilot practically gone for he died soon after.

The ambulance rushed up in time to take the two gunners, who were still alive, to Ely Hospital. One died even before they got there. I believe the other died later.

The second crash happened during an early morning take-off. As the Lancaster lifted from the runway an engine caught fire. Possibly wishing to clear the way for the following machine, the pilot tried to turn, which was fatal. He hadn't enough height and slipped into the ground.

The stricken machine caught fire as it hit and the bombs started to explode. By good fortune no cookie was being carried. If he had jettisoned his load he would probably have made a safe crash landing somewhere, but he was not entirely clear of the airfield and the living sites and this must have deterred him. As Murray said, the machine came down quite near the buildings that housed the WAAF but they were all at work or there might have been worse casualties.

The huts and buildings of this site were covered with tarpaulins and makeshift repairs were in progress when I returned. Houses in the neighbourhood that had suffered damage were already in the hands of the builders and no trace of the wrecked aircraft remained less than a week after it had happened.

Bad as this news sounded, there was more to come.

I had a telephone call from Mildenhall. Neville Parry, on that same Bremen operation that Jacobs had done, had been forced to bale out and nothing further was known.

This news affected me even more strongly for Neville and I had stuck together very closely all through the early days, ACRC Heaton Park, Canada and back to Harrogate before being sent on our separate ways. We corresponded and telephoned regularly and had much in common.

Meanwhile the whole character of the air war began to change, for it was now obvious that the end could not be delayed much longer. The Squadron found itself doing an entirely new sort of job, dropping supplies of food at The Hague to the Dutch, who were supposed to be starving. The crews called it the "grocery run" and navigators logged "Spam gone", instead of the more customary "Bombs away." The purpose of our sandbag dropping now became obvious.

The route that had to be followed was arranged by the enemy, who was still in occupation of large pockets of Holland. Bombers flew over at 1,500 feet and dropped supplies from 500 feet so the crews could easily see the scramble for any container that dropped outside the cordoned area and could appreciate the wild enthusiastic waving of the populace.

The most peculiar feature of these trips, they said, was that the enemy sent up a red light to warn anyone who might be straying off track, instead of opening fire.

Chapter 22

THE SHOUTING AND THE TUMULT DIES

I found a temporary job in the analysis room. The process of splitting up our crew had already begun for our papers had been sent to Group Headquarters as a preliminary to posting. Already, it was rumoured, Turner was going to a ground communications station in Europe. Blenkin and I had another interview with the Wing Commander concerning our application to fly Mosquitoes. He referred us to Group who were extremely vague about it. Doubtless, we were not the only aspirants.

Finally they gave us more leave while they made up their minds about our future.

A letter came from Mrs Parry giving me the good news that Melville was safe. Later on I had his own letter, which I quote:

"Herewith a fuller account of my adventures. I'm afraid they will take some days to write - not because of their length but because I am encased in the modern equivalent of the Iron Maiden; at least it feels like that. Excuse the diary form. I have to write for very short periods then relax for an hour and I am trying to get a few words to all my friends and relations to whom I write letters.

"April 22nd, afternoon. Set course Bremen. Leading the Squadron.

"18.20 hours, approximately. Running up on target. Flak very heavy. (Must adjourn, cramp in legs and throat.)

"18.25 hours, approx. Flak very close - too close. Felt a sharp pain in my left eye which started to water as I thought. I was too preoccupied with the radar screen and pulses to think about it.

"18.27. Direct hit on the port outer. I was surprised to find the screen go dead and was about to call the skipper when I noticed the wireless operator making his way to the rear with parachute on. The kite seemed OK from inside.

"Panicky bastard!" thought I. Immediately the skipper's voice: "Feather it, Mac!" The kite was juddering and shaking furiously.

"Jettison bombs, Pete!" says the skipper. We were still roughly on the same heading so the bombs must have fallen just north of the target if not on it.

"This is it, lads! Out you go - best of luck," called the skipper. (All this happened in a very short time.)

I made my way to the front. The bombardier was struggling with the hatch. Open. The engineer was not there, but was behind the skipper, his parachute opened in the kite."

(Here Melville's condition forced him to adjourn his writing for his injured state would not allow him any effort.)

"The bomb aimer opened the hatch and went out. I followed feet first, counted five and looked up. I saw the kite ahead and above and without waiting any longer pulled the ripcord. The 'chute opened with a jerk that nearly killed me - my straps were too loose.

"Height 18,000 feet. Very cold - I had no gloves on. I looked around and saw three other 'chutes."

I started map-reading. On west of Weser - good; the wind will blow me into Allied lines. It had been North to North-West. My eye was still watering. I rubbed it and found my face covered in blood. I had a gash on the left eyelid and eyebrow, presumably from a flak splinter when I felt the pain in the kite.

"For want of occupation I commenced working out my time of descent and the distance I should cover at an average wind speed of 30 mph. Sixteen minutes fall and six to eight miles.

"Map-reading again. Shock! I found myself EAST of the Weser - the wind had backed to West. I am floating into Bremen."

(Another adjournment).

"5,000 - 6,000 feet. Machine gun and rifle fire below. I thought at first that I was floating into a small-arms battle, but a second later I heard the whine of bullets and saw my 'chute holed and two panels torn. Also a bullet nicked my forehead taking out a neat, but shallow grove, and no more. There is just a tiny scar left now.

"At about 1,000 feet I realized that I was falling very fast. I prepared myself for a heavy landing in the north-west suburbs of Bremen.

"But when I did land, in a ploughed field, I hit the deck with a terrific wallop. My legs were uninjured but my back and abdomen badly so. I was dragged in a dazed condition about 50 yards by the parachute. I released myself - attempted to stand - could just do so - more rifle shots - sat down.

"Twenty Volksturm and Wehrmacht came up in Mikardo-like costumes, with an equally varied assortment of arms. Like our Home Guard! They carried me to an air-raid shelter, dressed my head and stole everything I possessed while I was unconscious.

"Later I was taken to a car, to find my rear-gunner who had a cut hand and the uninjured wireless operator. Also a Wehrmacht officer and NCO. We were taken to a barracks in the town and sat outside the main building for two hours. Pain from my back and abdomen was rather grim by now.

"20.00 hours. The wireless operator was taken into the house. The rear gunner and I went by car to a Roman Catholic hospital in Bremen."

(He continued later).

"We were dumped with some guards into an air-raid shelter built above ground and left all night half sitting, half lying on some stone steps. We saw no medical officer.

"At about 23.00 hours we were bombed by our Mitchells and by

Mosquitoes at five-minute intervals all night - a very wearing and annoying experience this latter, and worse than the concentrated raid.

"Around six o'clock next morning a RAF bomb aimer, a prisoner, saw us and took us to a man who looked after the prisoners. The nuns were still helping there. We were 10 British and 1 American. She gave Paddy and me pyjamas and took away our clothes.

"08.00 hours. April 23rd, nearly fourteen hours after coming down, we had a drink of vile "coffee" with some black bread.

"And thus we lived for nearly a week; in pyjamas on the stone floor of the Air Raid shelter, with no medical treatment. My back was pretty grim but I could walk with difficulty if I had aid. For the last four days we were in the midst of the battle for the city. Our 25-pounders were shelling the district almost continuously, because there were a lot of German 88 millimetre guns about two hundred yards from us. The hospital was hit some twenty times but didn't catch fire. Our guns fired thousands of rounds and it was very fine shooting to have so very few shells on us.

"We had no water for the last three days and the food was shocking, but at last in came the British Tommies, smiling as usual, though tired and dirty.

"As soon as they were aware of our presence they brought us champagne and cigarettes. The Nazis in the hospital - it was originally run by them - were rounded up and we were shipped away to a forward dressing station somewhere in the town."

(Later)

"The nun who looked after us was a wonderful woman. We were patients, not prisoners to her and she did what little she was allowed to do and was as pleased as we were to see the Tommies come in.

"I had developed tonsillitis with a temperature of 102 degrees, for three days, and my back was none too comfortable. In the early stages I was in four different British Army hospitals. Then I got as far as the RAF hospital in Brussels where they X-rayed me. I had broken and put out of alignment three vertebrae in the small of my back and two ribs near the breastbone.

"So once again I was slapped into a plaster cast, solid as marble from neck to thighs and for two days (VE day and VE plus one) I was more uncomfortable than I have ever been in my life. Then I got a little more accustomed to the cast and could walk with care but not sit except on something very high.

"After twelve days I was transferred to England on a stretcher in a Dakota and so to Cosford for a week.

"Now they have sent me home for six weeks, since they can do no more for me until I have this infernal cast off. I have to wear it for three months. Hence my difficulties in writing. I cannot sit for any length of time. My back is arched and I cannot put my head forward. I look a grotesque sight, with my huge chest and abdomen and I am comfortable only when standing or lying down. I get pains in my left eye and had a glorious black eye and a bloodshot cornea for a fortnight.

"But I am not complaining. I'm still very thankful to have got off so lightly as I did and I'm sure I shall be OK in four or five months."

Melville was lucky to escape with his life. As subsequently proved, all his crew reached earth safely, some suffering from injuries received in the aircraft. Men in such circumstances count a wound of little moment if life itself remains and their release from the hands of the enemy came very quickly, so they were spared long months of prison camp.

Meanwhile, I found myself recalled from leave. The crew, with the exception of Frank, were all gone, posted from the Squadron. I spent two days packing up and handing in my equipment, with the sickening business of saying goodbye to everyone, which is an all too familiar part of war-time service life.

On Tuesday, May 29th, in the afternoon, I left the Navigation Section for the last time. As I came out a Lancaster rolled round the perimeter, taxiing on two motors. She passed me while I stood watching, with her rows of bombs painted on her nose for battle honours and the crew all at stations, and as she passed I saw the letters XN - F. It was Fox.

I gave a thumbs up to the mid-upper, who waved back.

The noise of motors rose and flooded the field as Fox went down the runway. It was a beautiful afternoon with the sky full of wild, tumbled cumulus and patches of blue with the westering sun shining through in bars. As she rose off the runway she climbed up into the glory of it. I stood silent, looking hard, with my eyes watering from the glare, until the Lancaster became a bleak speck in the distance, and vanished. Then I turned away.

The fate of every Lancaster has been recorded. Like so many others of these gallant machines Fox ended up in the breaker's yard.

Next day I left Chedburgh for good.

In July, I went on what the Air Force, with its aptitude for nicknames, described as a Cook's Tour. A round trip of the Ruhr for sightseeing flown at 1,000 feet. These trips were organized with the praiseworthy intention of enabling ground staff personnel to see some of the havoc to which their efforts had indirectly contributed. The faces of the crew with whom I flew were a study when their passengers arrived, including three little girls from the WAAF.

The machine was a Lancaster of No. 138 Squadron from Tuddenham. Rather uncharitably I got myself down in the bomb hatch because the best view might be had from there, and that is where the main escape hatch is placed. The navigator came down too, with a handful of maps, saying he was going to map-read for practice. Hang the Gee - we don't need that stuff!

When we got into low stratocumulus over the Channel and the moisture was beading up the perspex in front of us he put his mouth to my ear and I pulled back my helmet enough to hear him say he was going up to his table.

So I had the maps and the hatch to myself. I lay sprawled, with greyness in front of me and the water running back across the nose in quick, gadroon-like rays. Presently we made the clear. I found that if I sat on the bombardier's belly rest and put by feet forward one on either side of the sighting head of the bombsight there was nothing between me and the ground but the perspex and I could command an uninterrupted view forward and down, even if the position were somewhat precarious.

We made Aachen our starting point. It was a sudden shock to come over the hills upon the battered town, but it was still recognizably the city of Charlemagne. Then I thought of the leaflets we used to throw out. Here it was. *Die Lehre von Aachen.*

The aircraft followed the line of the railway to Duren, also battered, and then swung round along the road to Köln.

A few minutes later the skeleton city came into sight. This place, whose population before the war was within a few thousands of Manchester, now lay below us nothing more than a vast, still, graveyard. The pilot banked the machine and closely circled the town while someone took photographs out of a side window, of the place where Evers's crew and hundreds of other good fellows had met their end, where Harris had put on the first major effort, and the place of all places that had cost the Command dear. Now nothing seemed to move in the streets except a few military vehicles going towards a temporary bridge. There were literally no people about. The once magnificent cathedral still pointed its twin spires upward but it was ridiculous to say, as some reporters had held, that it had suffered very little damage for it could be seen as very little better than a shell, with gaping holes in the roof, battered fabric and a courtyard littered with broken rubble and blocks of stone. The barren ruin all around heightened its massive look and filled one with a certain awe that it stood as well as it did. But it is a fact that churches stand up to bombing because they are solidly built and have such thick walls. The roof frequently goes but in all the dead cities of Germany at that time the cruciform outlines of the churches still paid tribute to their faith.

The ruined bridges blocked the river which frothed around the crazy heaps of disrupted steelwork. The railway lines had disappeared from the marshalling yards. Streets were delineated often by nothing more than a few broken walls, ridiculous remnants jutting disconnectedly, pierced with the unnatural sockets of vanished windows.

We could not stay at Köln. We flew to Solingen, one-time steel town, where great pylons carried the power-lines over the hills, and to Wuppertal which lies in a deep valley, a long rambling town that had an overhead railway built above the river Wupper. The railway was out of action and many of its girders were down.

Hagen came into view. This town is built in the intersection of two valleys and it is cross-shaped in consequence. Being protected naturally by the hills and most difficult to hit, it seemed reasonably intact. The countryside is beautiful hereabouts, hilly, wooded and green having prosperous houses tucked into the valleys and looking nothing like the preconceived impression of the industrialized Ruhr.

This pleasant country reminded me of the Welsh border. It remained with us up to the Möhne dam.

The dam had long been repaired; the new concrete showed where Barnes Wallis's bombs had done their work. The rusty boom supporting torpedo nets still stretched across the lake and all around the area the empty flak pits bore witness to the nature of the defences and the difficulty of the job that No. 617 had done. As one circled and flew over the river valley it was possible to pick out the limits of the flood waters. Doubtless there was extensive flooding for some way below the dam, but either time heals quickly or my anticipation of damage were coloured by the optimism of the newspaper reports that had given us such a lift in 1943. Albert Speer seems to have shared the same view.

We went to Hamm. We knew we were coming to Hamm because the bomb craters started miles away and as the town was approached the fields were literally pock-marked. Some very bad bombing indeed judged by recent standards, had happened in these parts. It was unfair to judge by our standards, for Hamm was bombed from the beginning before radar enabled the navigators to know they were at the target. Bombing on ETA is chancy. The famous yards contained dozens of battered trucks and the scars of many old bomb-bursts but some lines were in order and there was the rather welcome sight of a train going through. I think it must have been of the Station Master of Hamm that the French composed that famous line: "*Il est coucou, le chef de gare!*" ... This gentleman is reported as having 4,000 railway men and 8,000 slave labourers constantly working to repair the havoc that increasingly heavy bombing raids caused. He must have been a worried man.

Dortmund and Borchum were smashed and damaged everywhere. It was becoming monotonous to see so much destruction when someone in the crew said:

"Essen coming up. Now you'll see what Krupps looks like!"

It is incredible to think that Allied experts recorded any of Krupps machinery serviceable when the area was over-run, for what lay below us was a dead husk, a twisted shell silent and smashed, with the bare ribs of its huge sheds red with rust. All Essen was red rust, and Krupps was Essen. My lasting impression of the place was of hugeness, great undertakings and enormous enterprises of iron overtaken by a Wellsian destruction. Some parts of a roof remained on one of the biggest works but the covering was punched in by a giant's blow. Meaningless shapes of old steel traced a senseless geometry in this place where so much feverish toil and industry had been put into the German war machine only a short time ago. I then wondered if Krupps would ever recover.

After the vastness of the chaos in Essen the town of Oberhausen seemed almost undamaged. Not very flattering to me since it had been my first daylight target. I noticed a refinery, unmistakable by reason of its inverted, bottle-shaped retorts, still in good condition. But the great river port of Duisburg had been very badly battered and here was the same tale of distorted girder work and smashed buildings, with the addition of overturned lighters and barges, and one or two quite large ships lying heeled over in the docks.

Last of all our aircraft went to Wesel.

Here, with nothing but a small town to receive the full fury of many attacks, destruction had reached its consummation for the heart was cut out of the place. The whole of the town proper was gone. A ring of shattered properties marked the suburbs but the centre was just a flat wilderness and even the roads were indistinguishable from the all pervading brownness of the ruin. Both the road and railway bridges were down. An impression of the desertedness struck one with a shock.

As we turned away from the stricken Ruhr it was a relief to look at green fields and the shining Rhein. But we were not finished yet.

The flat Dutch lands were rolling past below and the pilot decided to do some low-level flying. He dived the heavy bomber to tree-top level. The ground rushed past as we tore across the countryside and from my position the sight was far from comforting, especially as he had to pull the nose up to clear occasional obstructions. Blenkin would never have taken such liberties with a Lancaster. At least someone enjoyed it for peasants in the fields took off their caps and waved and pointed excitedly as the great black machine passed by.

We came upon the final tragedy, an exhibition the more painful because necessity forced it upon us at the expense of the friendly industrious Dutch. We came upon the island of Walcheren.

No. 3 Group had burst the sea walls to let in the floods that inundated the island. Now the water covered it as far as the eye could see. Yet it was not part of the sea for the stark remains of human habitation still projected valiantly from the water, as though determined to assert their claim to the land beneath. A line of tree stumps stood unmistakably where once a road had passed. Barns looked like Noah's Ark floating in a child's pond. Here and there the hamlets still stood, the lower rooms of the houses under water, sometimes a house more fortunate than others had escaped entirely because it was built on a knoll. Incredibly enough, the region was not entirely deserted for a boat could be seen with a man rowing in it and also, on a piece of dry land, some chickens. It was a picture such as is seen wherever a great flood occurs as a result of some natural disaster.

"Shocking - this!", I said over the intercom.

"Yes, bad enough ... but it's worse in north-west Holland where the

Jerries let the water in. You can see some land over towards Flushing in these parts but up there the inundations stretch for miles."

The sense of tragedy was oppressive. It seemed utterly wanton. I was glad when the aircraft started to climb for its homeward journey and Walcheren was left behind.

We entered a region of hazy luminosity which made it impossible to see where sky and sea began and it was necessary to put on sun glasses to protect the eyes from the glare of the intense light reflected by the water and refracted in the thin veil of mist and smoke that the off-shore wind brings from England. I knew we must be approaching the land and very soon we were circling and landing at Base.

The journey left me with certain knowledge of the terrible destruction of modern bombing, a knowledge that it was impossible to quantify while on actual operations. I had seen everywhere ruin, rust and desolation. Shells of houses by the thousand, and battered churches and public buildings. Industrial plants derelict; smashed gas holders that look so unsubstantial when they are crumpled. And broken bridges and smashed vessels littering the ports and rivers. Railway yards obstructed with burnt-out rolling stock and hardly a train anywhere, while on the fine roads the only thing moving was a bicycle here and there.

Yet, oddly enough, there was a remarkable survival of factory chimneys in all the Ruhr. A large stack is built to sway and this and its streamlined form must have saved many a chimney when the factory itself was blown up.

One felt that the value of the damage that had been done must be beyond computation.

A year later, in May 1946, I flew over Wesel at low level and recorded what I could then see. A tributary flows into the Rhein at the place, which is built into the fork of the two. There were two railway bridges and one road bridge, all still down, although the army had put up a Bailey. The heart of the town had been obliterated so thoroughly that even the usual shells of buildings were almost entirely missing and the appearance of a slight eminence on which the town had stood was almost entirely cleared. One large building remained in the western part, the shell of what was an important church. The suburbs that had appeared reasonably intact from several thousand feet proved to be well battered and a large factory in the suburbs on the Eastern side had been extensively damaged. The railyard on the outskirts showed signs of restored working by this time.

This morbid catalogue of ruin, monstrous as it is in its uniformity would not be complete without some comment on the state of the arch target of our yesterdays - Berlin.

In the spring of 1946 I had been remustered to my old job of controlling and was posted to Joint Air Traffic Control in Europe, when I had the opportunity of visiting the city. Not only could one walk in the city, but I had access to a Volkswagen with a German guide, and since at that time we were on quite amiable terms with the officers of the other Allied powers, was able to move about in the various zones. Berlin was a complete and utter shambles. Some of it, as the result of Russian gunfire but largely as a result of the attacks of Bomber Command. Scores of streets were nothing but heaps of rubble with twisted girders sticking grotesquely out of heaps of bricks. Among these heaps, women were searching to remove any of these that were intact, to be piled on the side and re-used for new building. Obviously, building materials would be scarce for many years. Skeleton walls stood, quite a lot of them, buttressed by a stout chimney breast perhaps. Life on a large scale still existed there, people found shelter in makeshift accommodation - cellars that remained, or made a habitation of a room or two that had survived the general damage to a building.

The Kaiser Wilhelm memorial had its bronzework ripped by blast. The Reichstag was battered and scarred, particularly by the Russian artillery fire and its courtyard was an incredible junk-heap of great stone blocks, old guns, derelict tanks and rusty wire. The Chancellery, one of Speer's major constructions, had received a neat direct hit right through the roof that then exploded in the basement. The fabric was smashed and the precious marble on the panelling was grimed with thick dust. Hitler's quarters were a heap of rubble.

Kurfürstendam and Unter den Lindin were avenues of disintegration. The Tiergarten a waste, dominated by a brand new Russian war memorial, in whose shadow the soldiers openly bartered with the German black marketeers.

In the open spaces there were the fantastically huge Todt-built concrete bunkers where thousands of the population had sheltered. Guns and Freyas were still there. The bunkers were virtually immune from bombing and the Russians were making attempts to blow them up.

The roads had been cleared and were mostly repaired and good. A restricted tramway service was running. The universal battering that had not spared the suburbs had left very few bridges intact. The underground railway, which appeared not to have run very deep in the earth had caved in here and there leaving great rents in the road.

When a building collapses during a bombing raid the roof and the floors and all the interior work seem to come down in a heap, forfeiting all semblance of shape and colour. Sometimes the debris is so pulverized as to appear nothing more than a mound of earthy dust, blasted back into the material from which it was made. Such mounds were everywhere.

The people did not seem unduly ill or pinched considering the ordeals they had been through. Human resilience and the powers of recovery are remarkable as the aftermath of modern war has shown in Europe. Few young men were to be seen and the civil police were poor specimens because all fit men had been swallowed by the battlefronts. The burden of recovery was falling initially on the women.

But when the rain came down one suddenly caught an indefinable odour coming up from the cellars of some of the wrecked buildings; a decaying, mouldering smell. A smell that stirred the imagination to wonder what was still down there, for how many dead lay under the ruins we shall probably never know.

INDEX

HIGH ADVENTURE - NAVIGATOR AT WAR

Index compiled by Stuart Craik

C

D

N

224

228

230

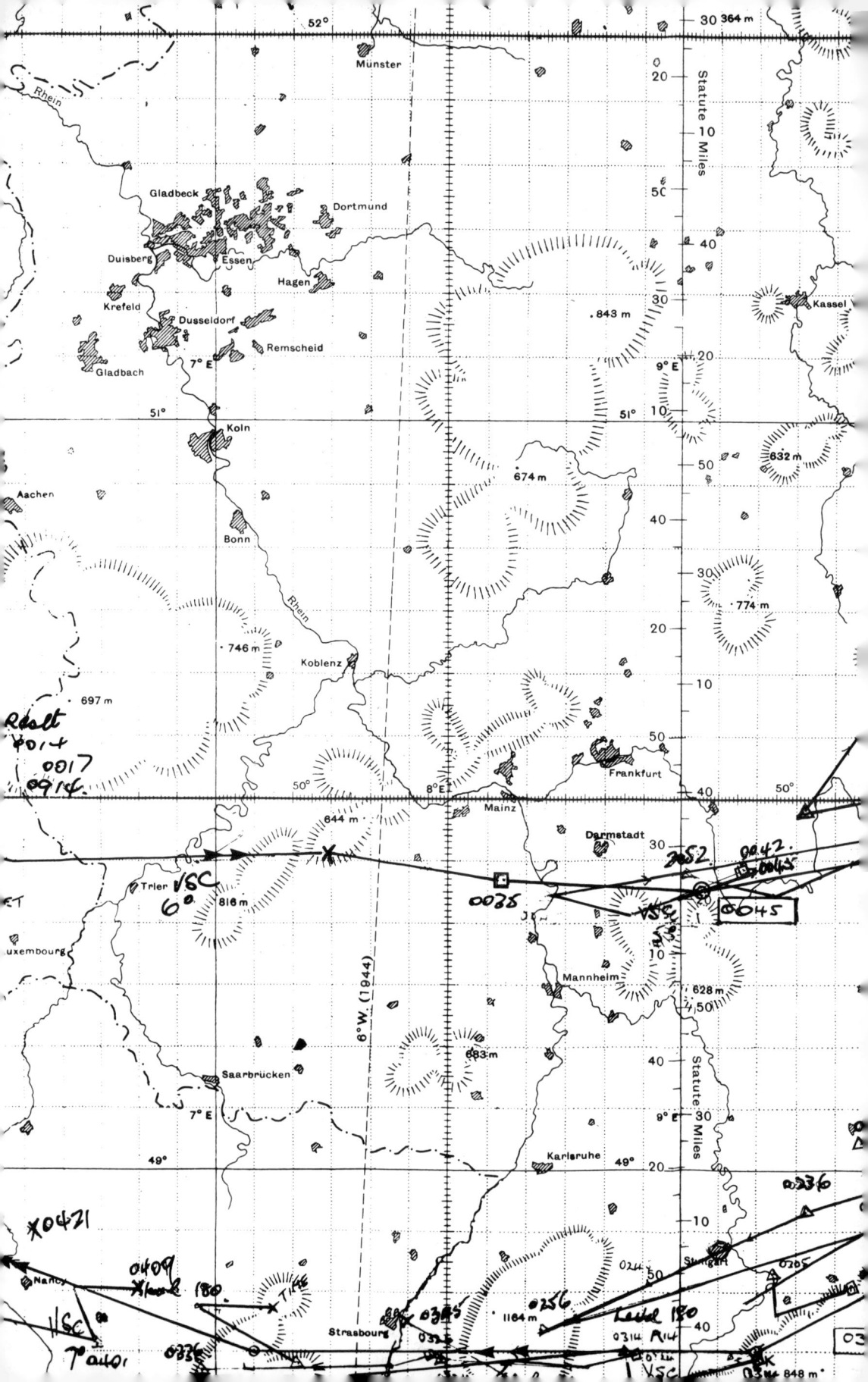

Münster

Rhein

Gladbeck   Dortmund

Duisberg   Essen   Hagen

Krefeld

Dusseldorf   Remscheid

Gladbach

Koln

Aachen

Bonn

. 746 m

697 m

Koblenz

Rhein

. 843 m

632 m

674 m

. 774 m

Kassel

Frankfurt

Mainz

Darmstadt

644 m

Trier

816 m

Mannheim

628 m

683 m

Luxembourg

Saarbrücken

Karlsruhe

1164 m

Strasbourg

Stuttgart

Nancy

52° 51° 50° 49°

7° E 8° E 9° E

6° W (1844)

Statute Miles

364 m

848 m

Handwritten annotations:

Reslt
0014
0017
0014

VSC 6°

0035

2252 0042 0045

0045

X0421

0409 Xkm 180

VSC Taylor

0336

0345

0236

Leith 180

0314 R14

VSC

0344 848 m

0205

0236

20 10 50 40 30

Münster

Gladbeck   Dortmund

Duisberg   Essen   Hagen
Krefeld
Düsseldorf   Remscheid
Gladbach   7° E

Köln

51°

Aachen

Bonn

Rhein

· 746 m   Koblenz

· 697 m

364 m   30
Statute Miles   20
50   10

Kassel

· 843 m   30
9° E   20
51°   10   50

· 674 m   40

· 632 m   50

30
· 774 m   20
10

Rest   50
014   40
0017   50°
0914   8° E   Mainz   Frankfurt

644 m   X   Darmstadt   352   0042   30
Trier VSC   0038   0045   VSC   0045
6°   816 m   J   10

6° W. (1944)   Mannheim   628 m
50

Luxembourg

Saarbrücken   683 m   40

7° E   9° E   30
49°   Karlsruhe   49°   20
Statute Miles

X0471   10

Nancy   0409   0236
X 180   Stuttgart   0205
TIME   0314   VSC   0244   0236   Lead 180
P 0401   0336   Strasbourg   0335   1164 m   0236   0314 R14   03
VSC   848 m